# Essential tables

## RATES OF INCOME TAX

*(ITA 2007, Pt 2, Ch 2)*

| Taxable income £ | Rate % | Tax £ | Cumulative £ |
|---|---|---|---|
| **2013–14** | | | |
| 0–32,010 | 20 | 6402.00 | 6,402.00 |
| 32,010–150,000 | 40 | 47,196.00 | 53,598.00 |
| Over 150,000 | 45 | – | – |
| **2012–13** | | | |
| 0–34,370 | 20 | 6,874.00 | 6,874.00 |
| 34,371–150,000 | 40 | 46,251.60 | 53,125.60 |
| Over 150,000 | 50 | – | – |
| **2011–12** | | | |
| 0–35,000 | 20 | 7,000.00 | 7,000.00 |
| 35,001–150,000 | 40 | 46,000.00 | 53,000.00 |
| Over 150,000 | 50 | – | – |
| **2010–11** | | | |
| 0–37,400 | 20 | 7,480.00 | 7,480.00 |
| 37,401–150,000 | 40 | 45,040.00 | 52,520.00 |
| Over 150,000 | 50 | – | – |
| **2009–10** | | | |
| 0–37,400 | 20 | 7,480.00 | 7,480.00 |
| Over 37,400 | 40 | – | – |
| **2008–09** | | | |
| 0–34,800 | 20 | 6,960.00 | 6,960.00 |
| Over 34,800 | 40 | – | – |
| **2007–08** | | | |
| 0–2,230 | 10 | 223.00 | 223.00 |
| 2,231–34,600 | 22 | 7,121.40 | 7,344.40 |
| Over 34,600 | 40 | – | – |

See further **Personal Taxation**, p 1.

# PERSONAL ALLOWANCES AND RELIEFS

*(ITA 2007, Pt 3)*

|  | 2013–14 £ | 2012–13 £ | 2011–12 £ | 2010–11 £ |
|---|---|---|---|---|
| **Personal allowance** | | | | |
| Age under 65 | | 8,105 | 7,475 | 6,475 |
| Born after 5 April 1948 | 9,440 | | | |
| Income limit for personal allowance | 100,000 | 100,000 | 100,000 | 100,000 |
| **Age-related allowances** | | | | |
| Personal allowance (age 65–74) | | 10,500 | 9,940 | 9,490 |
| Born between 5 April 1938 and 6 April 1948 | 10,500 | | | |
| Personal allowance (age 75 and over) | | 10,660 | 10,090 | 9,640 |
| Born before 6 April 1938 | 10,660 | | | |
| Income limit for age-related allowances | 26,100 | 25,400 | 24,000 | 22,900 |
| **Married couple's allowance** | | | | |
| Basic allowance | 3,040 | 2,960 | 2,800 | 2,670 |
| Age 75 or over | 7,915 | 7,705 | 7,295 | 6,965 |
| **Blind person's allowance** | 2,160 | 2,100 | 1,980 | 1,890 |
| **Rent-a-room relief** | 4,250 | 4,250 | 4,250 | 4,250 |

See further **Personal Taxation**, p 3.

# RATES OF CORPORATION TAX

*(CTA 2010, Pt 2, Ch 2, 3; Pt 3)*

|  | Financial Year commencing 1 April | | | |
|---|---|---|---|---|
|  | **2013** | **2012** | **2011** | **2010** |
| **Small Profits Rate** | 20% | 20% | 20% | 21% |
| Small Profits Rate can be claimed by qualifying companies with profits not exceeding | £300,000 | £300,000 | £300,000 | £300,000 |
| Marginal Relief Lower Limit | £300,000 | £300,000 | £300,000 | £300,000 |
| Marginal Relief Upper Limit | £1,500,000 | £1,500,000 | £1,500,000 | £1,500,000 |
| Standard fraction | 3/400 | 1/100 | 3/200 | 7/400 |
| Main rate of Corporation Tax | 23% | 24% | 26% | 28% |
|  | **2009** | **2008** | **2007** | **2006** |
| **Small Profits Rate** | 21% | 21% | 20% | 19% |
| Small Profits Rate can be claimed by qualifying companies with profits not exceeding | £300,000 | £300,000 | £300,000 | £300,000 |
| Marginal Relief Lower Limit | £300,000 | £300,000 | £300,000 | £300,000 |
| Marginal Relief Upper Limit | £1,500,000 | £1,500,000 | £1,500,000 | £1,500,000 |
| Standard fraction | 7/400 | 7/400 | 1/40 | 11/400 |
| Main rate of Corporation Tax | 28% | 28% | 30% | 30% |

See further **Taxation of Companies**, p 77.

# CGT RATES AND ANNUAL EXEMPTIONS

*(TCGA 1992, ss 3, 4, Sch 1)*

| Tax Year | Annual exempt amount | | Tax rate paid by | | |
| --- | --- | --- | --- | --- | --- |
| | Individuals, personal representatives (PR's) and trusts for disabled | General trusts | Individuals within: | | Trustees and PR's |
| | | | Basic rate band | Higher tax bands | |
| | £ | £ | % | % | % |
| 2013–14 | 10,900 | 5,450 | 18 | 28 | 28 |
| 2012–13 | 10,600 | 5,300 | 18 | 28 | 28 |
| 2011–12 | 10,600 | 5,300 | 18 | 28 | 28 |
| 2010–11 (23 June 2010 to 5 April 2011) | 10,100 | 5,050 | 18 | 28 | 28 |
| 2010–11 (6 April to 22 June 2010) | 10,100 | 5,050 | 18 | 18 | 18 |
| 2009–10 | 10,100 | 5,050 | 18 | 18 | 18 |
| 2008–09 | 9,600 | 4,800 | 18 | 18 | 18 |

See further **Capital Gains Tax**, p 91.

# Key Tax Dates

## Monthly

- 19<sup>th</sup> – Non-electronic payments of PAYE, Class 1 NIC and CIS deductions for the period ended 5<sup>th</sup> of the month should reach HMRC's Accounts Office by this date (*SI 2003/2682, reg 69(1)(b); SI 2005/2045, reg 7(1)(b)SI 2001/1004, Sch 4, reg 10(1)*).

- 22<sup>nd</sup> – Electronic payments of PAYE, Class 1 NIC and CIS deductions for the period ended 5<sup>th</sup> of the month should clear into HMRC's bank account by this date (*SI 2003/2682, reg 69(1)(a); SI 2001/1004, Sch 4, reg 10(1); SI 2005/2045, reg 7(1)(a)*).

## 6 April 2013

- RTI is compulsory for employers who have been invited by HMRC to join RTI, in practice all employers with up to 5,000 employees except for care and support employers and those with exemption on religious grounds (*SI 2003/ 2682 regs 2A, 67D*).

## 3 May 2013

- Employers must submit Form P46 (Car) if appropriate to report changes affecting car benefits during the quarter to 5 April 2013.

## 19 May 2013

- Employers (other than those already in RTI) must submit 2012–13 end of year PAYE returns (forms P35 and P38A, including 'nil' returns if appropriate, and P14) to HMRC (*SI 2003/2682, regs 73, 74*).

## 31 May 2013

- Employers must provide a 2012–13 form P60 to each employee who worked for them at 5 April 2013, and from whom the employer was required to deduct tax from relevant payments at any time during the tax year (*SI 2003/2682, reg 67*).

## 5 July 2013

- PAYE Settlement Agreements (PSAs) for 2012–13 must be agreed with HMRC (*SI 2003/2682, reg 112*).

## 6 July 2013

- Employers to submit returns of benefits and expenses (forms P11D and P9D) to HMRC for 2012–13 (*SI 2003/2682, reg 85*).

- Returns of Class 1A NICs (forms P11D(b)) for 2012–13 must reach HMRC (*SI 2001/1004, reg 80*).

- Employers must supply relevant employees with P11D(b), P11D and P9D information for 2012–13 (*SI 2003/2682, reg 94*).

- Annual returns for share schemes, forms 34, 35, 39 40, and form 42 (or equivalent) for reporting events relating to employment-related securities and options for the year to 5 April 2013 must reach HMRC (*ITEPA 2003, s 421J*).

## 19 July 2013

- Employer non-electronic payments of Class 1A NICs for 2012–13 on benefits returned on a declaration of expenses and benefits (form P11D(b)) must reach HMRC. The due date is 22 July for payments made by an approved electronic payment method (*SI 2001/1004, reg 71*).

## 31 July 2013

- The second payment on account of self assessment income tax (and Class 4 NIC) by individuals for 2012–13 must reach HMRC to avoid late payment interest charges (*TMA 1970, s 59A(2)*).

## 1 August 2013

- Individual taxpayers who have not paid their remaining tax liabilities for 2011–12 face a further 5% penalty, in addition to the 5% penalty suffered on amounts outstanding at 1 March 2013 (*FA 2009, Sch 56, para 3; SI 2011/702, art 3*).

## 2 August 2013

- Employers must submit Form P46 (Car) if appropriate to report changes affecting car benefits during the quarter to 5 July 2013.

## 31 August 2013

- If HMRC have not issued a 2012–13 income tax self-assessment notice to file until by now, the normal submission deadline of 31 October 2013 is extended to two months after the date on which the notice to file the tax return is issued (*TMA 1970, s 9(2)(b)*).

## 5 October 2013

- Any person chargeable to income tax or CGT for 2012–13 who has not received a notice to file a self assessment return must notify HMRC by this date that they are so chargeable (*TMA 1970, s 7(1)*).

## 6 October 2013

- RTI is compulsory for all employers except for care and support employers and those falling within with other exemptions (*SI 2003/2682 regs 2A, 67D*).

## 18 October 2013

- Employer non-electronic payments of income tax in respect of PAYE settlement agreements (PSAs) for 2012–13 should reach HMRC Accounts Office (*SI 2003/2682, reg 109(2)*) (the due date is extended to 22 October 2013 for payments made by an approved electronic payment method). This is also the normal due date for payment of Class 1B NIC liabilities in respect of PSAs for 2012–13 (or 22 October 2013 for electronic payments) (*SI 2001/1004, Sch 4 reg 13(1)*).

## 31 October 2013

- Paper (non-electronic) income tax self-assessment returns for 2012–13 must generally be filed. This applies to individuals, (*TMA 1970, s 8(1D)–(1F)*), trustees (*TMA 1970, s 8A(1B)–(1D)*) and partnerships which include one or more individuals (*TMA 1970, s 12AA(4A)–(4D)*).

- If HMRC do not issue a notice to file a 2012–13 self-assessment income tax return until after 31 October 2013, the return must be filed within three months from the date of the notice, whether the return is electronic or paper (*TMA 1970, ss 8(1G), 8A(1E), 12AA(4E)*).

- An employed taxpayer who submits a paper self assessment return for 2012–13 must do so by 31 October 2013 if they wish HMRC to collect a tax underpayment of less than £3,000 by adjustment to their future PAYE code where possible (*ITEPA 2003, s 684(3A); SI 2003/2682, reg 186(4)*).

## 2 November 2013

- Employers must submit Form P46 (Car) if appropriate to report changes affecting car benefits during the quarter to 5 October 2013.

## 30 December 2013

- An employed taxpayer who submits an electronic self assessment return for 2012–13 must do so by 30 December 2013 if they wish HMRC to collect a tax underpayment of less than £3,000 by adjustment to their future PAYE code where possible (*ITEPA 2003, s 684(3A); SI 2003/2682, reg 186(4)*).

## 31 January 2014

- Electronic income tax self-assessment returns for 2012–13 must normally be filed by this date, and any balancing payment of tax due for that year received by HMRC. However, if the notice to file was issued after 31 October 2013, the deadline for filing the return (whether electronically or on paper) is extended to three months from the date of issue of that notice (*TMA 1970, ss 8(1D)(b), 8(1G); 8A(1B)(b), 8A(1E); 12AA(4B), 12AA(4E)*).

- Any balancing payment of self assessment income tax (and Class 4 NIC, if applicable) for 2012–13 plus any capital gains tax for that year is normally payable by 31 January 2013. However, for 2012–13 tax returns where HMRC was notified of chargeability to tax by 5 October 2013 and the notice to file was issued after 31 October 2013, the payable date is extended to three months after the date on which the notice to file was issued (*TMA 1970, s 59B(3), (4)*).

- If a first payment on account is required for the tax year 2013–14, the payment of tax (and Class 4 NIC, if applicable) must reach HMRC by 31 January 2014 (*TMA 1970, s 59A(2)(a)*).

## 1 February 2014

- Most individual taxpayers who have not paid their remaining tax liabilities (and Class 4 NIC, if appropriate) for 2011–12 by this date face a further 5% penalty, in addition to the 5% penalties suffered on amounts outstanding at 1 March 2013 and 1 August 2013 (*FA 2009, Sch 56, para 3; SI 2011/702, art 3*).

## 2 February 2014

- Employers must submit Form P46 (Car) if appropriate to report changes affecting car benefits during the quarter to 5 January 2014.

## 1 March 2014

- Most individual taxpayers who have not paid their tax liabilities (and Class 4 NIC, if appropriate) for 2012–13 by this date face a 5% penalty (*FA 2009, Sch 56, para 3; SI 2011/702, art 3*).

## 5 April 2014

- The end of tax year 2013–14, and a crucial day for deciding whether to take particular action either before or after 5 April 2014 (eg utilising personal allowances, the CGT and IHT annual exemptions, etc).

## 6 April 2014

- RTI is compulsory for all employers who were previously exempt: eg care and support employers and those using special PAYE schemes for examination fee and electoral payments (*SI 2003/2682 reg 2A*).

## 30 April 2014

- Payment of IHT on lifetime transfers between 6 April and 30 September 2013 is due by this date (*IHTA 1984, s 226(1)*).

**Note**

The above list is for general information purposes only, and is not exhaustive.

# Bloomsbury's Tax Rates and Tables 2013/14

# Budget edition

## Compiled by:

Rebecca Cave FCA CTA MBA

## Contributing Editor:

Mark McLaughlin CTA (Fellow) ATT TEP

Welcome to *Tax Rates and Tables 2013/14* (Budget edition), published by Bloomsbury Professional.

Following very positive feedback, we are again producing this publication twice – in Budget and Finance Act editions. This Budget edition of *Tax Rates and Tables 2013/14* retains the successful format already established, but contains a significant amount of new material such as the RTI tables in Chapter 3, statutory payment rates in Chapter 16, and tables for child benefit and the state pension in Chapter 18. The tables relating to penalties and HMRC's investigation powers have been collected together in Chapter 17. The book has also been updated to reflect measures announced in the Budget of 20 March 2013. Everyone involved in this book is constantly striving for improvements in content and format. We would welcome your constructive comments or suggestions for future editions.

Many thanks to Mark McLaughlin for his invaluable contributions and also to everyone at Bloomsbury Professional who was involved in the publication, particularly Jane Bradford for her considerable skill and professionalism in bringing all the material together.

Finally, thank you for acquiring *Tax Rates and Tables 2013/14* (Budget edition). I hope that you find it very useful and practical.

*Rebecca Cave FCA CTA*
*Rebecca@ taxwriter.co.uk*
*April 2013*

# Bloomsbury Professional

**Bloomsbury Professional Ltd, Maxwelton House, 41–43 Boltro Road, Haywards Heath, West Sussex, RH16 1BJ**

© Bloomsbury Professional Ltd 2013
Bloomsbury Professional is an imprint of Bloomsbury Publishing Plc

A CIP Catalogue record for this book is available from the British Library.

ISBN 978 1 78043 151 2

Typeset by Phoenix Photosetting, Chatham, Kent
Printed and bound in Great Britain by Hobbs the Printers, Totton, Hampshire

# Personal Taxation

## RATES OF INCOME TAX

*(ITA 2007, Pt 2, Ch 2)*

| Taxable income £ | Rate % | Tax £ | Cumulative £ |
|---|---|---|---|
| **2013–14** | | | |
| 0–32,010 | 20 | 6,402.00 | 6,402.00 |
| 32,010–150,000 | 40 | 47,196.00 | 53,598.00 |
| Over 150,000 | 45 | – | – |
| **2012–13** | | | |
| 0–34,370 | 20 | 6,874.00 | 6,874.00 |
| 34,371–150,000 | 40 | 46,251.60 | 53,125.60 |
| Over 150,000 | 50 | – | – |
| **2011–12** | | | |
| 0–35,000 | 20 | 7,000.00 | 7,000.00 |
| 35,001–150,000 | 40 | 46,000.00 | 53,000.00 |
| Over 150,000 | 50 | – | – |
| **2010–11** | | | |
| 0–37,400 | 20 | 7,480.00 | 7,480.00 |
| 37,401–150,000 | 40 | 45,040.00 | 52,520.00 |
| Over 150,000 | 50 | – | – |
| **2009–10** | | | |
| 0–37,400 | 20 | 7,480.00 | 7,480.00 |
| Over 37,400 | 40 | – | – |
| **2008–09** | | | |
| 0–34,800 | 20 | 6,960.00 | 6,960.00 |
| Over 34,800 | 40 | – | – |
| **2007–08** | | | |
| 0–2,230 | 10 | 223.00 | 223.00 |
| 2,231–34,600 | 22 | 7,121.40 | 7,344.40 |
| Over 34,600 | 40 | – | – |

**Notes**

(1)   The basic rate limit is to be reduced from £32,010 (for 2013–14) to £31,865 (for 2014–15) (*Budget, 20 March 2013*).

(2)   The personal allowance for those born after 5 April 1948 will increase to £10,000 for 2014–15. Thus the higher rate threshold; the level of income at which taxpayers

start to pay 40% tax taking into account the personal allowance, will increase to £41,865 for 2014–15 (*Budget, 20 March 2013*).

(3)    The higher rate threshold will increase to £42,285 for 2015–16 (*Budget, 20 March 2013*).

## TAX RATES FOR SAVINGS AND DIVIDENDS

(*ITA 2007, ss 10–19*)

| Non-dividend savings income rates | 2013–14 | 2012–13 | 2011–12 | 2010–11 | 2009–10 | 2008–09 |
|---|---|---|---|---|---|---|
| Starting Rate | 10% up to £2,790 | 10% up to £2,710 | 10% up to £2,560 | 10% up to £2,440 | 10% up to £2,440 | 10% up to £2,320 |
| Basic Rate | 20% | 20% | 20% | 20% | 20% | 20% |
| Higher Rate | 40% | 40% | 40% | 40% | 40% | 40% |
| Additional Rate | 45% | 50% | 50% | 50% | – | – |

**Notes**

(1)    *Savings income* – A 10% starting rate of income tax applies to savings income only. If non-savings income exceeds this limit, the 10% starting rate for savings does not apply. If savings income does not exceed the basic rate limit, there is no additional tax to pay on savings income from which 20% tax has been deducted, but higher rate taxpayers are liable to income tax at 40% or 45% to the extent that savings income exceeds the higher or additional rate thresholds.

(2)    *Dividend income* – If gross dividend income does not exceed the basic rate threshold, the income tax rate is 10%. For the years 2010–11 to 2012–13, higher rate or additional rate taxpayers are liable to income tax at 32.5% or 42.5%, to the extent that dividend income exceeds the higher or additional rate thresholds.

(3)    The additional rate of income tax for 2013–14 is 45%, and the additional rate for dividend income for 2013–14 is set at 37.5% (*ITA 2007 s 8*).

(4)    The 10% non-repayable tax credit on dividends from UK resident companies can be calculated by applying a fraction of 1/9th to the net amount. In addition, from 6 April 2008 a non-repayable tax credit of 1/9th of the net dividend is available in respect of non–UK resident companies where the taxpayer's shareholding is less than 10%, if certain conditions are satisfied. The availability of a tax credit was extended to taxpayers with shareholdings of 10% or more, with effect from 22 April 2009 (*ITTOIA 2005, ss 397–397C*).

## TRUST RATES

(*ITA 2007, s 9*)

|  | **Trust rate** | **Dividend trust rate** |
|---|---|---|
| 2013–14 | 45% | 37.5% |
| 2010–11 to 2012–13 | 50% | 42.5% |
| 2004–05 to 2009–10 | 40% | 32.5% |

**Notes**

(1)    A 'standard rate band' applies to the first £1,000 of taxable income arising in 2006–07 and later years (for 2005–06, the starting rate band was £500). Income within this band is not taxable at the above trust rates, but is generally taxable at the (non-trust) rates applicable to the particular source of income (eg 10% for dividend income, or 20% for other savings income or non-savings income (eg rental and business profits). In the case of trusts made by the same settlor, the standard rate band is divided by the number of such trusts, subject to a minimum starting rate band of £200 (*ITA 2007, ss 491, 492*).

(2)    The above trust rates broadly apply to accumulated or discretionary trust income (*ITA 2007, s 479*). Trustees of an interest in possession trust are generally liable to income tax (for 2010–11 to 2013–14) at 10% in respect of dividend income, or 20% on other savings income or non-savings income), although certain capital receipts for trust law purposes are liable at the above trust rates (*ITA 2007, ss 481, 482*).

## PERSONAL ALLOWANCES AND RELIEFS

*(ITA 2007, Pt 3)*

|  | 2013–14 £ | 2012–13 £ | 2011–12 £ | 2010–11 £ |
|---|---|---|---|---|
| **Personal allowance** | | | | |
| Age under 65 | | 8,105 | 7,475 | 6,475 |
| Born after 5 April 1948 | 9,440 | | | |
| Income limit for personal allowance | 100,000 | 100,000 | 100,000 | 100,000 |
| **Age-related allowances** | | | | |
| Personal allowance (age 65–74) | | 10,500 | 9,940 | 9,490 |
| Born between 5 April 1938 and 6 April 1948 | 10,500 | | | |
| Personal allowance (age 75 and over) | | 10,660 | 10,090 | 9,640 |
| Born before 6 April 1938 | 10,660 | | | |
| Income limit for age-related allowances | 26,100 | 25,400 | 24,000 | 22,900 |
| **Married couple's allowance** | | | | |
| Basic allowance | 3,040 | 2,960 | 2,800 | 2,670 |
| Age 75 or over | 7,915 | 7,705 | 7,295 | 6,965 |
| **Blind person's allowance** | 2,160 | 2,100 | 1,980 | 1,890 |
| **Rent-a-room relief** | 4,250 | 4,250 | 4,250 | 4,250 |

**Notes**

(1)    *Reduction in personal allowances* – From 2010–11 onwards, personal allowances are reduced if 'adjusted net income' (as defined in *ITA 2007, s 58*) exceeds £100,000, by £1 for every £2 above the £100,000 threshold, irrespective of the taxpayer's age (*ITA 2007, s 35*).

(2)    *Personal allowances, 2014–15* – Legislation will be introduced in the *Finance Act 2014* to set the personal allowance for 2014–15 at £10,000 for those born after 5 April 1948.

(3) *Abatement of age-related allowances* – The age-related personal and married couple's allowances are subject to abatement to the extent that income exceeds the income limit, by £1 for every £2 of income above the limit. For tax years before 2010–11, allowances cannot be reduced below the basic personal allowance (or minimum amount of married couple's allowance) (*ITA 2007, ss 36, 37, 45*).

However, from 2010–11 age-related personal allowances for individuals can be reduced below the basic personal allowance if income exceeds £100,000.

(4) *Phasing out of age-related allowances* – From 2013–14, the age-related personal allowances will not be increased and their availability will be restricted to people born on or before:

- 5 April 1948 for the allowance worth £10,500; and

- 5 April 1938 for the allowance worth £10,660.

(5) *Married couple's allowance* – The rate of tax relief for the married couple's allowance is 10% (*ITA 2007, s 45*). The marriage must have taken place before 5 December 2005 and at least one party to the marriage must have been born before 6 April 1935.

# HIGH INCOME CHILD BENEFIT CHARGE (HICBC)

(*ITEPA 2003, ss 681B–681H*)

The amount of the high income child benefit charge is the appropriate percentage of child benefit. The 'appropriate percentage' is the lower of:

(a) 100%; or

(b) $\dfrac{\text{ANI} - \text{L}}{\text{X}}\%$

Where: ANI = adjusted net income;

L = £50,000;

X = £100.

**Notes**

(1) *General* – the HICBC apples to taxpayers whose 'adjusted net income' (as defined) exceeds £50,000 in a tax year and they or their partner is in receipt of child benefit. If the adjusted net incomes of both partners exceed £50,000, the charge applies to the partner with the highest income. The charge applies in certain circumstances, where the child is not living with the claimant but with an individual whose income is over £50,000 (*ITEPA 2003, s 681D*).

(2) *Effect* – The amount of HICBC is 1% of child benefit for every £100 of adjusted net income above £50,000. The charge is 100% of child benefit where adjusted net income exceeds £60,000. The amounts and percentages used in the formula are rounded down if not whole numbers.

(3) *Commencement* – HICBC applies in respect of any child benefit received for the week beginning 7 January 2013 and subsequent weeks.

(4)    *Election* – A taxpayer may elect not to receive child benefit in order to avoid the HICBC (*SSAA 1992, s 13A; SSA(NI)A 1992, s 11*).

(5)    *Declaration* – Taxpayers who are subject to the HICBC must declare the child benefit received by themselves or their partner on their self-assessment tax return for the relevant tax year. If the taxpayer is not already registered for self-assessment he or she must register by 5 October 2013 for the 2012–13 tax year.

(6)    *Further information* – For rates of child benefit see **Chapter 18: State Benefits**. For further information, see www.hmrc.gov.uk/childbenefitcharge/.

# STATUTORY RESIDENCE TEST

(*FB 2013, cl 215, Sch 43*)

## Basic rule

(*FB 2013, Sch 43, paras 3, 4*)

An individual is resident in the UK for a tax year if:

*   the **automatic residence test** is met; or

*   the **sufficient ties test** is met

If neither test is met, the individual is not resident in the UK for that tax year.

## Automatic residence test

(*FB 2013, Sch 43, para 5*)

The automatic residence test is met for a tax year if the individual:

*   meets any of the **automatic UK tests**; and

*   meets none of the **automatic overseas tests**.

Thus the individual will be automatically non-UK resident for a tax year in which any of the automatic overseas tests is met.

## Automatic overseas tests

(*FB 2013, Sch 43, paras 11–16*)

There are five automatic overseas tests:

(1)    *Day count (16-day test)* – The individual was UK resident for one or more of the three preceding tax years, and spent less than 16 days in the UK in the tax year in question (nb this test does not apply if the individual dies in the tax year).

(2)    *Day count (46-day test)* – The individual was UK resident for none of the three preceding tax years, and spent less than 46 days in the UK in the tax year in question.

(3)    *Work* – The individual works 'sufficient hours overseas' for the tax year with no 'significant breaks from overseas work', *and* the number of days in the tax year on which more than three hours' work was done in the UK is less than 31, *and* less than 91 days (excluding 'deemed days' – see notes below) are spent in the UK in the tax year (NB this test does not apply to international transportation workers).

(4)   *Deceased individuals* – The individual dies during the tax year, and spent less than 46 days in the UK during that tax year, *and* was UK resident for neither of the two preceding tax years or alternatively was not UK resident in the preceding tax year and the tax year before that was a 'split year' by virtue of case 1, 2 or 3 (see note 5 below).

(5)   *Deceased individuals (alternative test)* – The individual dies during the tax year, *and* was not resident in the UK in either of the two preceding tax years due to meeting the third automatic overseas test for those years or was not UK resident for the preceding tax year due to meeting the third automatic overseas test for that year and the tax year before that was a 'split year' by virtue of case 1 (see note 5 below), *and* the individual would meet the third automatic test for the tax year if the third automatic overseas test was subject to 'relevant modifications' as defined.

## Automatic UK tests

(*FB 2013, Sch 43, paras 6–10*)

There are four automatic UK tests:

(1)   *Day count* – At least 183 days are spent in the UK in the tax year in question.

(2)   *Home* – This test is met broadly if the individual has a 'home' in the UK during the tax year, *and* presence at that home in the year exceeds certain limits (ie the individual 'spends a sufficient amount of time' there, as defined), *and* while the individual has that home there is a period of 91 consecutive days (at least 30 days of which falls within the tax year in question) when either there is no overseas home or the individual has one or more overseas homes in which the individual 'spends no more than a permitted amount of time' as defined.

(3)   *Work* – This test is met broadly if the individual works 'sufficient hours in the UK' over a period of 365 days, with no 'significant breaks from UK work' (both as defined), *and* all or part of that period falls within the tax year, *and* more than 75% of the total number of days in the 365 day period when the individual does more than three hours' work are days when more than three hours' work is done in the UK, *and* there is at least one day in the tax year when the individual does more than three hours' work in the UK (NB this test does not apply to international transportation workers).

(4)   *Deceased individuals* – An individual who dies during the tax year is UK resident if they were UK resident for each of the three preceding tax years by virtue of meeting the automatic UK residence test, *and* assuming they were not UK resident for the tax year in question the preceding tax year would not have been a 'split year' (see notes below), *and* they had a home in the UK when they died.

## Sufficient ties test

(*FB 2013, Sch 43, para 17*)

The sufficient ties test is met for a tax year if the individual:

- meets none of the automatic UK tests *and* none of the automatic overseas tests; but
- has 'sufficient UK ties' for that year.

## UK ties

(*FB 2013, Sch 43, paras 31–38*)

The UK ties for the purposes of the **sufficient UK ties** tests below are as follows:

(a)    Family tie;

(b)    Accommodation tie;

(c)    Work tie;

(d)    90-day tie;

(e)    Country tie.*

*This test only needs to be considered for a tax year if the individual was UK resident for one or more of the preceding three tax years.

## Sufficient UK ties

*(FA 2013, Sch 43, paras 18–20)*

*(a)    UK ties sufficient if individual was UK resident for one or more of the three tax years before the tax year under consideration*

| Days spent in the UK in the tax year under consideration | Number of UK ties sufficient |
|---|---|
| 16–45 days | At least 4 ties |
| 46–90 days | At least 3 ties |
| 91–120 days | At least 2 ties |
| Over 120 days | At least 1 tie |

*(b)    UK ties sufficient if individual was UK resident for none of the three tax years before the tax year under consideration*

| Days spent in the UK in the tax year under consideration | Number of UK ties sufficient |
|---|---|
| 46–90 days | All 4 ties |
| 91–120 days | At least 3 ties |
| Over 120 days | At least 2 ties |

**Notes**

(1)    *General* – The statutory residence test (SRT) legislation applies to individuals for income tax and capital gains tax purposes, and for inheritance tax and corporation tax purposes to the extent that an individual's residence status is relevant to them. As well as determining whether individuals are resident in the UK for those purposes, there are also provisions about 'split years' and periods when individuals are temporarily non-resident.

(2)    *Deceased persons* – The 'sufficient UK ties' tests also apply to individuals who die during the tax year under consideration, but subject to specified modifications in some cases (*FB 2013, Sch 43, para 20*).

(3)    *'Deemed' days in the UK* – If an individual is not present in the UK at the end of a day, that day does not generally count as a day spent in the UK. However, this is subject to a 'deeming rule', which applies if certain conditions are satisfied. The effect of this deeming rule is broadly to treat subsequent 'qualifying days' (ie when the individual was present in the UK at some point during the day without being present at the end of that day) in the tax year over a 30 day threshold as days spent in the UK (nb the deeming rule does not apply for the purposes of deciding if there

is a 90 day tie when determining if there are 3 UK ties, which is a condition for the deeming rule to apply) (*FB 2013, Sch 43, paras 22, 23*).

(4)  *Definitions* – Key concepts including 'home', 'work', 'full-time work' and the above 'UK ties' are defined in the SRT legislation (*FB 2013, Sch 43, paras 21–30*).

(5)  *Split-year treatment* – An individual is generally either UK resident or non-UK resident for a full tax year under the SRT. However, if an individual either leaves the UK to live or work abroad, or comes from abroad to live or work in the UK, the tax year may be split into two parts (ie a UK part and an overseas part) in certain circumstances (*FB 2013, Sch 43, Pt 3*). The individual is charged to UK tax on the UK part as a UK resident, and (for most purposes) on the overseas part as a non-UK resident. There are special charging rules for income and gains if split-year treatment applies. The provisions specify eight sets of circumstances ('cases') where an individual who is UK resident for a tax year may be eligible for split year treatment. Cases 1 to 3 involve actual or deemed departure from the UK, and cases 4 to 8 involve actual or deemed arrival in the UK. The cases broadly deal with the following circumstances:

*Leaving the UK*

Case 1 – Starting to work overseas (ie 'satisfies the overseas work criteria' as defined);

Case 2 – Accompanying partner (eg spouse);

Case 3 – Leaving the UK to live abroad;

*Coming to the UK*

Case 4 – Coming to live in the UK;

Case 5 – Starting to work in the UK (ie the taxpayer works 'sufficient hours in the UK');

Case 6 – Coming to the UK after work overseas;

Case 7 – Accompanying partner; and

Case 8 – Having a home in the UK.

Split-year treatment does not apply to individuals acting as personal representatives, and only applies in a limited way to individuals acting as trustees of a settlement. Nor are the split-year treatment rules intended to affect whether an individual is regarded as UK resident for the purposes of any double taxation arrangements (*FB 2013, Sch 43, paras 41–42*).

(6)  *Commencement* – The SRT generally has effect for the tax year 2013–14 and later years (*FB 2013, Sch 43, para 151*).

(7)  *Transitional provisions and election* – Transitional provisions apply if an individual is considering residence status for the tax years 2013–14, 2014–15 or 2015–16 (or the application of the split-year rules to those years), and it is necessary for that purpose to determine the individual's residence status for a tax year before 2013–14 (a 'pre-commencement tax year'). The individual's residence status for a pre-commencement tax year is normally determined in accordance with the rules applicable for that tax year, as opposed to the SRT. However, the individual may make a written election to HMRC to determine his or her residence status for a pre-commencement year in accordance with the SRT instead. The election must be made no later than the first anniversary of the tax year to which it applies. The election is irrevocable (*FB 2013, Sch 43, para 152*).

(8) *Further guidance* – HMRC published a draft guidance note on the SRT on 18 December 2012, based on the draft legislation published on 11 December 2012 (www.hmrc.gov.uk/budget-updates/11dec12/stat-res-test-note.pdf). Further guidance is expected to follow, based on the final legislation as enacted by Parliament. The Government produced an interactive online tool for determining residence status (www.hm-treasury.gov.uk/consult_statutory_residence_test.htm) as part of the consultation process for the SRT. However, it is not presently known whether the online tool will be updated or provide a definitive answer as to an individual's residence status.

# CAP ON INCOME TAX RELIEFS

*(FB 2013, cl 16, Sch 3)*

| Title and description of relief | Legislation |
| --- | --- |
| Trade loss relief against general income (aka 'sideways loss relief') | *ITA 2007, s 64* |
| Early years trade losses relief – available in the first four years of the trade, profession or vocation | *ITA 2007 , s 72* |
| Post-cessation trade relief – for qualifying payments/events within seven years of the permanent cessation of the trade. | *ITA 2007, s 96* |
| Property loss relief against general income – property business losses arising from capital allowances or agricultural expenses | *ITA 2007, s 120* |
| Post-cessation property relief – for qualifying payments/events within seven years of the permanent cessation of the UK property business | *ITA 2007, s 125* |
| Employment loss relief | ITA 2007, s 128 |
| Former employees deduction for liabilities | *ITEPA 2003, s 555* |
| Share loss relief, see note 2 | *ITA 2007, s 131* |
| Losses on deeply discounted securities – only for losses on gilt strips and listed securities held since 26 March 2003 | *ITTOIA 2005 ss 446–488, 453–456* |
| Qualifying loan interest – on loans to buy an interest in certain types of company, or in a partnership | *ITA 2007, Pt 8 Ch 1* |

**Notes**

(1) *General* – The cap is applied on the above income tax reliefs claimed by individuals with effect from 6 April 2013. For anyone seeking to claim more than £50,000 in reliefs, the cap is set at the greater of £50,000 and 25% of adjusted total income *(ITA 2007, s 24A)*.

(2) *Exclusions for EIS and SEIS* – The cap does not apply to share loss relief where the shares are qualifying EIS or SEIS shares *(ITA 2007, s 24A(7)(d))*.

(3) *Overlap relief* – The cap does not apply to overlap relief allowed under *ITTOIA 2005, s 205 or 220*.

(4) *Business premises renovation* – The cap does not apply to business premises renovation allowance under *CAA 2001, Pt 3A*.

(5) *Same trade* – The cap does not apply to deductions for trade or property loss relief or post-cessation trade or property relief made from profits of the same trade or property business *(ITA 2007, s 24A(7)(b))*.

## COMMONWEALTH AND LONDON GAMES

*Finance Act 2013* will include provisions for a limited tax exemption in connection with the Glasgow 2014 Commonwealth Games and the London Anniversary Games. UK resident athletes will pay income tax in the UK as normal. Non-resident competitors will be exempt from UK tax on any income arising from their appearance in the relevant games, but will remain liable to tax in their home country (*Budget, 20 March 2013*).

In a change with effect from 1 July 2012 that applies more generally to payments or transfers made to non-UK resident entertainers, sportspersons or people connected with them in relation to activities performed in the UK, the limit below which the aggregate of such payments may be made without deduction of income tax at source is increased from £1,000 to the amount of the personal allowance for income tax (*SI 2012/1359*).

## SELF ASSESSMENT TAX RETURN FILING DATES: INDIVIDUALS AND TRUSTEES

*(TMA 1970, ss 8, 8A)*

| Type of tax return | Filing date |
|---|---|
| Paper returns (non-electronic) | 31 October following the end of the tax year (*TMA 1970, ss 8(1D)(a), 8A(1B)(a)*) |
| Electronic returns | 31 January following the end of the tax year (*ss 8(1D)(b), 8A(1B)(b)*). |
| Return (or notice to file) issued after 31 July but before 31 October following the end of the tax year | 3 months from the date of the return/ notice for paper returns, or 31 January for electronic returns (*TMA 1970, ss 8(1F), 8A(1D)*). |
| Return (or notice to file) issued after 31 October following the end of the tax year | 3 months from the date of the return/notice (whether paper or electronic) (*TMA 1970, ss 8(1G), 8A(1E)*). |

**Notes**

(1) *PAYE coding* – Individuals filing returns electronically who owe tax of less than £3,000 and wish HMRC to collect the liability through a reduction in their PAYE coding for the next tax year must file their tax return online by 30 December, instead of 31 January.

(2) *Partnerships* – The above filing dates also apply to partnerships with individual members (*TMA 1970, s 12AA(4)–(4E)*). Separate provisions apply in the case of partnerships involving one or more companies (*TMA 1970, s 12AA(5)–(5E)*).

(3) *Must be paper* – The following tax returns cannot be submitted online and must be submitted in paper form by 31 January following the tax year end:

- SA700 – Non-resident Company Tax Return
- SA970 – Trustees of Registered Pension Schemes
- SA200 – Short tax return

(4) *Needs commercial software* – The following types of tax return and supplementary pages to the SA100 cannot be submitted online using the HMRC free software so will require commercial software:

- SA800 – partnership tax return
- SA900 – Trust and estate return
- SA102M – Ministers of religion
- SA102MP – Members of Westminster Parliament
- SA102MLA – members of Northern Ireland Assembly
- SA102MSP – Members of Scottish Parliament
- SA102WAM – Members of the National Assembly for Wales
- SA103L – Lloyds underwriters
- SA107 – Trust income
- SA109 – Residence and remittance basis

# SELF ASSESSMENT: DUE DATES FOR PAYMENT OF TAX

*(TMA 1970, ss 59A, 59B)*

*1st payment on account* – On or before 31 January in the tax year.

*2nd payment on account* – On or before 31 July following the end of the tax year.

*Balancing payment* – On or before 31 January next following the tax year of assessment. This is also the due date for any capital gains tax (for which payments on account are not required). However, if a return (or a notice to file) was not issued until after 31 October following the end of the tax year and the taxpayer has notified chargeability by 5 October, the due date for the final payment (including any capital gains tax) is 3 months from the issue of the return/notice *(TMA 1970, s 59B(3), (4))*.

**Notes**

(1)   Payments on account are not required where:
- More than 80% of the previous year's tax liability was covered by tax deducted at source and dividend tax credits; or
- the previous year's liability (net of tax deducted at source) was less than £1,000 *(SI 1996/1654, SI 2008/838)*.

# SELF ASSESSMENT PENALTY PROVISIONS

See **Chapter 17**.

## Interest payable on overdue income tax, national insurance contributions and capital gains tax etc

| Period from | Rate % |
|---|---|
| 29 September 2009 | 3.0 |
| 24 March 2009 to 28 September 2009 | 2.5 |
| 27 January 2009 to 23 March 2009 | 3.5 |

*continued*

11

| Period from | Rate |
|---|---|
| | % |
| 6 January 2009 to 26 January 2009 | 4.5 |
| 6 December 2008 to 5 January 2009 | 5.5 |
| 6 November 2008 to 5 December 2008 | 6.5 |
| 6 January 2008 to 5 November 2008 | 7.5 |
| 6 August 2007 to 5 January 2008 | 8.5 |
| 6 September 2006 to 5 August 2007 | 7.5 |
| 6 September 2005 to 5 September 2006 | 6.5 |
| 6 September 2004 to 5 September 2005 | 7.5 |
| 6 December 2003 to 5 September 2004 | 6.5 |
| 6 August 2003 to 5 December 2003 | 5.5 |
| 6 November 2001 to 5 August 2003 | 6.5 |
| 6 May 2001 to 5 November 2001 | 7.5 |
| 6 February 2000 to 5 May 2001 | 8.5 |

**Note**

The interest regime in *FA 2009, ss 101–103* ('Late payment interest on sums to be paid by HMRC', 'Repayment interest on sums to be paid by HMRC' and 'Rates of interest') applies with effect from 31 October 2011, for the purposes of self-assessment payments and repayments (*SI 2011/701*).

## Rates of interest on repayments of income tax, national insurance contributions and capital gains tax etc*

| Period from | Rate |
|---|---|
| | % |
| 29 September 2009 | 0.50 |
| 27 January 2009 to 28 September 2009 | 0.00 |
| 6 January 2009 to 26 January 2009 | 0.75 |
| 6 December 2008 to 5 January 2009 | 1.50 |
| 6 November 2008 to 5 December 2008 | 2.25 |
| 6 January 2008 to 5 November 2008 | 3.00 |
| 6 August 2007 to 5 January 2008 | 4.00 |
| 6 September 2006 to 5 August 2007 | 3.00 |
| 6 September 2005 to 5 September 2006 | 2.25 |
| 6 September 2004 to 5 September 2005 | 3.00 |
| 6 December 2003 to 5 September 2004 | 2.25 |
| 6 August 2003 to 5 December 2003 | 1.50 |
| 6 November 2001 to 5 August 2003 | 2.25 |
| 6 May 2001 to 5 November 2001 | 3.00 |
| 6 February 2000 to 5 May 2001 | 4.00 |

* See note to table '**Interest payable on overdue income tax, national insurance contributions and capital gains tax etc**' above.

# TIME LIMITS – ASSESSMENTS, CLAIMS ETC

## Normal time limits (individuals) – Direct taxes

*(TMA 1970, ss 34, 43; FA 2008, s 118, Sch 39)*

| Tax year | Claim by |
|----------|----------|
| 2006–07 | 5 April 2011 |
| 2007–08 | 5 April 2012 |
| 2008–09 | 5 April 2013 |
| 2009–10 | 5 April 2014 |
| 2010–11 | 5 April 2015 |
| 2011–12 | 5 April 2016 |
| 2012–13 | 5 April 2017 |

**Notes**

(1) Claims or elections should be made on the tax return or by an amendment to the return. Except where otherwise specified, a relief claim for income tax and capital gains purposes must be made within four years after the end of the tax year (or accounting period, for companies). This time limit generally applies for direct tax purposes from 1 April 2010.

(2) The time limit for claims by individuals prior to April 2010 was generally within five years from 31 January following the year of assessment to which it relates (unless otherwise specified).

# DISCOVERY ASSESSMENTS

*(TMA 1970, ss 29, 34, 36)*

## Time limits

| Circumstances | Time Limit |
|---------------|------------|
| Loss of tax not due to careless or deliberate behaviour <br> *(TMA 1970, s 34)* | 4 years from the end of the year of assessment |
| Loss of tax due to careless behaviour of person or agent etc <br> *(TMA 1970, s 36(1), (1B))* | 6 years from the end of the year of assessment |
| Loss of tax due to deliberate behaviour by person or agent etc <br><br> *(TMA 1970, s 36(1A), (1B))* | 20 years from the end of the year of assessment |

**Notes**

(1) *General* – The above time limits were introduced by *FA 2008, Sch 39* ('Time limits for assessments, claims etc'). For periods prior to the introduction of the above time limits (in *SI 2009/403*), the normal time limit for assessments is five years after 31 January next following the year of assessment. For 'fraudulent or negligent

13

conduct' the time limit is 20 years after 31 January next following the year of assessment.

(2)    *Scope* – Separate 'discovery' assessment provisions and time limits apply in certain circumstances, such as the following:

- Failure to provide information about an avoidance scheme;

- Failure to notify liability to the tax (*TMA 1970, ss 34, 118(2); ss 36(1A), (1B)*); and

- Discovery assessment on personal representatives of a deceased person in respect of years/periods up to the date of death (*TMA 1970, 40(1), (2)*).

A table of assessment time limits for income tax and capital gains tax purposes is included in HMRC's Compliance Handbook (at CH56100).

# Expenses and benefits

## COMPANY CAR BENEFIT CHARGES
*(ITEPA 2003, s 139; FA 2010, ss 58, 59; FA 2011, s 51)*

### Table of appropriate percentages from 6 April 2012 to 5 April 2014

| $CO_2$ emissions (g/km) not exceeding (see Note 1 below) | 2013–14 | 2012–13 |
|---|---|---|
| 0 | 0 | 0 |
| 75 | 5 | 5 |
| 94 | 10 | 10 |
| 99 | 11 | 10 |
| 100 | 12 | 11 |
| 105 | 13 | 12 |
| 110 | 14 | 13 |
| 115 | 15 | 14 |
| 120 | 16 | 15 |
| 125 | 17 | 16 |
| 130 | 18 | 17 |
| 135 | 19 | 18 |
| 140 | 20 | 19 |
| 145 | 21 | 20 |
| 150 | 22 | 21 |
| 155 | 23 | 22 |
| 160 | 24 | 23 |
| 165 | 25 | 24 |
| 170 | 26 | 25 |
| 175 | 27 | 26 |
| 180 | 28 | 27 |
| 185 | 29 | 28 |
| 190 | 30 | 29 |
| 195 | 31 | 30 |
| 200 | 32 | 31 |
| 205 | 33 | 32 |
| 210 | 34 | 33 |
| 215 | 35 | 34 |
| 220 and above | 35 | 35 |

**Notes**

(1)  *Round down* – Before applying the appropriate percentage listed above, the emissions figure should be rounded down to the nearest multiple of five, except that rounding does not apply to cars with emissions below 95g/km in 2013–14 (100g/km in 2012–13).

(2)  *Diesel cars* – These are subject to the 3% supplement up to a maximum of 35% (see **Diesel cars** below).

## Table of appropriate percentages from 6 April 2014 to 5 April 2017

| $CO_2$ emissions (g/km) | 2016–17 Petrol and Diesel | 2015–16 Petrol | 2015–16 Diesel | 2014–15 Petrol | 2014–15 Diesel |
|---|---|---|---|---|---|
| 0 | N/A | N/A | N/A | 0 | 0 |
| 0–50 | 7 | 5 | 8 | N/A | N/A |
| 51–75* | 11 | 9 | 12 | 5 | 8 |
| 76–94 | 15 | 13 | 16 | 11 | 14 |
| 95–99 | 16 | 14 | 17 | 12 | 15 |
| 100–104 | 17 | 15 | 18 | 13 | 16 |
| 105–109 | 18 | 16 | 19 | 14 | 17 |
| 110–114 | 19 | 17 | 20 | 15 | 18 |
| 115–119 | 20 | 18 | 21 | 16 | 19 |
| 120–124 | 21 | 19 | 22 | 17 | 20 |
| 125–129 | 22 | 20 | 23 | 18 | 21 |
| 130–134 | 23 | 21 | 24 | 19 | 22 |
| 135–139 | 24 | 22 | 25 | 20 | 23 |
| 140–144 | 25 | 23 | 26 | 21 | 24 |
| 145–149 | 26 | 24 | 27 | 22 | 25 |
| 150–154 | 27 | 25 | 28 | 23 | 26 |
| 155–159 | 28 | 26 | 29 | 24 | 27 |
| 160–164 | 29 | 27 | 30 | 25 | 28 |
| 165–169 | 30 | 28 | 31 | 26 | 29 |
| 170–174 | 31 | 29 | 32 | 27 | 30 |
| 175–179 | 32 | 30 | 33 | 28 | 31 |
| 180–184 | 33 | 31 | 34 | 29 | 32 |
| 185–189 | 34 | 32 | 35 | 30 | 33 |
| 190–194 | 35 | 33 | 36 | 31 | 34 |
| 195–199 | 36 | 34 | 37 | 32 | 35 |
| 200–204 | 37 | 35 | 37 | 33 | 35 |
| 205–209 | 37 | 36 | 37 | 34 | 35 |
| 210 and above | 37 | 37 | 37 | 35 | 35 |

*Band is 1–75 for 2014–15.

**Notes**

(1)  *For 2014–15* – The appropriate percentage for company cars emitting more $CO_2$ than 75g/km is increased by one percentage point to a maximum of 35% (*FA 2012, s 17*).

(2)  *For 2015–16* – Two new appropriate percentage bands are introduced for company cars emitting 0–50g/km of $CO_2$ and for emissions of 51–75g/km of $CO_2$ (*Budget, 20 March 2013*).

(3)  *For 2016–17* – The appropriate percentages of list price for the 0–50g/km will be 7%, and for the 51–75g/km band the appropriate percentage will be 11%. All other appropriate percentages will rise by two percentage points to a maximum of 37%. The 3% diesel supplement is removed (*Budget, 20 March 2013*).

(4)  *Future changes – Finance Bills* for 2014 to 2016 will provide that for 2017–18 there will be a three percentage point differential between the 0–50 and 51–75g/km bands and between the 51–75 and 76–94g/km bands. In 2018–19 and 2019–20 there will be a two percentage point differential between those bands (*Budget, 20 March 2013*).

## Table of appropriate percentages from 6 April 2005 to 5 April 2012

(*ITEPA 2003, s 139*)

| CO$_2$ emissions g/km | 2011–12 | 2010–11 | 2008–09 to 2009–10 | 2005–06 to 2007–08 |
|---|---|---|---|---|
| 75 | 5% | 5% | N/A | N/A |
| 120 | 10% | 10% | 10% | 15% |
| 125 | 15% | 15% | 15% | 15% |
| 130 | 16% | 15% | 15% | 15% |
| 135 | 17% | 16% | 15% | 15% |
| 140 | 18% | 17% | 16% | 16% |
| 145 | 19% | 18% | 17% | 17% |
| 150 | 20% | 19% | 18% | 18% |
| 155 | 21% | 20% | 19% | 19% |
| 160 | 22% | 21% | 20% | 20% |
| 165 | 23% | 22% | 21% | 21% |
| 170 | 24% | 23% | 22% | 22% |
| 175 | 25% | 24% | 23% | 23% |
| 180 | 26% | 25% | 24% | 24% |
| 185 | 27% | 26% | 25% | 25% |
| 190 | 28% | 27% | 26% | 26% |
| 195 | 29% | 28% | 27% | 27% |
| 200 | 30% | 29% | 28% | 28% |
| 205 | 31% | 30% | 29% | 29% |
| 210 | 32% | 31% | 30% | 30% |
| 215 | 33% | 32% | 31% | 31% |
| 220 | 34% | 33% | 32% | 32% |
| 225 | 35% | 34% | 33% | 33% |
| 230 | 35% | 35% | 34% | 34% |
| 235 or more | 35% | 35% | 35% | 35% |

## Notes

(1)  *General* – The income tax charge is based on percentage of car's list price graduated according to the level of $CO_2$ emissions measured in grams per kilometre (g/km) and rounded down to the nearest 5g/km.

17

(2)   *Ultra-low emissions* – For the appropriate percentages in 2010–11 and later years, see **Ultra-low emission cars** below.

(3)   *Car not available* – The car benefit is proportionately reduced if the company car is only available for part of the year, where the benefit ceases part way through a tax year (and is not reinstated in that year), or where the benefit of the company car is shared (*ITEPA 2003, ss 143, 148*).

## Diesel cars

*(ITEPA 2003, s 141)*

There is a 3% supplement on diesel cars to a maximum of 35%, subject to the following:

- before 5 April 2006, no supplement applies to diesel cars first registered before 1 January 2006 that met the Euro IV emissions standard;

- from 6 April 2006, the supplement applies to all diesel cars first registered from 1 January 2006 (EIM24810);

- from 6 April 2011, the diesel supplement applies to all diesel cars (as to diesel supplements generally, see EIM24855).

- future *Finance Bills* will provide that the 3% supplement for diesel cars will be abolished from 6 April 2016 (Budget, 21 March 2012).

## Qualifying low emissions cars (QUALECs)

*(ITEPA 2003, s 139(3A); FA 2010, s 59)*

(1)   From 6 April 2008 to 5 April 2012 a lower tax charge applies if the car is a QUALEC.

(2)   A car is a QUALEC if its $CO_2$ emissions figure does not exceed the qualifying limit for the year (120g/km from 2008–09).

(3)   Where the car qualifies as a QUALEC, the appropriate percentage is 10% (for petrol cars, but with a 3% supplement for diesels). See below as to ultra-low emission cars.

## Ultra-low emission cars

*(ITEPA 2003, s 139; FA 2010, s 59)*

From 6 April 2010 to 5 April 2015, a reduced appropriate percentage of 5% applies for company cars with an approved $CO_2$ emissions figure not exceeding 75g/km (*ITEPA 2003, s 139(1B)*).

## Alternative fuel cars (from 6 April 2011 to 6 April 2015)

*(ITEPA 2003, ss 137, 140; SI 2001/1123 as amended; EIM24730)*

| Type of car | Discounted charge |
| --- | --- |
| Zero-emission cars (including Electric only) | Appropriate percentage of list price (no adjustment) |

| Type of car | Discounted charge |
|---|---|
| Diesel cars (all Euro standards) | Appropriate percentage of list price plus 3% supplement |
| All other | Appropriate percentage of list price (no adjustment) |

**Notes**

(1) *Zero percentage* – This applies to cars which cannot produce $CO_2$ emissions under any circumstances when driven, for tax years 2010–11 to 2014–15 inclusive (*ITEPA 2003, s 140(3A)*).

(2) *Simplified arrangements* – These apply for alternative fuels apply from 2011–12 (*SI 2010/695*). The 3% diesel supplement will apply to all diesel powered cars until 6 April 2016, and alternative fuel reductions generally cease to be available, although see note 1 above regarding cars which cannot produce $CO_2$ emissions, such as electric cars (see EIM24730).

## Cars registered with no $CO_2$ emission figures

(*ITEPA 2003, ss 140–142; see also EIM24950, EIM24975*)

| Cylinder capacity of car | Registered on or after 1 January 1998 | Registered before 1 January 1998 |
|---|---|---|
| 1,400 cc or less | 15% | 15% |
| Over 1,400 cc to 2,000 cc | 25% | 22% |
| Over 2,000 cc | 35% | 32% |

**Note**

A 3% addition applies to diesel cars to a maximum of 35%.

## Fuel benefit charges

(*ITEPA 2003, ss 149–153*)

*Car fuel benefit multiplier*

| Tax year | £ | Tax year | £ |
|---|---|---|---|
| 2013–14 | 21,100 | 2009–10 | 16,900 |
| 2012–13 | 20,200 | 2008–09 | 16,900 |
| 2011–12 | 18,800 | 2007–08 | 14,400 |
| 2010–11 | 18,000 | 2006–07 | 14,400 |

**Notes**

(1) *Nil fuel benefit* applies in the following circumstances:

- if the employee is required to make good the full cost of all fuel provided for private use and actually does so;

- if fuel is made available only for business travel (*ITEPA 2003, s 151*);

(2)  *Reductions* – The fuel benefit is proportionately reduced if the company car is only available for part of the year, where the benefit ceases part way through a tax year (and is not reinstated in that year), or where the benefit of the company car is shared (*ITEPA 2003, ss 152–153*).

(3)  *Cash equivalent* – The benefit charge for fuel provided for private motoring is calculated by applying the appropriate percentage to the relevant multiplier in the table above. The 'appropriate percentage' is broadly that used to calculate the car benefit (*ITEPA 2003, s 150*). The following tables show the resulting cash equivalent of the car fuel benefit.

| $CO_2$ emissions (g/km) not exceeding | Petrol | | Diesel | |
|---|---|---|---|---|
| | **2012–13** | **2013–14** | **2012–13** | **2013–14** |
| | £ | £ | £ | £ |
| 0 | 0 | 0 | 0 | 0 |
| 75 | 1,010 | 1,055 | 1,616 | 1,688 |
| 94 | 2,020 | 2,110 | 2,626 | 2,743 |
| 99 | 2020 | 2,321 | 2,626 | 2,954 |
| 100 | 2,222 | 2,532 | 2,828 | 3,165 |
| 105 | 2,424 | 2,743 | 3,030 | 3,376 |
| 110 | 2,626 | 2,954 | 3,232 | 3,587 |
| 115 | 2,828 | 3,165 | 3,434 | 3,798 |
| 120 | 3,030 | 3,376 | 3,636 | 4,009 |
| 125 | 3,232 | 3,587 | 3,838 | 4,220 |
| 130 | 3,434 | 3,798 | 4,040 | 4,431 |
| 135 | 3,636 | 4,009 | 4,242 | 4,642 |
| 140 | 3,838 | 4,220 | 4,444 | 4,853 |
| 145 | 4,040 | 4,431 | 4,646 | 5,064 |
| 150 | 4,242 | 4,642 | 4,848 | 5,275 |
| 155 | 4,444 | 4,853 | 5,050 | 5,486 |
| 160 | 4,646 | 5,064 | 5,252 | 5,697 |
| 165 | 4,848 | 5,275 | 5,454 | 5,908 |
| 170 | 5,050 | 5,486 | 5,656 | 6,119 |
| 175 | 5,252 | 5,697 | 5,858 | 6,330 |
| 180 | 5,454 | 5,908 | 6,060 | 6,541 |
| 185 | 5,656 | 6,119 | 6,262 | 6,752 |
| 190 | 5,858 | 6,330 | 6,464 | 6,963 |
| 195 | 6,060 | 6,541 | 6,666 | 7,174 |
| 200 | 6,262 | 6,752 | 6,868 | 7,385 |
| 205 | 6,464 | 6,963 | 7,070 | 7,385 |
| 210 | 6,666 | 7,174 | 7,070 | 7,385 |
| 215 | 6,868 | 7,385 | 7,070 | 7,385 |
| 220 and above | 7,070 | 7,385 | 7,070 | 7,385 |

| CO₂ emission grams per kilometre | Petrol | | | Diesel | | |
|---|---|---|---|---|---|---|
| | **2011–12** £ | **2010–11** £ | **2009–10** £ | **2011–12** £ | **2010–11** £ | **2009–10** £ |
| 120 | 1,880 | 1,800 | 1,690 | 2,444 | 2,340 | 2,197 |
| 125 | 2,820 | 2,700 | 2,535 | 3,384 | 3,240 | 3,042 |
| 130 | 3,008 | 2,700 | 2,535 | 3,572 | 3,240 | 3,042 |
| 135 | 3,196 | 2,880 | 2,535 | 3,760 | 3,420 | 3,042 |
| 140 | 3,384 | 3,060 | 2,704 | 3,948 | 3,600 | 3,211 |
| 145 | 3,572 | 3,240 | 2,873 | 4,136 | 3,780 | 3,380 |
| 150 | 3,760 | 3,420 | 3,042 | 4,324 | 3,960 | 3,549 |
| 155 | 3,948 | 3,600 | 3,211 | 4,512 | 4,140 | 3,718 |
| 160 | 4,136 | 3,780 | 3,380 | 4,700 | 4,320 | 3,887 |
| 165 | 4,324 | 3,960 | 3,549 | 4,888 | 4,500 | 4,056 |
| 170 | 4,512 | 4,140 | 3,718 | 5,076 | 4,680 | 4,225 |
| 175 | 4,700 | 4,320 | 3,887 | 5,264 | 4,860 | 4,394 |
| 180 | 4,888 | 4,500 | 4,056 | 5,452 | 5,040 | 4,563 |
| 185 | 5,076 | 4,680 | 4,225 | 5,640 | 5,220 | 4,732 |
| 190 | 5,264 | 4,860 | 4,394 | 5,828 | 5,400 | 4,901 |
| 195 | 5,452 | 5,040 | 4,563 | 6,016 | 5,580 | 5,070 |
| 200 | 5,640 | 5,220 | 4,732 | 6,204 | 5,760 | 5,239 |
| 205 | 5,828 | 5,400 | 4,901 | 6,392 | 5,940 | 5,408 |
| 210 | 6,016 | 5,580 | 5,070 | 6,580 | 6,120 | 5,577 |
| 215 | 6,204 | 5,760 | 5,239 | 6,580 | 6,300 | 5,746 |
| 220 | 6,392 | 5,940 | 5,408 | 6,580 | 6,300 | 5,915 |
| 225 | 6,580 | 6,120 | 5,577 | 6,580 | 6,300 | 5,915 |
| 230 | 6,580 | 6,300 | 5,746 | 6,580 | 6,300 | 5,915 |
| 235 | 6,580 | 6,300 | 5,915 | 6,580 | 6,300 | 5,915 |

## Mileage allowances

*Advisory fuel rates for company cars*

(www.hmrc.gov.uk/cars/fuel_company_cars.htm)

| Engine size | Rate per Mile | | |
|---|---|---|---|
| | **Petrol** | **Diesel** | **LPG** |
| **From 1 March 2013** | | | |
| Up to 1,400 cc | 15p | | 10p |
| 1,401–2,000 cc | 18p | | 12p |
| Over 2,000 cc | 26p | | 18p |
| Up to 1,600 cc | | 13p | |
| 1,601–2,000 cc | | 15p | |
| Over 2,000 cc | | 18p | |
| **From 1 December 2012** | | | |
| Up to 1,400 cc | 15p | | 11p |
| 1,401–2,000 cc | 18p | | 13p |
| Over 2,000 cc | 26p | | 18p |

*continued*

| Engine size | Rate per Mile | | |
|---|---|---|---|
| | **Petrol** | **Diesel** | **LPG** |
| Up to 1,600 cc | | 12p | |
| 1,601–2000 cc | | 15p | |
| Over 2,000 cc | | 18p | |
| **From 1 September 2012** | | | |
| Up to 1,400 cc | 15p | | 10p |
| 1,401–2,000 cc | 18p | | 13p |
| Over 2,000 cc | 26p | | 17p |
| Up to 1,600 cc | | 12p | |
| 1,601–2,000 cc | | 15p | |
| Over 2,000 cc | | 18p | |
| **From 1 June 2012** | | | |
| Up to 1,400 cc | 15p | | 11p |
| 1,401–2,000 cc | 18p | | 13p |
| Over 2,000 cc | 26p | | 19p |
| Up to 1,600 cc | | 12p | |
| 1,601–2000cc | | 15p | |
| Over 2,000 cc | | 18p | |
| **From 1 March 2012** | | | |
| Up to 1,400 cc | 15p | | 10p |
| 1,401–2,000 cc | 18p | | 12p |
| Over 2,000 cc | 26p | | 18p |
| Up to 1,600 cc | | 13p | |
| 1,601–2,000cc | | 15p | |
| Over 2,000 cc | | 19p | |
| **From 1 December 2011** | | | |
| Up to 1,400 cc | 15p | | 10p |
| 1,401–2,000 cc | 18p | | 12p |
| Over 2,000 cc | 26p | | 18p |
| Up to 1,600 cc | | 12p | |
| 1,601–2,000 cc | | 15p | |
| Over 2,000 cc | | 18p | |
| **From 1 September 2011** | | | |
| Up to 1,400 cc | 15p | | 11p |
| 1,401–2,000 cc | 18p | | 12p |
| Over 2,000 cc | 26p | | 18p |
| Up to 1,600 cc | | 12p | |
| 1,601–2,000 cc | | 15p | |
| Over 2,000 cc | | 18p | |
| **From 1 June 2011** | | | |
| Up to 1,400 cc | 15p | | 11p |
| 1,401–2,000 cc | 18p | | 13p |
| Over 2,000 cc | 26p | | 18p |
| Up to 1,600 cc | | 12p | |
| 1,601–2,000 cc | | 15p | |
| Over 2,000 cc | | 18p | |

| Engine size | Rate per Mile | | |
|---|---|---|---|
| | **Petrol** | **Diesel** | **LPG** |
| **From 1 March 2011** | | | |
| 1,400 cc or less | 14p | 13p | 10p |
| 1,401–2,000 cc | 16p | 13p | 12p |
| Over 2,000 cc | 23p | 16p | 17p |
| **From 1 December 2010** | | | |
| 1,400 cc or less | 13p | 12p | 9p |
| 1,401–2,000 cc | 15p | 12p | 10p |
| Over 2,000 cc | 21p | 15p | 15p |
| **From 1 June 2010** | | | |
| 1,400 cc or less | 12p | 11p | 8p |
| 1,401–2,000 cc | 15p | 11p | 10p |
| Over 2,000 cc | 21p | 16p | 14p |
| **From 1 December 2009** | | | |
| 1,400 cc or less | 11p | 11p | 7p |
| 1,401–2,000 cc | 14p | 11p | 8p |
| Over 2,000 cc | 20p | 14p | 12p |
| **From 1 July 2009** | | | |
| 1,400 cc or less | 10p | 10p | 7p |
| 1,401–2,000 cc | 12p | 10p | 8p |
| Over 2,000 cc | 18p | 13p | 12p |
| **From 1 January 2009** | | | |
| 1,400 cc or less | 10p | 11p | 7p |
| 1,401–2,000 cc | 12p | 11p | 9p |
| Over 2,000 cc | 17p | 14p | 12p |
| **From 1 July 2008** | | | |
| 1,400 cc or less | 12p | 13p | 7p |
| 1,401 cc to 2,000 cc | 15p | 13p | 9p |
| Over 2,000 cc | 21p | 17p | 13p |
| **From 1 January 2008** | | | |
| 1,400 cc or less | 11p | 11p | 7p |
| 1,401–2,000 cc | 13p | 11p | 8p |
| Over 2,000 cc | 19p | 14p | 11p |

**Notes**

(1)   *Quarterly updates* – Since March 2011 the advisory fuel rates are reviewed quarterly and updated as necessary from 1 March, 1 June, 1 September and 1 December.

(2)   *Hybrids* – Petrol hybrid cars are treated as petrol cars for this purpose.

(3)   *VAT* – HMRC accept these figures for VAT purposes, ie a business can reclaim the VAT element on the amount attributable to fuel of mileage allowances paid to employees or subcontractors.

(4)   *Earlier years* – Earlier advisory fuel rates can be found at www.hmrc.gov.uk/cars/ advisory-fuel-archive-2002-07.htm

*Approved mileage allowance payments (AMAPs) rates for private vehicles*
*(ITEPA 2003, ss 229–232, 235, 236)*

| | Rate per business mile | | | |
| | From 2011–12 | | 2002–3 to 2010–11 | |
| | First 10,000 miles | Over 10,000 miles | First 10,000 miles | Over 10,000 miles |
|---|---|---|---|---|
| Cars | 45p | 25p | 40p | 25p |
| Allowance for each passenger making the same trip | 5p | 5p | 5p | 5p |
| Motorcycles | 24p | 24p | 24p | 24p |
| Bicycles | 20p | 20p | 20p | 20p |

**Notes**

(1)  *Additional claims* – Where the employer pays less than the authorised rate, the employee may claim tax relief (mileage allowance relief) on the difference.

(2)  *Passengers* – The additional rate applying when carrying passengers was extended to volunteers with effect from 6 April 2011.

## Company vans

*(ITEPA 2003, ss 154–164)*

| Tax Year | Cash equivalent of benefit | |
| | private use of van | fuel for private use |
|---|---|---|
| 2013–14 | £3,000 | £564 |
| 2012–13 | £3,000 | £550 |
| 2011–12 | £3,000 | £550 |
| 2010–11 | £3,000 | £550 |
| 2009–10 | £3,000 | £500 |
| 2008–09 | £3,000 | £500 |
| 2007–08 | £3,000 | £500 |

**Notes**

(1)  *No emissions* – For the tax years 2010–11 to 2014–15 inclusive, the cash equivalent will be nil for vans which cannot produce $CO_2$ emissions under any circumstances when driven (*ITEPA 2003, s 155(2)*). The cash equivalent for use of the van will revert to £3,000 for the tax year 2015–16 onwards.

(2)  *No benefit* – No charge arises if the restricted private use condition is satisfied (see *ITEPA 2003, s 155(4)*).

(3)  *Older vans* – Before 6 April 2007 there were different cash equivalent rates for vans aged under four years and those aged over four years.

(4)  *The fuel benefit* – This charge for private journeys in a company van was introduced from 2007–08, (*ITEPA 2003, ss 160–164*).

## Buses

*(ITEPA 2003, ss 242, 243)*

(1)  *Works buses* – No income tax charge arises on the provision for employees of a works transport service, if the following conditions are satisfied:

(a)  the service is available generally to employees of the employer (or each employer) concerned;

(b)  the main use of the service is for qualifying journeys by those employees; and

(c)  the service–

(i)  is used only by the employees for whom it is provided or their children, or

(ii)  is substantially used only by those employees or children.

(2)  *Public buses* – No charge to tax arises in respect of support provided for public bus services, if the following conditions are satisfied:

(a)  the service is available to employees generally;

(b)  it is used for qualifying journeys by employees of one or more employers; and

(c)  either:

(i)  it is a local bus service; or

(ii)  the bus must be provided to other passengers on terms that are as favourable as the terms on which the bus is provided to employees.

## TRAVEL AND SUBSISTENCE

## Daily subsistence rate

(See HMRC's Employment Income Manual, at *EIM05231*)

| Description | Rate (maximum) £ | Detail |
|---|---|---|
| Breakfast | 5 | Irregular early starters |
| One meal (5 hour) | 5 | Away for at least 5 hours |
| Two meals (10 hour) | 10 | Away for at least 10 hours |
| Late evening meal | 15 | Irregular late finishers |

## Incidental overnight expenses and benefits

*(ITEPA 2003, ss 240, 241)*

| From | Permitted amount per night | |
|---|---|---|
| | In UK | Overseas |
| | £ | £ |
| 6 April 1995 | 5 | 10 |

**Note**

The allowance applies to employees' minor personal expenditure. The above figures represent the maximum daily amounts whilst on business-related activities. If exceeded the whole amount provided is taxable.

## Lorry drivers' overnight subsistence allowance

(HMRC's Employment Income Manual, at *EIM66110*)

| Year ended 31 December: | Permitted amount per night £ |
|---|---|
| 2012 | 33.85 |
| 2011 | 32.20 |
| 2010 | 30.75 |
| 2009 | 30.75 |
| 2008 | 29.85 |
| 2007 | 28.62 |
| 2006 | 27.55 |

## MOBILE PHONES

(*ITEPA 2003, s 319; see also EIM21779*)

(1)   *One phone policy* – No chargeable benefit arises (from 2006–07 onwards) on employer-provided mobile phones. The exemption is restricted to one mobile phone per employee. There is no exemption for mobile phones provided for family members.

(2)   *Top-up vouchers* – There is no tax charge under *ITEPA 2003, s 62* (general earnings) or *ITEPA 2003, Pt 3, Ch 4* (vouchers and credit tokens) on the provision of top-ups for a mobile phone which is owned by the employer and provided to the employee.

(3)   *What is a mobile phone?* – For these purposes 'mobile phone' includes smartphones but not devices that are solely PDAs, tablets or laptop computers.

## CHILDCARE VOUCHERS

(*ITEPA 2003, ss 270A, 318A; SI 2013/513*)

| Year | Weekly Limit basic rate | Higher rate taxpayer | Additional rate taxpayer |
|---|---|---|---|
| 2013–14 | £55 | £28 | £25 |
| 2012–13 | £55 | £28 | £22 |
| 2011–12 | £55 | £28 | £22 |
| 2010–11 | £55 | £55 | £55 |
| 2009–10 | £55 | £55 | N/A |
| 2008–09 | £55 | £55 | N/A |
| 2007–08 | £55 | £55 | N/A |

**Notes**

(1)   *Pre April 2011* – Employees who joined the employer-provided childcare voucher scheme before 6 April 2011, and are still employed by that employer, continue to receive a benefit of £55 per week, whatever their marginal rate of tax.

(2)   *New voucher scheme* – From Autumn 2015 parents will be able to buy childcare vouchers through an online scheme, with the cost subsidised by the Government at the rate of £20 for every £80 paid by the parent, up to a limit of £1,200 per child (ie 20% of yearly childcare costs up to £6,000). The employer-provided system of childcare vouchers will be phased out (Treasury press release: www.hm-treasury. gov.uk/press_29_13.htm).

## RELOCATION EXPENSES

(*ITEPA 2003, ss 271–289*)

(1)   Exemption for qualifying removal expenses and benefits up to a maximum of £8,000 on a change of residence.

(2)   The relief from an employment income charge applies to relocation expenses in relation to payments made or expenses provided in connection with the engagement of a new employee or the change of duties or place of work of an existing employee.

## TERMINATION PAYMENTS

(*ITEPA 2003, Pt 6, Ch 3*)

| Tax year | Threshold |
|---|---|
| From 1998–99 onwards | £30,000 |

**Notes**

(1)   *Exemption* – A payment or benefit given in respect of the termination of an office or employment by the death of the holder is exempted from a tax charge under the above termination payment provisions.

(2)   *No exemption* – The termination payment provisions do not apply if the payment or benefit is otherwise chargeable to income tax, such as payments chargeable under *ITEPA 2003, s 394* if a non-approved or employer-financed retirement benefits scheme exists.

## SCHOLARSHIPS

(*ITEPA 2003, ss 211–215; SP 4/86*)

| Period | Specified amount |
|---|---|
| From 1 September 2007 | £15,480 |
| From 1 September 2005–31 August 2007 | £15,000 |
| From 6 April 1992–31 August 2005 | £7,000 |

## ACTUAL OFFICIAL RATE OF INTEREST – EMPLOYMENT RELATED LOANS

(*ITEPA 2003, s 181*)

| Period | Rate % |
|---|---|
| From 6 April 2010 | 4.00 |
| 1 March 2009–5 April 2010 | 4.75 |
| 6 April 2007–28 February 2009 | 6.25 |
| 6 January 2002–5 April 2007 | 5.00 |

## AVERAGE OFFICIAL RATES OF INTEREST – EMPLOYMENT RELATED LOANS

(*ITEPA 2003, s 182*)

| Year | Average official rate % |
|---|---|
| 2012–13 | 4.00 |
| 2011–12 | 4.00 |
| 2010–11 | 4.00 |
| 2009–10 | 4.75 |
| 2008–09 | 6.10 |
| 2007–08 | 6.25 |

**Note**

The average official rates of interest are used if the loan was outstanding throughout the year and the normal averaging method of calculation is being used.

## FLAT RATE EXPENSES

(*ITEPA 2003, s 367; EIM32712*)

| Occupation | | | Deduction from 2008–09 onwards £ | Deduction from 2004–05 to 2007–08 £ |
|---|---|---|---|---|
| Agriculture | | All workers | 100 | 70 |
| Airlines | | Uniformed flight deck crew | 850 | 850 |
| Aluminium | A | Continual casting operators, process operators, de-dimplers, driers, drill punchers, dross unloaders, firemen (see Note 3 below), furnace operators and their helpers, leaders, mouldmen, pourers, remelt department labourers, roll flatteners | 140 | 130 |

| Occupation | | | Deduction from 2008–09 onwards | Deduction from 2004–05 to 2007–08 |
|---|---|---|---|---|
| | | | £ | £ |
| Aluminium – *contd* | B | Cable hands, case makers, labourers, mates, truck drivers and measurers, storekeepers | 80 | 60 |
| | C | Apprentices | 60 | 45 |
| | D | All other workers | 120 | 100 |
| Banks and Building societies | | Uniformed employees | 60 | 45 |
| Brass and copper | | All workers | 120 | 100 |
| Building | A | Joiners and carpenters | 140 | 105 |
| | B | Cement works and roofing (asphalt) labourers | 80 | 55 |
| | C | Labourers and navvies | 60 | 45 |
| | D | All other workers | 120 | 85 |
| Building materials | A | Stone-masons | 120 | 85 |
| | B | Tilemakers and labourers | 60 | 45 |
| | C | All other workers | 80 | 55 |
| Clothing | A | Lacemakers, hosiery bleachers, dyers, scourers and knitters, knitwear bleachers and dyers | 60 | 45 |
| | B | All other workers | 60 | 45 |
| Constructional engineering (see Note 4) | A | Blacksmiths and their strikers, burners, caulkers, chippers, drillers, erectors, fitters, holders up, markers off, platers, riggers, riveters, rivet heaters, scaffolders, sheeters, template workers, turners, welders | 140 | 115 |
| | B | Banksmen labourers, shop-helpers, slewers, straighteners | 80 | 60 |
| | C | Apprentices and storekeepers | 60 | 45 |
| | D | All other workers | 100 | 75 |
| Electrical and electricity supply | A | Those workers incurring laundry costs only (generally CEGB employees) | 60 | 45 |
| | B | All other workers | 120 | 90 |
| Trades ancillary to Engineering | A | Pattern makers | 140 | 120 |
| | B | Labourers, supervisory and unskilled workers | 80 | 60 |
| | C | Apprentices and storekeepers | 60 | 45 |

*continued*

| Occupation | | | Deduction from 2008–09 onwards | Deduction from 2004–05 to 2007–08 |
|---|---|---|---|---|
| | | | £ | £ |
| Trades ancillary to Engineering – *contd* | D | Motor mechanics in garage repair shop | 120 | 100 |
| | E | All other workers | 120 | 100 |
| Fire service | | Uniformed firefighters and fire officers | 80 | 60 |
| Food | | All workers | 60 | 45 |
| Forestry | | All workers | 100 | 70 |
| Glass | | All workers | 80 | 60 |
| Healthcare | A | Ambulance staff on active service (ie excluding staff who take telephone calls or provide clerical support) | 140 | 110 |
| | B | Nurses and midwives, chiropodists, dental nurses, occupational speech physios and therapists, phlebotomists, radiographers | 100 | 70 |
| | C | Plaster room orderlies, hospital porters, ward clerks, sterile supply workers, hospital domestics, hospital catering staff | 100 | 60 |
| | D | Laboratory staff, pharmacists, pharmacy assistants | 60 | 45 |
| | E | Uniformed ancillary staff – maintenance workers, grounds staff, drivers, parking attendants and security guards, receptionists and other uniformed staff | 60 | 45 |
| Heating | A | Pipe fitters and plumbers | 120 | 100 |
| | B | Coverers, laggers, domestic glaziers, heating engineers and their mates | 120 | 90 |
| | C | All gas workers, all other workers | 100 | 70 |
| Iron Mining | A | Fillers, miners and underground workers | 120 | 100 |
| | B | All other workers | 100 | 75 |
| Iron and steel | A | Day labourers, general labourers, stockmen, time-keepers, warehouse staff and weighmen | 80 | 60 |

| Occupation | | | Deduction from 2008–09 onwards | Deduction from 2004–05 to 2007–08 |
|---|---|---|---|---|
| | | | £ | £ |
| Iron and steel – *contd* | B | Apprentices | 60 | 45 |
| | C | All other workers | 140 | 120 |
| Leather | A | Curriers (wet workers), fellmongering workers, tanning operatives (wet) | 80 | 55 |
| | B | All other workers | 60 | 45 |
| Particular engineering (see Note 5) | A | Pattern makers | 140 | 120 |
| | B | All chainmakers; cleaners, galvanisers, tinners and wire drawers in the wire drawing industry; tool-makers in the lock making industry | 120 | 100 |
| | C | Apprentices and storekeepers | 60 | 45 |
| | D | All other workers | 80 | 60 |
| Police force | | Police officers (ranks up to and including Chief Inspector) | 140 | 110 (2007–08) 55 (2004–05 to 2006–07) |
| Precious metals | | All workers | 100 | 70 |
| Printing | A | Letterpress Section – Electrical engineers (rotary presses), electrotypers, ink and roller makers, machine minders (rotary), maintenance engineers (rotary) | 140 | 105 |
| | B | Bench hands (P & B), compositors (LP), readers (LP), T & E Section wireroom operators, warehousemen (PBM) | 60 | 45 |
| | C | All other workers | 100 | 70 |
| Prisons | | Uniformed prison officers | 80 | 55 |
| Public service | A | Dock and inland waterways: | | |
| | | – Dockers, dredger drivers, hopper steerers | 80 | 55 |
| | | – All other workers | 60 | 45 |
| | B | Public transport: | | |
| | | – Garage hands (including cleaners and mechanics) | 80 | 55 |
| | | – Conductor and drivers | 60 | 45 |

*continued*

| Occupation | | | Deduction from 2008–09 onwards | Deduction from 2004–05 to 2007–08 |
|---|---|---|---|---|
| | | | £ | £ |
| Quarrying | | All workers | 100 | 70 |
| Railways | A | (See the appropriate category for craftsmen, eg engineers, vehicle builders etc.) | 100 | 70 |
| | B | All other workers | 100 | 70 |
| Seamen | A | Carpenters on passenger liners | 165 | 165 |
| | B | Carpenters on cargo vessels, tankers, coasters and ferries | 140 | 130 |
| Shipyards | A | Blacksmiths and their strikers, boilermakers, burners, carpenters, caulkers, drillers, furnacemen (platers), holders up, fitters, platers, plumbers, riveters, sheet iron workers, shipwrights, tubers, welders | 140 | 115 |
| | B | Labourers | 80 | 60 |
| | C | Apprentices and storekeepers | 60 | 45 |
| | D | All other workers | 100 | 75 |
| Textiles and textile printing | A | Carders, carding engineers, overlookers and technicians in spinning mills | 120 | 85 |
| | B | All other workers | 80 | 60 |
| Vehicles | A | Builders, railway wagon etc. repairers and railway wagon lifters | 140 | 105 |
| | B | Railway vehicle painters and letterers, railway wagon etc. builders' and repairers' assistants | 80 | 60 |
| | C | All other workers | 60 | 45 |
| Wood and furniture | A | Carpenters, cabinet makers, joiners, wood carvers and woodcutting machinists | 140 | 115 |
| | B | Artificial limb makers (other than in wood), organ builders and packaging case makers | 120 | 90 |
| | C | Coopers not providing own tools, labourers, polishers and upholsterers | 60 | 45 |
| | D | All other workers | 100 | 75 |

**Notes**

(1)     *Flat rate expense* – For most classes of industry a tax deduction is given for certain amounts 'representing the average annual expenses incurred by employees of the class to which the employee belongs in respect of the repair and maintenance of work equipment'. The term 'flat rate expense allowance' is often used for this purpose.

(2)     *'Workers' and 'all other workers'* – These are references to manual workers or to workers who have to pay for the upkeep of tools and special clothing.

(3)     *'Firemen'* – Means persons engaged to light and maintain furnaces.

(4)     *'Constructional engineering'* – Means engineering undertaken on a construction site, including buildings, shipyards, bridges, roads and other similar operations.

(5)     *'Particular engineering'* – Means engineering undertaken on a commercial basis in a factory or workshop for the purposes of producing components such as wire, springs, nails and locks.

(6)     *Occupations not listed* – If the occupation is not listed in the table, a standard amount of £60 can be claimed for the laundry costs of uniforms or protective clothing (www.hmrc.gov.uk/incometax/relief-tools.htm#2).

*3*

# PAYE, RTI, student loans and CIS

## PAYE AND RTI

## REAL TIME INFORMATION (RTI)

### RTI procedures

(*SI 2003/2682, regs 67B–67H*)

| What is not changing | New with RTI |
|---|---|
| Application of PAYE to employees' pay does not change. | The reporting of deductions and payments must be made online, generally on or before the day the employee is paid. |
| Payment dates for PAYE remain:<br><br>• for cheques as 19th of the month; or<br><br>• for electronic payments: 22nd of the month. | HMRC will be able to match the employer's liability for PAYE to the payments made by the employer each month, and HMRC's Debt Management department will chase up underpayments in real time. |
| PAYE coding notices are issued in the same way | Employees may receive more accurate PAYE codes, but not until 2014. |
| Forms P60 and P45 given to employees/ex-employees. | Forms P14, P35, P38A, P38S, P46s all removed. P45s are not sent to HMRC. |
| Expenses and benefits reported on forms P11D and P9D. | The simplified PAYE scheme used for domestic staff and carers will close from April 2014. |
| Construction industry scheme (CIS) operation and reports are made in the same fashion. | Companies who are CIS subcontractors will need to report CIS deductions on the EPS each month to off-set the CIS tax against PAYE due. |

**Notes**

(1)   *General* – Real time information (RTI) is a new way to report pay and deductions made under PAYE, (see RTI reports below).

(2)   *RTI & Universal Credit* – RTI is required in order to implement universal credit which will replace tax credits and certain other state benefits from October 2013 onwards (see **Chapter 15**).

(3)   *Benefits of RTI* – RTI should improve the accuracy of PAYE, as there will be fewer tax under and overpayments for individuals at the end of the tax year.

(4)    *Further information* – For further guidance on RTI see www.hmrc.gov.uk/payerti/
index.htm.

## Joining dates for RTI

| Employers | RTI joining dates |
|---|---|
| In RTI pilot | Specified dates in April, July, November 2012 and January 2013. |
| With 5,000 or more employees | Dates as agreed with HMRC between November 2012 and October 2013. |
| Under 5,000 employees | First pay date on or after 6 April 2013. |
| New employers | On registering for PAYE, or can defer to April 2013. |

### Notes

(1)    *Commencement dates* – HMRC will invite employers to join RTI on particular dates; this invitation cannot be refused.

(2)    *Data Alignment* – Employers need to align their payroll data with that of HMRC in the first report under RTI, so should strive to have all employee details correct. It is particularly important to have accurate; national insurance numbers, full names and dates of birth for each employee.

## New data items for RTI

*(SI 2003/ 2682, reg 67CA, Sch A1, para 21, 38)*

| Data | What and why |
|---|---|
| Hours worked | Needed for all employees; the number of hours the employee is contracted to work within the bands: <br><br> A    Up to 15.99 hours <br><br> B    16 to 29.99 hours <br><br> C    30 hours or more <br><br> D    Other |
| Passport number | Where this is collected as part of checks to ensure the person is entitled to work in the UK. |
| BACS hash code | Where employees are paid by BACS a four character code must be added into the BACS payment file. BACS software may have to be updated to include this code. |

## RTI Reports

*(SI 2003/2682, reg 67B–67H)*

| Reports | Function and submission period |
| --- | --- |
| Full payment submission (FPS) | Must be submitted on or before the date on which employees are paid, but see notes below for exceptions. |
| Employer Alignment Submission (EAS) | To align employee records with HMRC records before any other information is submitted under RTI. Only required for payrolls of over 250 employees. |
| Employer Payment Summary (EPS) | Each month, preferably between 6$^{th}$ and 19$^{th}$ of the month following payment to employees. A nil EPS will need to be submitted where no payments have been made to employees. |
| National Insurance Number verification request (NVR) | To verify or obtain a National Insurance number for new employees. Can only be submitted after an EAS or the first FPS has been submitted. |
| Early Year Update (EYU) | After 19 April following tax year end, to correct any of the year to date totals submitted in the final FPS for the previous tax year. |

**Notes**

(1)   *Small employers* – Employers with fewer than 50 employees will be permitted to submit the FPS at the time of their regular payroll run, as long as this is before the end of the tax month (5$^{th}$). This relaxation is due to apply until 5 October 2013 but further concessions may be announced before the end of that period (www.hmrc. gov.uk/news/rti-small-businesses.htm).

(2)   *Cash payments to casuals* – Where the employee is paid in cash for work done on the day at a time when it would be impractical to make an RTI report, the FPS can be submitted on the earliest of the next regular RTI report date, or seven days after the payment date.

(3)   *Notional payments* – Where there is no transfer of money from the employer to the employee, such as an award of shares, the RTI report can be made at the earliest of the time the employer operates PAYE on the notional payment or 14 days after the end of the tax month.

(4)   *Further information* – All situations in which HMRC will permit the FPS to be submitted after the date of payment are listed here: www.hmrc.gov.uk/payerti/on-or-before.pdf

## PAYE thresholds

*(SI 2003/2682, reg 9)*

|  | 2013–14 | 2012–13 | 2011–12 | 2010–11 | 2009–10 | 2008–09 | 2007–08 |
|---|---|---|---|---|---|---|---|
|  | £ | £ | £ | £ | £ | £ | £ |
| Weekly | 182 | 156 | 144 | 125 | 125 | 116 | 100 |
| Monthly | 787 | 675 | 623 | 540 | 540 | 503 | 435 |
| Annual | 9,440 | 8,105 | 7,475 | 6,475 | 6,475 | 6,035 | 5,225 |

**Notes**

(1)  *Tax thresholds* – The above thresholds are the level of earnings at which income tax becomes payable, but NICs will be due at lower thresholds (see **Chapter 14**).

(2)  *PAYE requirement* – The employer must operate a PAYE scheme and report under RTI once an employee earns over the lower earnings limit (LEL), which is £109 per week for 2013–14.

## PAYE codes

*(SI 2003/2682, reg 7)*

| PAYE code | Application |
|---|---|
| L | For those eligible for the basic personal allowance. Also used for 'emergency' tax codes – see note 2 |
| P | For individuals born between 6 April 21938 and 5 April 1948 and eligible for the full personal age-related allowance |
| Y | For individuals born before 5 April 1938 and eligible for the full personal age-related allowance |
| T | Used where HMRC are reviewing other items in tax code (eg the income-related reduction in the personal allowance) Also used if allowances have been used up or reduced to nil ('0T') |
| K | Used where total coding 'deductions' (eg other income) exceed allowances. Up to 50% gross pay can be deducted using a K code. |
| BR | Used when all income is taxable at the basic rate |
| D0 | Used when all income is taxable at the higher rate (eg due to a second job or pension) |
| D1 | Used if earnings in one employment exceed £150,000, all earnings from a second employment will be taxed at the additional rate (from 2011–12) |
| NT | Used when no tax is to be deducted from the income or pension |
| OT | Used as default PAYE tax code to deduct tax at the basic, higher and additional rates in certain circumstances (eg for new employees without form P45 and with no P46 or starter information, and for pension income of a person still in receipt of employment income) (from 2011–12) |

**Notes**

(1)  *Use of codes* – PAYE codes are used by employers or pension providers to calculate the amount of tax, if any, to be deducted from an individual's pay or pension.

(2)    *'Emergency' codes* – The emergency tax code for 2013–14 is 944L

(3)    *Further information* – For guidance on PAYE tax codes see: HMRC leaflet E12 or www.hmrc.gov.uk/incometax/codes-basics.htm.

## Returns

*(SI 2003/2682, regs 67, 73, 74, 85, 90)*

| Forms | Due Date |
|---|---|
| P14, P35, P38A *(SI 2003/2682, regs 73, 74)* | 19 May following the end of the tax year. For employers using RTI these end of year returns are no longer required. |
| P60 (to employee) *(SI 2003/2682, reg 67)* | 31 May following the end of the tax year. |
| P9D, P11D, P11D(b) *(SI 2003/2682, reg 85; SI 2001/1004, reg 80)* | 6 July following the end of the tax year. |
| P46 (Car) *(SI 2003/2682, reg 90)* | 28 days following the end of the relevant tax quarter, which end on:<br><br>• 5 July<br><br>• 5 October<br><br>• 5 January<br><br>• 5 April. |

## Late PAYE returns: Current regime

(1)    **PAYE returns** – The penalties for late filing of forms P35 and P14 as follows *(TMA 1970, s 98A)*:

    (a)    *Up to 12 months late* – £100 for each 50 employees (or part thereof) for each month the failure continues;

    (b)    *Over 12 months late* – penalty up to the amount of PAYE etc due and unpaid at 19 April following year end.

(2)    **Benefits and expenses** – The penalties for late filing of forms P11D and P9D are as follows *(TMA 1970, s 98(1)(b))*

    (a)    Initial penalty of up to £300 per form;

    (b)    Continuing penalty of up to £60 for each day on which the penalty continues after imposition of initial penalty.

(3)    **Returns of Class 1A NIC** – Separate penalty provisions apply to the late filing of form P11D(b), which are similar to the above penalties for the late filing of PAYE returns *(SI 2001/1004, reg 81(2))*.

## Penalties for late PAYE returns: under RTI

*(FA 2009, s 106, Sch 55)*

| RTI report: | For tax years: 2012–13 and 2013–14 | 2014–15 onwards |
|---|---|---|
| FPS filed in-year | No late penalty | One late report in the year is ignored. |
| Final FPS for the year | Late penalty if FPS submitted after 19 April following the tax year | See notes below. |

**Notes**

(1) *Commencement* – A new penalty regime for the failure to make or deliver PAYE returns under RTI by the filing deadline will be introduced by *FA 2013* into *FA 2009, s 106, Sch 55, paras 6B–6D*, to take effect from 2014/15.

(2) *Grace period* – No late filing penalty will apply for an 'initial period'. Each PAYE scheme will also be allowed one default without a penalty being charged (an unpenalised default). HMRC will determine the length of the initial period and the size of the late filing penalties to be set by regulations. HMRC also have power to determine the circumstances in which an unpenalised default or the initial period will be disapplied *(FA 2009, Sch 55, para 6C)*.

(3) *Amount* – The size of the late filing penalty will depend on the size of the PAYE scheme.

(4) *Frequency* – Only one penalty will apply per month even if FPS reports are submitted more frequently. Penalties will be charged quarterly.

(5) *Tax-geared penalties* – Where the report is more than three months late a penalty of 5% of the amount showing on the missing returns applies *(FA 2009, Sch 55 para 6D)*.

(6) *Appeals* – Employers with a reasonable excuse will be able to submit appeals to get penalties cancelled.

## Penalties for incorrect returns

*(FA 2007, s 97, Sch 24, para 1)*

| Behaviour | Unprompted disclosure | | Prompted disclosure | |
|---|---|---|---|---|
| | Maximum penalty | Minimum penalty | Maximum penalty | Minimum penalty |
| Careless | 30% | 0% | 30% | 15% |
| Deliberate but not concealed | 70% | 20% | 70% | 35% |
| Deliberate and concealed | 100% | 30% | 100% | 50% |

**Notes**

(1) *Commencement* – The above penalty regime applies to inaccuracies in returns due to be filed from 1 April 2009 where the tax period begins from 1 April 2008.

(2) *Previous regime* – For earlier tax years, the maximum penalty for incorrect PAYE returns is 100% of the difference between the amount payable under the return

and the amount payable had the return been correct. For incorrect forms P9D and P11D, the maximum penalty is up to £3,000 per incorrect form (*TMA 1970, ss 98, 98A*).

(3)   *RTI regime* – Penalties for inaccurate FPS reports submitted under RTI will apply from Royal Assent of *Finance Act 2013*. One penalty notice may cover multiple inaccuracies penalties in a year (*FA 2007 Sch 24, paras 1ZA–1ZD*).

(4)   *Further information* – For guidance on penalties for RTI reporting, see www.hmrc.gov.uk/payerti/reporting/late-reporting.htm.

## Late payments of PAYE

(*FA 2009, s 107, Sch 56*)

*Default penalties*

| Number of times payments late in the tax year | Penalty % | Amount to which penalty percentages apply |
|---|---|---|
| 1 | No penalty (as long as the payment is less than 6 months late – see below) | Total amount that is late in the tax year (ignoring the first late payment in that tax year) |
| 2–4 | 1% | |
| 5–7 | 2% | |
| 8–10 | 3% | |
| 11 or more | 4% | |

**Notes**

(1)   *Further penalties* – In addition to the above, a 5% penalty is imposed:

- Where monthly or quarterly payments remain unpaid after six months; and again,
- where payments remain outstanding after 12 months.

Such penalties apply even where only one payment in the tax year is late.

(2)   *Commencement* – The penalty regime for failure to pay PAYE and NIC on time commenced on 6 April 2010 (*SI 2010/466, art 3*). It applies to late payments relating to 2010–11 onwards, including student loan and construction industry scheme deductions (see **Late CIS payments** below), and annual payments of employers' Class 1A and 1B NIC (see CH152100). The late payment penalty regime applies to all employers and contractors, regardless of the number of employees or subcontractors.

(3)   *Small employers* – A small employer who makes quarterly payments can only have a maximum of four failures in a tax year, so the maximum initial default penalty rate is 1% (CH152550). However, further penalties may still arise (see note (1)).

(4)   *Appeals, reductions, etc* – The imposition and/or amount of penalty are subject to an appeal procedure. HMRC may also reduce a penalty due to 'special circumstances' at its discretion. Penalties are suspended if the contractor has an agreement for

deferred payment in place (ie a 'time to pay' arrangement) with HMRC, which is not broken. Liability to a penalty does not arise if there is a 'reasonable excuse' for the failure (*FA 2009, Sch 56, paras 9, 10, 13, 16*).

(5) *Future penalties* – From 2014–15 the penalty regime is amended such that penalties apply to each late payment relating to a tax year, not for each payment due within the year (*FB 2013, Sch 48 paras 10–14*).

## PAYE electronic communications – penalties: relevant annual returns

(*SI 2003/2682, regs 210A, 210AA*)

| Number of employees for whom particulars should have been included | 2010–11 and subsequent years | 2009–10 | 2004–5 to 2008–09 |
|---|---|---|---|
| 1–5 | £100 | £0 | £0 |
| 6–49 | £300 | £100 | £0 |
| 50–249 | £600 | £600 | £600 (nil for 2004–05) |
| 250–399 | £900 | £900 | £900 |
| 400–499 | £1,200 | £1,200 | £1,200 |
| 500–599 | £1,500 | £1,500 | £1,500 |
| 600–699 | £1,800 | £1,800 | £1,800 |
| 700–799 | £2,100 | £2,100 | £2,100 |
| 800–899 | £2,400 | £2,400 | £2,400 |
| 900–999 | £2,700 | £2,700 | £2,700 |
| 1,000 or more | £3,000 | £3,000 | £3,000 |

### Note

The above penalties apply to failures to comply with *SI 2003/2682, reg 205* (ie in relation to the mandatory use of electronic communications), in respect of a failure to deliver 'specified information' (from 2011–12; previously 'relevant annual returns'), ie forms P35 and P14 (*SI 2003/2682, regs 206A, 207*).

## PAYE electronic communications – penalties: specified information

(*SI 2003/2682, reg 210B*)

| Penalty | Number of items of specified information the employer has failed to deliver in the tax quarter | | |
|---|---|---|---|
| | Tax year ending 5 April 2014 and subsequent years | Tax years ending 5 April 2012 and 2013 | Tax year ending 5 April 2011 |
| £0 | n/a | 1–2 | 1–5 |
| £100 | 1–49 | 3–49 | 6–49 |
| £300 | 50–149 | 50–149 | 50–149 |

| Penalty | Number of items of specified information the employer has failed to deliver in the tax quarter | | |
|---|---|---|---|
| | Tax year ending 5 April 2014 and subsequent years | Tax years ending 5 April 2012 and 2013 | Tax year ending 5 April 2011 |
| £600 | 150–299 | 150–299 | 150–299 |
| £900 | 300–399 | 300–399 | 300–399 |
| £1,200 | 400–499 | 400–499 | 400–499 |
| £1,500 | 500–599 | 500–599 | 500–599 |
| £1,800 | 600–699 | 600–699 | 600–699 |
| £2,100 | 700–799 | 700–799 | 700–799 |
| £2,400 | 800–899 | 800–899 | 800–899 |
| £2,700 | 900–999 | 900–999 | 900–999 |
| £3,000 | 1,000 or more | 1,000 or more | 1,000 or more |

**Notes**

(1) *General* – The above penalties apply to failures by employers to deliver specified information.

(2) *'Specified information'* – This means form P45 (Parts 1 or 3), form P46 or form P46 (Pen) (*SI 2003/2682, reg 207*).

## PAYE surcharges (to 5 April 2010)

| Specified percentage for each default in a surcharge period | |
|---|---|
| Default number | % |
| 1 | 0.00 |
| 2 | 0.00 |
| 3 | 0.17 |
| 4 | 0.17 |
| 5 | 0.17 |
| 6 | 0.33 |
| 7 | 0.33 |
| 8 | 0.33 |
| 9 | 0.58 |
| 10 | 0.58 |
| 11 | 0.58 |
| 12 and over | 0.83 |

**Notes**

(1) *Repeal* – The default surcharge provisions (*SI 2003/2682, reg 203*) were repealed with effect from 6 April 2010.

(2) *Transitional provisions* – These surcharge provisions continue to have effect in relation to surcharges arising in respect of late payments of tax where the tax was

chargeable in respect of a tax period ending on or before 5 April 2010 (*SI 2010/466, art 4(3)*).

## PAYE and Class 1 NIC etc – monthly accounting periods

(*SI 2003/2682, reg 69*)

| Tax Period | Tax Month | Payment due (Electronic) | Payment due (Other) |
|---|---|---|---|
| 6 Apr–5 May | 1 | 22 May | 19 May |
| 6 May–5 Jun | 2 | 22 June | 19 June |
| 6 Jun–5 Jul | 3 | 22 July | 19 July |
| 6 Jul–5 Aug | 4 | 22 August | 19 August |
| 6 Aug–5 Sep | 5 | 22 September | 19 September |
| 6 Sept–5 Oct | 6 | 22 October | 19 October |
| 6 Oct–5 Nov | 7 | 22 November | 19 November |
| 6 Nov–5 Dec | 8 | 22 December | 19 December |
| 6 Dec–5 Jan | 9 | 22 January | 19 January |
| 6 Jan–5 Feb | 10 | 22 February | 19 February |
| 6 Feb–5 Mar | 11 | 22 March | 19 March |
| 6 Mar–5 Apr | 12 | 22 April | 19 April |

**Notes**

(1) *Large employers* – Employers with 250 or more employees are required to pay PAYE liabilities electronically. HMRC recommend that all employers pay electronically.

(2) *Electronic payments* – These must be cleared through HMRC's bank account within 17 days after the end of the tax period. This is generally the 22nd of the following month, as indicated above. However, if the 22nd falls on a weekend or a bank holiday, the payment must reach HMRC on the previous working day.

(3) *Non-electronic payments* – These are due 14 days following the end of the tax period. Thus employers who pay by post must ensure that payment reaches HMRC no later than 19th of the month. HMRC treat payments as being received on the day that the cheque is received (see www.hmrc.gov.uk/paye/file-or-pay/payments/deadlines.htm).

## PAYE and Class 1 NIC etc – quarterly accounting periods

(*SI 2003/2682, reg 70*)

| Tax Period | Tax Month | Payment due (Electronic) | Payment due (Other) |
|---|---|---|---|
| 6 Apr–5 Jul | 1–3 | 22 July | 19 July |
| 6 Jul–5 Oct | 4–6 | 22 October | 19 October |
| 6 Oct–5 Jan | 7–9 | 22 January | 19 January |
| 6 Jan–5 Apr | 10–12 | 22 April | 19 April |

**Notes**

(1)   *Quarterly payment* – Employers who have reasonable grounds for believing that the 'average monthly amount' will be less than £1,500 can ask HMRC to for permission to pay quarterly. Call the HMRC payment enquiry line: 0845 366 7816 to discuss quarterly or annual payments.

(2)   *Reporting* – Nil monthly or quarterly PAYE payments can be reported online: www.hmrc.gov.uk/payinghmrc/paye-nil.htm

## Interest on PAYE paid late

*(SI 2003/2682, regs 82, 83)*

(1)   Where an employer has not paid to HMRC the net tax payable under PAYE within 14 days of the end of the tax year (or 17 days, if the payment is made electronically), the unpaid tax carries interest at the prescribed rate from the reckonable date until the date of payment.

(2)   Interest payable on PAYE paid late is in addition to and separate from any penalties for late payment of PAYE.

(3)   Certain repayments of tax to the employer after the end of the tax year to which it relates also attract interest.

## Student Loans

*(SI 2009/470, reg 29; SI 2011/784, reg 6)*

| Year | Percentage | Threshold | | |
|------|-----------|-----------|---|---|
| | | Annual | Monthly | Weekly |
| 2013–14 | 9% | £16,365 | £1,363.75 | £314.71 |
| 2012–13 | 9% | £15,795 | £1,316.25 | £303.75 |
| 2011–12 | 9% | £15,000 | £1,250.00 | £288.46 |
| 2010–11 | 9% | £15,000 | £1,250.00 | £288.46 |
| 2009–10 | 9% | £15,000 | £1,250.00 | £288.46 |
| 2008–09 | 9% | £15,000 | £1,250.00 | £288.46 |
| 2007–08 | 9% | £15,000 | £1,250.00 | £288.46 |

**Notes**

(1)   *General* – Employers are responsible for deducting student loan repayments due to the Student Loan Company and passing the payment to HMRC.

(2)   *Threshold* – The 'threshold' (see above) is the amount of the gross earnings for NICs purposes, above which the student loan repayments become due. The amount of repayment is calculated as the stated percentage of earnings over that threshold. From April 2016 this threshold will be set at £21,000 and will be increased every year in line with earnings inflation.

(3)   *Reporting* – Student loan deductions must be reported within RTI, but the loan deductions data will be passed to the Student Loan Company just once after the end of the tax year.

(4)    *Further guidance* – Guidance for employers on the deduction of student loans is found in HMRC leaflet E17(2013).

## CONSTRUCTION INDUSTRY SCHEME (CIS)

### CIS returns

(*FA 2004, s 70; SI 2005/2045, reg 4*)

- *Filing date* – Contractors are required to submit monthly returns to HMRC, no later than 14 days after the end of every tax month. Returns may be submitted on paper (form CIS300) or electronically.

- *'Nil' returns* – Contractors who have not paid any subcontractors in the previous tax month must nevertheless submit 'nil' returns, unless HMRC have been notified that no further payments will be made, in which case HMRC may cease to require monthly returns for up to six months, or until payments to subcontractors recommence (www.hmrc.gov.uk/cis/returns/returns-records.htm#4).

### Late CIS returns (from October 2011)

(*FA 2009, s 106; Sch 55, paras 7–13*)

| Period | Penalty |
|---|---|
| Up to 2 months late | £100 |
| More than 2 months late | £200 |
| More than 6 months late | Greater of:<br>• 5% of tax liability; and<br>• £300 |
| More than 12 months late<br>Other cases (ie not included below)<br>(also see below for returns relating only to persons registered for gross payment)<br>Information [deliberately]* withheld: | Greater of:<br>• 5% of tax liability; and<br>• £300 |
| Deliberate but not concealed | Greater of:<br>• 70% of tax liability; and<br>• £1,500 |
| Deliberate and concealed | Greater of:<br>• 100% of tax liability; and<br>• £3,000 |
| More than 12 months late – Information [deliberately]* withheld: Return relating only to persons registered for gross payment | |
| Deliberate but not concealed | £1,500 |
| Deliberate and concealed | £3,000 |

* 'Deliberately' inserted (by *F(No 3)A 2010, s 26, Sch 10 paras 1, 5, 6* with effect from 6 October 2011 (*SI 2011/2391*).

**Notes**

(1) *Commencement* – The penalty regime for failing to make CIS returns under *FA 2009, Sch 55* takes effect from October 2011. The first return to attract a penalty under *Sch 55* will be the return due for the month ended 5 November 2011 (see CH61120).

(2) *Contractors new to CIS* – For contractors who have not submitted any previous returns and are filing their first returns late, an upper limit of £3,000 applies to the total 'fixed' penalties (ie. £100 and £200) arising. The £3,000 upper limit does not replace any 'tax geared' penalties, but the £300 minimum penalties that would otherwise be charged where the tax geared penalty is less than £300 is removed (*FA 2009, Sch 55, para 13*).

## Late CIS returns (to October 2011)

(*TMA 1970, s 98A*)

The penalties for late filing of monthly CIS returns were as follows:

- Up to 12 months late – £100 for each 50 employees (or part thereof) for each month the failure continues; and

- Over 12 months late – Up to £3,000.

**Notes**

(1) *New regime* – A new penalty regime for the late filing of CIS returns applies from October 2011 (see above).

(2) *Calculation of penalties* – In some cases, penalties based on the new rules may be lower than those charged under the above regime. As a transitional measure, contractors who were charged penalties for the late filing of a monthly CIS return before October 2011 could ask HMRC to calculate penalties under the new penalty regime and reduce their penalties accordingly if this calculation resulted in a lower amount (see www.hmrc.gov.uk/cis/penalties-late-returns.htm).

## CIS payments

(*FA 2004, s 62; SI 2005/2045, regs 7, 8*)

- *Payment dates* – Contractors are normally required to make monthly payments to HMRC of deductions from contract payments, within 17 days after the end of the tax period if made electronically, or otherwise within 14 days after the end of the tax period.

- *Quarterly payments* – A contractor who has reasonable grounds for believing that the 'average monthly amount' will be less than £1,500 can choose to pay tax on a quarterly basis (ie for quarters ending 5 July, 5 October, 5 January and 5 April).

## Late CIS payments

(*FA 2009, s 107, Sch 56, paras 6–8*)

- *Penalties* – A penalty regime applies to the failure to make CIS payments on time. For a table of penalties, see **Late payments of PAYE** above.

- *Scope* – The potential penalties for a tax year comprise 'default' penalties for unpaid CIS deductions at the penalty date, and two further penalties for CIS deductions which are more than 6 and 12 months late. Penalties apply for the failure to pay all or part of the amounts due. HMRC guidance and worked examples regarding the late payment regime for CIS purposes are contained in HMRC's Compliance Handbook (CH153000 onwards).

- *Commencement* – The penalty regime for failure to make CIS payments on time in *FA 2009, Sch 56* applies with effect from 6 April 2010 (*SI 2010/466, art 3*).

- *Appeals, reductions, etc* – The imposition and/or amount of penalty are subject to an appeal procedure. HMRC may also reduce a penalty due to 'special circumstances' which does not include inability to pay. Penalties are suspended if the contractor has an agreement with HMRC for deferred payment (ie a 'time to pay' arrangement) and complies with its terms. Liability to a penalty does not arise if there is a 'reasonable excuse' for the failure (*FA 2009, Sch 56, paras 9, 10, 13, 16*).

*4*

# Shares and Share options

## APPROVED SHARE INCENTIVE PLANS (SIPs)

*(ITEPA 2003, Pt 7, Ch 6, Sch 2; ITTOIA 2005, ss 392–396, 405–408, 770; SI 2001/1004, reg 22(8), Sch 3, Pt 9, para 7)*

| Type of share | When shares acquired | Shares taken from plan during the first 3 years | Shares taken from plan during years 3–5 | Shares taken from plan after 5 years |
|---|---|---|---|---|
| Free shares and Matching shares | No income tax or NICs to pay on the value of the shares *(ITEPA 2003, s 490)* | Income tax payable on the market value of the shares when taken out of the plan *(ITEPA 2003, s 505(2))* | Income tax payable on the lower of market value of the shares:<br>• When awarded, or<br>• When taken out of plan<br>*(ITEPA 2003, s 505(3))* | No income tax or NICs to pay |
| Partnership shares | No income tax or NICs to pay on the money used to buy the shares *(ITEPA 2003, s 492)* | Income tax payable on the market value of the shares when taken out of the plan *(ITEPA 2003, s 506(2))* | Income tax payable on the lower of:<br>• the pay used to buy the shares, or<br>• the market value of the shares when taken out of the plan<br>*(ITEPA 2003, s 506(3))* | No income tax or NICs |

| Type of share | When shares acquired | Shares taken from plan during the first 3 years | Shares taken from plan during years 3–5 | Shares taken from plan after 5 years |
|---|---|---|---|---|
| Dividend shares | No income tax or NICs on dividends used to buy dividend shares<br><br>*(ITEPA 2003, ss 490(1(b), 493, 496; ITTOIA 2005, s 770(2))* | Dividends used to buy shares are taxed as a dividend in the year the shares are taken out of the plan<br><br>*(ITTOIA 2005, ss 394(2), 407(2))* | No income tax or NICs | No income tax or NICs |

**Notes**

(1)  *Approved scheme* – A SIP is an HMRC approved plan which offers tax and National Insurance advantages. The SIP must satisfy various conditions, and the company should send details of its SIP to HMRC for formal approval prior to starting the plan *(ITEPA 2003, Sch 2, Pt 10)*.

(2)  *All employees* – Participation in the SIP cannot be restricted to particular groups or individuals. However, companies can exclude employees who have not worked for the company for a minimum period of time. Individual companies can set their own minimum limit, but it cannot be longer than 18 months *(ITEPA 2003, Sch 2, paras 7, 8, 16)*.

(3)  *NI exemption* – There is generally no National Insurance liability when an employee acquires shares from a SIP. However, a Class 1 NIC liability (and an income tax charge) may arise if the employee leaves the company, or takes shares out of the plan, within five years of joining it (see National Insurance Manual, NIM06806-06807).

## ENTERPRISE MANAGEMENT INCENTIVES (EMI)

*(ITEPA 2003, Pt 7, Ch 9, Sch 5)*

## Taxation

*(ITEPA 2003, Pt 7, Ch 9)*

The tax and National Insurance contributions implications of EMI options include the following:

- *Grant of EMI option* – No income tax or NICs arise on the grant of a qualifying EMI option.

- *Exercise of EMI option* – If the option is exercised within ten years of the date of grant and there has been no disqualifying event, no income tax or NIC charges arise provided that the employee buys the shares at a price at least equal to market value on the day the option was granted. If the option is a replacement option, it must be exercised within ten years of grant of the original option in order to qualify for tax relief (*ITEPA 2003, ss 529–530*).

An income tax charge may arise on the exercise of a qualifying EMI option in the following circumstances, and a NIC liability may also arise if the shares are 'readily convertible assets' (as defined in *ITEPA 2003, s 702*; see *NIM06835*):

- the option was granted at a discount to market value (ie the option price is less than the market value at the date of grant) (*ITEPA 2003, s 531*); or

- the option is exercised more than 40 days after a disqualifying event (*ITEPA 2003, s 532*).

- *Capital Gains Tax* (CGT) – A sale of qualifying EMI shares is potentially subject to CGT. However, EMI shares can qualify for entrepreneurs' relief on disposal if they were acquired on or after 6 April 2012. The period of holding the EMI option is counted towards the 12-month holding period to qualify for entrepreneurs' relief (*FB 2013, Sch 23*).

- *National Insurance Contributions* – As to the circumstances in which a liability arises (under *SSCBA 1992, s 4(4)*) in respect of EMI shares or options, see *NIM06810*.

## General requirements

(*ITEPA 2003, Sch 5, Pt 2*)

- *Purpose* – The EMI option must be granted for qualifying purposes (see *Sch 5, para 4*);

- *Maximum employee entitlement* – An employee may be granted qualifying options over shares with a total value not exceeding a specific statutory maximum (*Sch 5, paras 5–6*); for qualifying EMI options granted before 16 June 2012 the maximum is £120,000, and for those granted on or after that date it is £250,000 (*SI 2012/1360*);

- *Maximum company limit* – The total value of shares under EMI options granted by the company must not exceed £3 million (*Sch 5, para 7*).

## Qualifying companies

(*ITEPA 2003, Sch 5, Pt 3*)

- *Independence and qualifying subsidiaries* – The company must satisfy certain requirements (in *Sch 5, paras 8–11B*) as appropriate;

- *Gross assets* – The value of the company's gross assets must not exceed £30 million at the date the EMI option is granted (if the company is a member of a group of companies, the limits are applied to the gross assets of the group as a whole) (*Sch 5, para 12*);

- *Number of employees* – The company must have fewer than 250 'full-time equivalent employees' at the date on which a qualifying EMI option is granted (this requirement applies to employees of a parent company and all its qualifying subsidiaries) (*Sch 5, para 12A*);

- *Trading activities* – A qualifying trade must be carried on (*Sch 5, paras 13–23*).

## Eligible employees

*(ITEPA 2003, Sch 5, Pt 4)*

● *Employment* – The individual must be an employee of the company whose shares are the subject of the options (or for a group, employees of a qualifying subsidiary *(Sch 5, para 25)*;

● *Working time* – The employee must be required to spend on average at least 25 hours per week or, if less, 75% of working time on the business of the company whose shares are subject to the EMI option or a qualifying subsidiary *(Sch 5, paras 26–27)*.

● *No material interest* – The employee must not have a material interest in the company whose shares are under option, or (if that company is a parent company) in any group company. A 'material interest' is either beneficial ownership of, or the ability to control directly or indirectly, more than 30% of the ordinary share capital of the company, or where the company is a close company, possession of or entitlement to acquire rights that would give more than 30% of the assets available for distribution on a winding up *(Sch 5, paras 28–33)*.

## Requirements relating to options

*(ITEPA 2003, Sch 5, Pt 5)*

● *Type of shares* – The option must be a right to acquire shares that are part of the ordinary share capital of the company, are fully paid up and are not redeemable *(Sch 5, para 35)*.

● *Exercise of option* – It must be possible for the option to be exercised within ten years from the date of grant *(Sch 5, para 36)*.

● *Terms of option to be agreed in writing* – The option must be a written agreement between the person granting the option and the employee, which contains the information specified in *Sch 5, para 37*.

● *Options not transferable* – The option terms must prohibit the option holder from transferring their rights under it. If the option terms allow for its exercise after the option holder's death, the option cannot be exercised more than one year after the date of death *(Sch 5, para 38)*.

### Notes

(1) EMIs are tax advantaged share options. They are designed to help small, higher risk companies recruit and retain employees. Guidance on the EMI scheme conditions is included in HMRC's Employee Share Schemes User Manual (www.hmrc.gov.uk/manuals/essum/ESSUM50000.htm).

(2) Notice of the option must be given within 92 days after its grant *(ITEPA 2003, Sch 5, para 44)*. HMRC provide a form (EMI 1) to notify grants of EMI options, and this is available on HMRC's website (www.hmrc.gov.uk/shareschemes/emi/emi-10-09.pdf).

(3) Employers operating an EMI scheme must submit an annual return to HMRC before 7 July in the following tax year *(ITEPA 2003, Sch 5, para 52)*. HMRC provide an annual return form (EMI 40), which is available on HMRC's website (www.hmrc.gov.uk/shareschemes/emi40-2012.pdf).

# COMPANY SHARE OPTION PLANS (CSOPs)

*(ITEPA 2003, Pt 7, Ch 8, Sch 4)*

## Taxation

*(ITEPA 2003, ss 524, 526)*

*Grant of option* – A tax charge can arise if an option is granted at a discount (ie the consideration (if any) for the grant of the option and the amount payable on exercise is less than the market value of the relevant shares) (*s 526*).

*Exercise of option* – No income tax charge arises if the following conditions are satisfied (s 524):

- The option is exercised in accordance with the provisions of the scheme at a time when the scheme is approved; and

- The avoidance of tax or National Insurance Contributions is not the main purpose (or one of the main purposes) of any arrangement under which the option was granted or exercised; and

- One of the following conditions is met:

  - The option is exercised on after the third anniversary of the date of grant and not later than the tenth anniversary of that date; or

  - The option is exercised before the third anniversary of the date of grant and is so exercised by virtue of a 'good leaver' provision included in the scheme (*s 524(2A)*; see ESSUM48200).

For options granted before 9 April 2003, the option must be exercised not less than three years or more than ten years after the date of grant (without exception) and not less than three years after a previous exempt exercise of another option under the same or another approved company share option scheme.

*Capital Gains Tax* – A disposal of shares is a chargeable occasion for capital gains tax purposes.

*National Insurance Contributions* – HMRC guidance on CSOPs for National Insurance Contributions purposes is contained in the National Insurance Manual at NIM06809.

## Scheme requirements

*(ITEPA 2003, Sch 4)*

The requirements for CSOP schemes to be approved by HMRC include the following:

- *General* – The scheme must meet the purpose of providing benefits in the form of share options to employees and directors, and must not include features that are neither essential nor reasonably incidental to that purpose.

  No participant can be granted approved options with a market value of more than £30,000 (calculated at the date of grant) (*Sch 4, Pt 2*).

- *Eligible employees* – The scheme rules must provide that the individual is a full-time director or a 'qualifying employee' of the scheme organiser (or constituent company in a group scheme). Participation in the scheme is not open to individuals if they and/or their associates have (or have had in the previous 12 months) a material interest in a close company whose shares are being used in the scheme, or in certain other companies. 'Material interest' is defined in the legislation, but broadly means more than 25% of the ordinary share capital of the company, or more than 25% of the assets which would be available for distribution among the participators (*Sch 4, Pt 3*).

- *Scheme shares* – The CSOP scheme must satisfy various requirements relating to shares that may be subject to share options. For example, eligible shares must be fully paid up and not redeemable. Options cannot be granted over shares in a company which is under the control of a listed company with effect from 24 September 2010, subject to transitional provisions (*Sch 4, Pt 4*).

- *Share options* – The scheme must meet certain requirements relating to the share options, may make provisions in relation to the acquisition cost of the shares subject to the option and the non-transferability of those options, and provisions as to when they may be exercised in specified circumstances (eg following the participant's death) (*Sch 4, Pt 5*).

- *Exchange of options* – The scheme rules may allow for an exchange of options on a company reorganisation, if certain conditions are satisfied (*Sch 4, Pt 6*).

**Notes**

(1)   A CSOP scheme is a share option plan arranged by a company, which provides for share options to be granted to employees and directors. The company can only grant options if HMRC has approved the scheme (*ITEPA 2003, Sch 4 Pt 7*).

(2)   HMRC has produced an informal checklist in respect of CSOP scheme requirements to be satisfied, for approval or review purposes (www.hmrc.gov.uk/manuals/essum/essum47903.htm).

## SAVE AS YOU EARN (SAYE) SCHEMES
(*ITEPA 2003, Pt 7, Ch 7, Sch 3*)

## Taxation
(*ITEPA 2003, Pt 7, Ch 7*)

*Grant of option* – No income tax charge arises on the grant of an approved SAYE share option. If options are accidentally granted at a discount to the market value of the shares on the agreed valuation date in excess of the permitted 20%, such options should be treated as not having been granted in accordance with the provisions of an approved SAYE share option scheme and so will attract no tax advantages (*ESSUM39350*).

*Exercise of option* – No income tax charge arises on the exercise of the share option if the following conditions are satisfied (*s 519*):

- The option is exercised in accordance with the provisions of the SAYE scheme at a time when the scheme is approved; and

- The avoidance of tax or National Insurance Contributions is not the main purpose (or one of the main purposes) of any arrangement under which the option was granted or exercised; and

- One of the following conditions is met:

  - The option is exercised on or after the third anniversary of the date on which it was granted; or

  - The option is exercised before the third anniversary of the date of grant in certain defined circumstances such as injury, disability or redundancy.

*Interest and bonuses* – No income tax liability arises on interest and any bonus payable under a certified SAYE savings arrangement (*ITTOIA 2005, ss 702–703*).

*Capital Gains Tax* – A disposal of shares is a chargeable occasion for capital gains tax purposes.

*National Insurance Contributions* – No liability arises when the proceeds of the savings are used to buy shares. As to the National Insurance Contributions position generally, see *NIM06808*.

## Scheme requirements

(*ITEPA 2003, Sch 3*)

*General* – The scheme must meet the purpose of providing benefits in the form of share options to employees and directors, and must not include features that are neither essential nor reasonably incidental to that purpose. The scheme must provide that every individual who meets certain eligibility criteria may participate (eg an employee (whether full-time or part-time) or full-time director of the scheme organiser or (in the case of a group) of a constituent company, who has been an employee or director at all times during a qualifying period (specified in the scheme rules) not exceeding five years). Participation in the scheme must be on similar terms (*Sch 3, Pt 2*).

*Eligible employees* – The scheme rules must provide that the individual is a current director or employee of the scheme organiser (or constituent company in a group scheme). Participation in the scheme is not open to individuals if they and/or their associates have (or have had in the previous 12 months) a material interest in a close company whose shares are being used in the scheme, or in certain other companies. 'Material interest' is defined in the legislation, but broadly means more than 25% of the ordinary share capital of the company, or more than 25% of the assets which would be available for distribution among the participators (*Sch 3, Pt 3*).

*Scheme shares* – SAYE option scheme shares must form part of the ordinary share capital of the scheme organiser or certain other companies, and must satisfy various other eligibility requirements (eg the shares must be fully paid up and not redeemable), and must not be subject to any restrictions other than those attaching to all shares of the same class, or which are permitted by the approved SAYE option schemes legislation (*Sch 3, Pt 4*).

*Linked savings arrangements* – The scheme must provide for shares acquired by exercising SAYE scheme options to be bought with funds up to the amount of repayments and interest under a certified SAYE savings arrangement approved by HMRC. Individuals may contract to make monthly contributions over a three or five year period, and may choose to leave the contributions in their accounts for an additional two years (ESSUM34170–34180). The scheme must also provide for an individual's contributions to the approved savings arrangement to be sufficient (as far as possible) to secure repayment of the exercise price of the share options granted under the scheme.

The maximum contribution that may be permitted is £250 per month. The minimum contribution allowed under the scheme cannot exceed £10 per month (nb the current SAYE Prospectus imposes a minimum monthly contribution of £5 per month under a savings contract (see ESSUM34510) *(Sch 3, Pt 5)*.

*Share options that may be granted under the scheme* – The SAYE scheme must satisfy various requirements, including in relation to the exercise price of the option shares, the non-transferability of share options, when the options can be exercised and the 'specified age' of the individual for the purposes of the scheme *(Sch 3, Pt 6)*.

*Exchange of share options* – The scheme rules may allow for an exchange of options on a company reorganisation, if certain conditions are satisfied *(Sch 3, Pt 7)*.

**Notes**

(1) *Motivation* – A SAYE scheme allows a company to grant eligible employees and directors an option to purchase the company's shares in the future at a price determined at the time of invitation.

(2) *Approval required* – SAYE option schemes are subject to approval by HMRC *(Sch 3, Pt 8)*. HMRC has produced a specimen set of scheme rules and other specimen documentation relating to SAYE schemes in the Employee Share Schemes User Manual (ESSUM38810–38814). A model SAYE Prospectus is also available from: www.hmrc.gov.uk/shareschemes/model-saye-prospectus.pdf.

(3) *Bonus rates* – The bonus rate applicable to a SAYE share option scheme is set at the time the savings contract is entered into, and is unaffected by any subsequent change to the rate. The rates are calculated from market swap rates quoted in the Financial Times the rates are published here: www.hmrc.gov.uk/shareschemes/saye-bonus-rates.htm *(ITEPA 2003, Sch 3, Pt 5)*

(4) *Interest rates* – The interest rates for SAYE schemes for early withdrawal and otherwise are published here: www.hmrc.gov.uk/shareschemes/historical-bonus-rates.pdf.

## EMPLOYEE SHAREHOLDER STATUS

*(FB 2013, cl 54, Sch 22)*

(1) *General* – Certain CGT, income tax and National Insurance exemptions will be available to individuals who take up shares acquired through the adoption of an 'employee shareholder' employment status under the *Growth and Infrastructure Bill (cl 27)*. This clause inserts *s 205A* into the *Employment Rights Act 1996*, which broadly provides that if the company and individual agree to the individual being an employee shareholder, the company must issue or allot shares worth at least £2,000. However, the House of Lords voted against *cl 27* in the Bill on 20 March 2013, so the future of employee shareholder status looks uncertain.

(2) *Employment rights* – By taking up employee shareholder status the employee opts out of certain employment rights, including:

- Unfair dismissal, apart from when this is automatically unfair or relates to anti-discrimination law;

- Right to request studying or training;

- Right to flexible working;

- Statutory redundancy pay; and

- The employee must give 16 weeks' notice (instead of 8 weeks) when returning from maternity or adoption leave.

(3)  *CGT exemption limit* – The capital gains tax exemption applies to qualifying shares issued or allotted to an employee under an employee shareholder agreement with a total 'unrestricted market value' not exceeding £50,000 on receipt. The shares cease to be exempt from CGT when the employee disposes of them (*TCGA 1992, ss 236B–236G*).

(4)  *Income tax and NI exemption* – The first £2,000 of shares awarded to an employee taking up employee shareholder status will be free of income tax and NICs, and the employee is deemed to have paid £2,000 for the shares acquired (*ITEPA 2003, ss 226A–226D*).

No income tax charge arises under *ITTOIA 2005, Pt 4, Ch 3* ('Tax on dividends etc from UK companies') if the shares are sold back to the company (i.e. on a payment by the company for a purchase own shares from the individual) in respect of shares in that company which are exempt employee shareholder shares, if the individual is not an employee (or office holder) of the employer company or associated company at the time of disposal (*ITTOIA 2005, s 385A*).

(5)  *Conditions* – All the tax exemptions are subject to qualifying conditions. These include that the employee who receives the shares must not have a 'material interest' in the company (or its parent company) when the share is issued or allotted or within one year previously, and must not be connected with an individual with such an interest (*ITEPA 2003, s 226D; TCGA 1992, s 236D*).

The employee is not treated as disposing of an asset by relinquishing rights under an employee shareholder agreement, and employee shareholder shares are treated as being acquired for no consideration.

(6)  *Corporation tax* – The deemed payment of £2,000 for income tax purposes is disregarded for various purposes relating to the corporation tax deduction under *CTA 2009, Pt 12* ('Other relief for employee share acquisitions') available to a company when an employee shareholder acquires shares.

(7)  *Commencement* – The exemptions will apply to shares received through the adoption of employee shareholder status on or after 1 September 2013, but see note 1) above.


## REFORM OF SHARE SCHEMES

### Approved share schemes

Following the Office of Tax Simplification (OTS) review into tax advantaged share schemes the Government will replace the system of HMRC approval of share schemes with self-certification of share schemes by the companies that use them. Legislation for this change will be introduced in the *Finance Bill 2014* (*Budget, 20 March 2013*).

## Unapproved share schemes

The Government will consult on how to take forward recommendations made by the OTS in their review of unapproved share schemes (*Budget, 20 March 2013*).

# 5

# Pensions, Investment income etc

## PENSIONS

*(FA 2004, Pt 4, Schs 28–36)*

Tax relief is available on contributions to registered pension schemes (subject to potential relief restrictions; see below) as follows (*FA 2004, s 190*):

- up to 100% of relevant UK earnings for a tax year; or
- up to £3,600 per annum if relevant UK earnings are lower than this amount.

**Notes**

(1) A relevant UK individual is entitled to tax relief in respect of 'relievable pension contributions'. These exclude contributions after the individual has reached age 75, and any contributions by the individual's employer (*FA 2004, s 188(3)*).

(2) Additional contributions may be made in excess of the above limits, but no further tax relief is available.

(3) Normal minimum pension age is 55 from 6 April 2010 (members of certain professions and occupations can retire earlier; see below).

(4) Tax relief for pension contributions is subject to potential restrictions (see below).

(5) Contracting out through a defined contribution scheme is abolished with effect from 6 April 2012. Contracting out for other pension schemes will be abolished from 6 April 2016 (*Budget, 20 March 2013*).

## RESTRICTIONS ON RELIEF

*(FA 2004, ss 218, 228, 215, 227)*

### Annual and lifetime allowances

*(FA 2004, ss 218, 228)*

|  | 2013–14 | 2012–13 | 2011–12 | 2010–11 | 2009–10 | 2008–09 |
|---|---|---|---|---|---|---|
|  | £ | £ | £ | £ | £ | £ |
| Annual Allowance | 50,000 | 50,000 | 50,000 | 255,000 | 245,000 | 235,000 |
| Lifetime Allowance | 1,500,000 | 1,500,000 | 1,800,000 | 1,800,000 | 1,750,000 | 1,650,000 |

## Annual allowance charge

*(FA 2004, s 227)*

- *Rate of charge* – From 2011–12, the annual allowance charge is levied at the 'appropriate rate' (ie broadly the individual's marginal tax rate). An individual with an annual allowance charge of over £2,000 will in most cases be able to elect for his pension scheme to pay the liability instead, with scheme benefits being actuarially reduced accordingly *(FA 2004, s 237B)*.

  For 2010–11, the annual allowance charge was 40% of the amount by which the total pension input amount exceeded the annual allowance.

- *Carry forward of unused annual allowance* – Any unused annual allowance for up to three tax years preceding 'the current tax year' may be added to the annual allowance available for the current tax year, if it arises for a tax year in which the individual was a member of a registered pension scheme (even if the pension input amount for that year was nil). Unused allowances for 2008–09, 2009–10 and 2010–11 can be carried forward to 2011–12. The earliest years' unused allowance is used first. However, for these purposes the annual allowance is treated as being £50,000 for each of 2008–09, 2009–10 and 2010–11 *(FA 2004, s 228A)*.

## Lifetime allowance charge

*(FA 2004, s 215)*

- 25% of the amount by which total pension savings exceed the lifetime allowance, if taken as a pension; or

- 55% of the excess if taken as a lump sum.

- Transitional provisions in *Finance Act 2011* provide protection from the lifetime allowance charge from 6 April 2012 for individuals with pension savings which were based on the expectation that the lifetime allowance would remain at the previous level of £1.8 million, where certain conditions are satisfied *(FA 2011, s 67, Sch 18)*.

## TAX CHARGES ON PAYMENTS FROM REGISTERED PENSION SCHEMES

*(FA 2004, Pt 4, Ch 5)*

| Charge | Rates |
|---|---|
| Lifetime allowance charge *(FA 2004, s 215)* | See **Lifetime allowance charge**<br>• 55% – if the amount over the lifetime allowance is paid as a lump sum<br>• 25% – if the amount over the lifetime allowance is not taken as a lump sum |

*continued*

| Charge | Rates |
|---|---|
| Annual allowance charge (**Note 2**) | See **Annual allowance charge** |
| (*FA 2004, s 227*) | 20%; 40%; 50% |
| Unauthorised payments charge | 40% |
| (*FA 2004, s 208*) | |
| Unauthorised payments surcharge | 15% |
| (*FA 2004, s 209*) | |
| Short service refund lump sum charge | From 2010–11: |
| (*FA 2004, s 205; SI 2010/536*) | • 20% on first £20,000; |
| | • 50% on amount over £20,000 |
| | To 2009–10: |
| | • 20% on first £10,800; |
| | • 40% on amounts over £10,800 |
| Serious ill-health lump sum charge (**Note 3**) | 55% |
| (*FA 2004, s 205A*) | |
| Special lump sum death benefits charge | 55% |
| (*FA 2004, s 206*) | |
| Authorised surplus payments charge | 35% |
| (*FA 2004, s 207*) | |
| Scheme sanction charge | 5%–40% |
| (*FA 2004, s 240*) | |
| De-registration charge | 40% |
| (*FA 2004, s 242*) | |

**Notes**

(1)  *Lifetime allowance charge* – Transitional provisions in *Finance Act 2011* provide protection from the lifetime allowance charge from 6 April 2012 for individuals with pension savings which were based on the expectation that the lifetime allowance would remain at the previous level of £1.8 million, where certain conditions are satisfied (*FA 2011, s 67, Sch 18*).

(2)  *Annual allowance charge* – The annual allowance charge (from 2011–12) is at the appropriate rate on the excess of the 'total pension input amount' (see *FA 2004, s 229*) over the annual allowance for the tax year. The 'appropriate rate' is the basic rate of income tax (20%) to the extent that the excess (when added to 'reduced net income') does not exceed the individual's basic rate limit for the year, the higher rate (40%) above the basic rate limit up to the higher rate limit, and the additional rate (50%) to the extent of any amount in excess of the higher rate limit for the tax year. For previous tax years, the charge is 40% on the excess of pension inputs over the annual allowance.

An individual with an annual allowance charge of over £2,000 will in most cases be able to elect for his pension scheme to pay the liability instead, with scheme benefits being actuarially reduced accordingly (*FA 2004, s 237B*).

For 2010–11, the annual allowance charge was 40% of the amount by which the total pension input amount exceeded the annual allowance.

(3) *Serious ill-health lump sum charge* – The charge (in *FA 2004, s 205A*) was introduced with effect for 2011–12 and subsequent tax years, in respect of lump sums paid on or after 6 April 2011 (*FA 2011, Sch 16, para 102*).

# PROFESSIONS AND OCCUPATIONS WITH PROTECTED RETIREMENT AGES

(*FA 2004, Sch 36, paras 21, 23; SI 2005/3451, reg 3, Sch 2*)

- Athletes,
- Badminton players,
- Boxers,
- Cricketers,
- Cyclists,
- Dancers,
- Divers (saturation, deep sea and free swimming)
- Footballers,
- Golfers,
- Ice hockey players,
- Jockeys – flat racing,
- Jockeys – national hunt,
- Members of the Reserve Forces,
- Models,
- Motor cycle riders (Motocross or road racing),
- Motor racing drivers,
- Rugby League players,
- Rugby Union players,
- Skiers (downhill),
- Snooker or billiards players,
- Speedway riders,
- Squash players,
- Table tennis players,
- Tennis players (including real tennis)
- Trapeze artists, and
- Wrestlers

**Notes**

(1)   *Normal retirement age* – Retirement benefits can generally only be taken from a registered pension scheme from minimum pension age of 55 (prior to 6 April 2010 this was 50). Lower pension ages for certain qualifying occupations were generally abolished from 6 April 2006.

(2)   *Protected age* – The above occupations and profession have protected pre-existing rights to take benefits under a personal pension scheme or retirement annuity contract before the age of 50. This is the individual's protected pension age (HMRC Registered Pension Schemes Manual, RPSM03106035).

## INDIVIDUAL SAVING ACCOUNTS (ISAs)

*(ITTOIA 2005, Pt 6, Ch 3; SI 1998/1870, reg 4)*

|  | 2013–14 | 2012–13 | 2011–12 | 2010–11 |
|---|---|---|---|---|
|  | Age 18 and over | Age 18 and over | Age 18 and over | Age 18 and over |
| Overall limit | £11,520 | £11,280 | £10,680 | £10,200 |
| Cash limit | £5,760 | £5,640 | £5,340 | £5,100 |
| Junior ISA | Under 18 £3,720 | Under 18 £3,600 | Under 18 £3,600 | – |

**Notes**

(1)   *Young people* – Whether or not a person aged 16 to 18 already holds a Junior ISA (see Note 2 below), they may invest in an adult cash ISA up to the cash limit, but not in a stocks and shares ISA.

(2)   *Junior ISA* (JISA) – These became available from 1 November 2011 to UK resident children (under 18s) who do not have a Child Trust Fund (CTF) account. The investment limit can be divided between cash and stocks and shares JISA. When the holder reaches the age of 18, a JISA becomes an adult ISA *(ITTOIA 2005, s 695A)*.

## INVESTMENTS FOR CHILDREN BY PARENTS

*(ITTOIA 2005, s 629)*

- The 'settlements' anti-avoidance provisions apply to the income of a relevant child, which would otherwise be income of the settlor. A 'relevant child' is the settlor's minor child (including a stepchild), who is neither married nor in a civil partnership. The child's income is deemed to be that of the parent for income tax purposes.

- However, if the child's settlement income from the parent does not exceed £100, the legislation does not apply in that tax year. This £100 limit for the tax year applies separately to each parent.

- When a parent contributes to a JISA on behalf of their child or to a child trust fund account (CTF) the funds are not considered to be settlement income from the parent (see ISA guidance notes: www.hmrc.gov.uk/isa/isa-guidance-notes.pdf).

- If a parent contributes to an adult cash ISA on behalf of their child the funds contributed are considered to be settlement income under *ITTOIA 2005, s 629*, so the ISA income will be considered to the parent's income if it exceeds £100 per tax year.

## ENTERPRISE INVESTMENT SCHEME (EIS)

*(ITA 2007, Pt 5)*

### EIS income tax relief annual limit

*(ITA 2007, s 158)*

| Shares issued | Maximum investment per tax year | Rate of relief |
|---|---|---|
| From 2012–13 | £1,000,000 | 30% |
| From 2011–12 | £500,000 | 30% |
| From 2008–09 | £500,000 | 20% |
| From 2006–07 | £400,000 | 20% |
| From 2004–05 | £200,000 | 20% |

**Notes**

(1) *Maximum annual investment* – The maximum EIS annual investment limit for individuals is increased to £1,000,000 with effect from 6 April 2012 (*ITA 2007, s 158*).

(2) *Minimum subscription* – A £500 minimum subscription upon which relief is available in a tax year applies until 2011–12, but this is removed with effect from 2012–13. The restriction does not apply to subscriptions made through an approved investment fund (*ITA 2007, s 157(2), (3)*).

(3) *Carry back of EIS relief (ITA 2007, s 158(4))* – EIS relief is available for the tax year in which the shares are issued.

However, for shares issued from 2009–10 onwards, the investor may claim to treat some or all of the shares as issued in the year preceding that in which the shares were issued. There is no limit on the amount which may be carried back, subject to the overriding relief limit for that earlier year.

For shares issued up to and including the tax year 2008–09, where the shares are issued before 6 October in the tax year, up to half can be treated as having been issued in the previous tax year, subject to the following limits:

- 2006–07 to 2008–09 – £50,000;
- 1998–99 to 2005–06 – £25,000.

## SEED ENTERPRISE INVESTMENT SCHEME (SEIS)

*(TCGA1992, ss150E–150G & ITA 2007, Pt 5A)*

| Shares issued in: | Maximum investment in the tax year | Rate of income tax relief | Rate of CGT reinvestment relief |
|---|---|---|---|
| 2016/17 | £100,000 | 50% | Nil |
| 2015/16 | £100,000 | 50% | Nil |
| 2014/15 | £100,000 | 50% | Nil |
| 2013/14 | £100,000 | 50% | 50% |
| 2012/13 | £100,000 | 50% | 100% |

**Notes**

(1) *General* – The SEIS is a tax-advantaged venture capital scheme similar to EIS. It is designed to incentivise investment in small, early stage companies. A claim for SEIS is broadly available to individuals ('qualifying investors') who subscribe for relevant shares in a 'qualifying company' where certain requirements are satisfied. The SEIS applies to 'smaller' companies, broadly those with 25 or fewer employees and assets of up to £200,000. An upper limit applies to the total amount of investments in the issuing company of £150,000.

(2) *Scope* – SEIS income tax relief applies to shares issued on or after 6 April 2012 and before 6 April 2017 (subject to any extension by Treasury order).

(3) *Income tax relief* – The income tax relief is given upon making a claim as a reduction in the individual's tax liability for the current tax year. Alternatively, a claim can be made to treat the shares as having been issued in the preceding tax year (but not so as to treat them as acquired before 2012–13). This carry-back election is also effective for CGT reinvestment relief (HMRC Venture Capital Manual VCM45010).

(4) *CGT reinvestment relief* – This relief is given for gains from disposals made in the same tax year as the SEIS shares are subscribed for, or treated as subscribed for if the carry-back election is used. This relief only applies for gains arising in 2012–13 and/or 2013–14 *(TCGA 1992, Sch 5BB)*.The reinvestment relief is dependent upon the income tax relief being available for the SEIS shares acquired, and will be withdrawn if the income tax relief is later withdrawn for those shares.

## VENTURE CAPITAL TRUSTS (VCT)

*(ITA 2007, Pt 6)*

## VCT relief annual limit

(ITA 2007, ss 262–263)

| Shares issued | Maximum annual investment | Rate of relief |
|---|---|---|
| From 6 April 2006 | £200,000 | 30% |
| From 6 April 2004 | £200,000 | 40% |
| From 6 April 2000 | £100,000 | 20% |

**Notes**

(1) *Income tax relief* – VCT income tax relief is given for the tax year in which the shares are issued by the VCT. The relief available is the lower of 30% (from 6 April 2006) on amounts up to the above maximum, and the amount which reduces the individual's income tax liability to nil.

(2) *Dividend exemption* – Individual investors are exempt from income tax on dividends in respect of ordinary VCT shares acquired with the above maximum amounts, provided that the shares were acquired for genuine commercial reasons and not for a tax avoidance purpose (*ITTOIA 2005, Pt 6, Ch 5*).

(3) *CGT exemption* – Disposals of VCT shares by individual investors are exempt from CGT (and losses are not allowable) where the shares were acquired within the above permitted maximum amounts, and if certain other conditions are satisfied (*TCGA 1992, ss 151A, 151B*).

(4) Changes to VCT rules relaxed the definition of qualifying company so that it must have fewer than 250 employees (previously 50), and gross assets of no more than £15 million (previously £7 million) before investment and £16 million (previously £8 million) thereafter; and increased the maximum annual amount of State-aided risk capital (including EIS and VCT) that can be invested in an individual company to £5 million (previously £2 million). These changes took effect from 17 July 2012 (*FA 2012, Sch 8, paras 18–22*).

# LEASE PREMIUMS

## Short leases

(*ITTOIA 2005, s 277; CTA 2009, s 217*)

$$P \times \frac{(50 - Y)}{50}$$

Where–

P is the premium, and

Y is the number of complete periods of 12 months (other than the first) comprised in the effective duration of the lease.

**Notes**

(1) A short lease is broadly a lease with 50 years or less to run.

(2) The amount calculated using the above formula is treated as a property business receipt for the tax year or accounting period in which the lease is granted.

(3) The amount of the premium for the grant of a short lease which is brought into account as a property business receipt is deducted from the consideration taken into account for capital gains purposes, in accordance with *TCGA 1992, Sch 8, paras 5, 7*.

(4) The percentages of short lease premium charged as a property business receipt and taken into account for capital gains purposes are summarised in the table below (see PIM1205):

| Length of lease in years | Percentage of premium taxable as receipt of property business | Percentage of premium chargeable as a capital gain |
|---|---|---|
| More than 50 | 0 | 100 |
| 50 | 2 | 98 |
| 49 | 4 | 96 |
| 48 | 6 | 94 |
| 47 | 8 | 92 |
| 46 | 10 | 90 |
| 45 | 12 | 88 |
| 44 | 14 | 86 |
| 43 | 16 | 84 |
| 42 | 18 | 82 |
| 41 | 20 | 80 |
| 40 | 22 | 78 |
| 39 | 24 | 76 |
| 38 | 26 | 74 |
| 37 | 28 | 72 |
| 36 | 30 | 70 |
| 35 | 32 | 68 |
| 34 | 34 | 66 |
| 33 | 36 | 64 |
| 32 | 38 | 62 |
| 31 | 40 | 60 |
| 30 | 42 | 58 |
| 29 | 44 | 56 |
| 28 | 46 | 54 |
| 27 | 48 | 52 |
| 26 | 50 | 50 |
| 25 | 52 | 48 |
| 24 | 54 | 46 |
| 23 | 56 | 44 |
| 22 | 58 | 42 |
| 21 | 60 | 40 |
| 20 | 62 | 38 |
| 19 | 64 | 36 |
| 18 | 66 | 34 |
| 17 | 68 | 32 |
| 16 | 70 | 30 |
| 15 | 72 | 28 |
| 14 | 74 | 26 |
| 13 | 76 | 24 |
| 12 | 78 | 22 |

| Length of lease in years | Percentage of premium taxable as receipt of property business | Percentage of premium chargeable as a capital gain |
|---|---|---|
| 11 | 80 | 20 |
| 10 | 82 | 18 |
| 9 | 84 | 16 |
| 8 | 86 | 14 |
| 7 | 88 | 12 |
| 6 | 90 | 10 |
| 5 | 92 | 8 |
| 4 | 94 | 6 |
| 3 | 96 | 4 |
| 2 | 98 | 2 |
| 1 or less | 100 | 0 |

## Long Leases

- Where the payment relates to a lease of more than 50 years, a premium is treated as being within the lease premium regime if it falls within *ITTOIA 2005 s 303, rule 1* or *CTA 2009, s 243.*

- For leases granted on and after 1 April 2013 for companies, and on and after 6 April 2013 for unincorporated businesses, the lease premium relief is limited (*FB 2013, Sch 26*).

## Leases which are wasting assets

*(TCGA 1992, Sch 8, para 1)*

A short lease is a wasting asset. The allowable expenditure attributable to a short lease therefore reduces over its term. The rate at which the expenditure is written off is fixed in accordance with the table in *TCGA 1992, Sch 8, para 1* (see **Chapter 8: Capital Gains Tax**).

## RELIEF FOR PREMIUMS PAID

*(ITTOIA 2005, s 61; CTA 2009, s 63)*

### (a) Tenant occupies the whole of the land

$$\frac{A}{TRP}$$

Where:

A is the unreduced amount of the taxed receipt; and

TRP is the number of days in the receipt period of the taxed receipt.

## (b)  Tenant occupies part of the land

$$\frac{F \times A}{TRP}$$

Where:

F is the fraction of the land occupied (calculated on a just and reasonable basis); and

A and TRP have the same meaning as in (a) above.

**Notes**

(1)   In the case of land used in a trade, the income element of a short lease premium is allowable as a deduction from the tenant's business profits for income tax or corporation tax purposes. The above formulae are used to calculate the allowable proportion of the 'taxed receipt' (broadly the amount of the lease taxed on the landlord as a rental business receipt) available as a deduction for the tenant. Relief is also available if the land is sub-let.

(2)   The formula in (a) above is relevant if the tenant occupies the whole of the land for trading purposes. The formula in (b) applies if only part of the land is so used.

## COMMUNITY INVESTMENT TAX RELIEF (CITR)

*(ITA 2007, Pt 7; CTA 2010, Pt 7)*

- CITR applies to investments in accredited Community Development Finance Institutions (CDFIs) made on or after 17 January 2002. Investing individuals (or companies) can claim tax relief of up to 25% of the amount of the investment. To obtain maximum relief under the scheme, the investment must be held for at least five years (or accounting periods).

- The tax relief is spread over the five-year term of the investment, giving tax relief of 5% of the 'invested amount' per year *(ITA 2007, s 335(2); CTA 2010, s 220(3))*.

- CITR is given as a reduction in the investor's tax liability, and is limited to the amount of that liability (ie it cannot reduce a liability below zero).

- Relief is claimed for the tax year or accounting period in which the investment falls and the four subsequent tax years or accounting periods *(ITA 2007, s 335(3); CTA 2010, s 220(4))*.

- The 'invested amount' in the case of loans is determined as follows *(ITA 2007, s 337(2); CTA 2010, s 222(2))*:

   ○   Tax year of investment – the average capital balance for the first year of the five-year period;

   ○   Next tax year – the average capital balance for the second year of the five-year period;

   ○   Subsequent years – the average capital balance for the 12-month period beginning with the anniversary of the investment date in the tax year (or accounting period) (or if less, the average capital balance for the six months beginning 18 months after the investment date).

- The conditions to be satisfied in relation to a loan include that the loan must not have been made on terms that allow repayments as follows (*ITA 2007, s 345(3); CTA 2010, s 226(3)*):

  ○ During the first two years of the five year period – any of the loan capital advanced;

  ○ During the third year – more than 25% of the loan capital outstanding at the end of those two years;

  ○ Before the end of the fourth year – more than 50% of that loan capital;

  ○ Before the end of the period – more than 75% of that loan capital.

- From April 2013 there are restrictions for corporate investors of the amounts of relief they can receive under CITR. Also for both individual and corporate investors any unused relief can be carried forward (*FB 2013, Sch 25*).

*6*

# Taxation of business profits

## CASH BASIS FOR SMALL BUSINESSES

*(FB 2013, cl 17, Sch 4)*

● From 6 April 2013 certain businesses can elect to calculate profits/losses for tax purposes on the basis of the cash received and expenses paid out, known as the cash basis.

● This cash basis replaces the existing cash basis used by barristers, with some transitional arrangements.

**Notes:**

(1) *Permitted turnover* – The cash basis is only available to businesses whose turnover is under the VAT registration threshold (£79,000 from 1 April 2013, see **Chapter 12: VAT**), or for Universal Credit claimants, where the turnover if up to twice the VAT registration threshold *(ITTOIA 2005, s 31B)*.

(2) *Excluded businesses* – The following businesses cannot use the cash basis:

● companies;

● LLPs;

● farmers using the herd basis;

● persons using profit averaging under *ITTOIA 2005, s 221*;

● persons carrying on a mineral extraction trade

● persons who have claimed business premises renovation allowance or R&D allowance; and

● Lloyd's underwriters.

(3) *Leaving the cash basis* – Once a business is using the cash basis it can carry on doing so until its annual turnover is twice the VAT registration threshold (£158,000 from April 2013). Alternatively the business may leave the cash basis when its commercial circumstances change such that the cash basis is no longer appropriate.

(4) *Loan interest* – The deduction for loan interest paid is limited to £500 per year, although a full deduction for hire purchase costs is permitted *(ITA 2007, s 384A*, inserted by *FB 2013, Sch 4)*.

(5) *Losses* – Under the cash basis losses can only be carried forward to the next tax year. No sideways or carry back of loss relief is permitted *(ITA 2007, s 74E)*.

(6) *Accounting year* – The business can make up its accounts to any date in the year and use the cash basis.

(7)    *Further information* – Guidance for the self-employed is provided in the HMRC helpsheet: www.hmrc.gov.uk/budget-updates/11dec12/2014-2016-helpsheet.pdf. Technical guidance is provided here: www.hmrc.gov.uk/budget-updates/march 2013/simpler-income-tax-tech-note.pdf

The simplified reporting requirement (three line accounts) for the income tax Self Assessment return continue to be aligned with the VAT registration threshold (*Budget, 21 March 2012*; for VAT registration threshold see **Chapter 12**).

## FIXED RATE DEDUCTIONS

(*ITTOIA 2005, Ch 5A*, inserted by *FB 2013, Sch 5*)

**Optional use** – From 6 April 2013 any unincorporated trading business or profession, can use the following flat rate expenses to replace the calculation of actual costs incurred, whether or not the business opts to use the cash basis described above (*ITTOIA 2005, s 94B*).

**Not companies** – Any firm which includes a company as a partner is prohibited from using these flat rate deductions (*ITTOIA 2005, s 94C*).

## Motor expenses

| Vehicle and usage | Rate per mile |
|---|---|
| Car – first 10,000 miles per year | 45p |
| Car – in excess of 10,000 miles per year | 25p |
| Motor cycle – all miles | 24p |

**Notes**

(1)    *Only deduction* – If the business uses the above mileage rates it cannot make any other deductions in respect of that vehicle.

(2)    *Excluded vehicles* – Goods vehicles or motorcycles acquired under the cash basis where a full deduction has been made for the cost, and vehicles for which capital allowances have previously been claimed cannot use these mileage rates (*ITTOIA 2003, s 94E*).

## Use of home for business purposes

| Number of hours used per month | Rate per month |
|---|---|
| 25–50 hours | £10 |
| 51–100 hours | £18 |
| 101 hours or more | £26 |

**Notes**

(1)    *General* – Businesses that use the home for business purposes can opt to use the above fixed deductions for the cost of using the home.

(2)    *Separate months* – The flat rate expense claimed can be different for each month, depending on the use in a particular month.

71

## Business premises used partly as a home

| Number of occupants who live in the premises | Rate per month |
|---|---|
| 1 | £350 |
| 2 | £500 |
| 3 or more | £650 |

**Notes**

(1)    *General* – Where business premises, such as a hotel or bed and breakfast business are used partly for private purposes as a home an adjustment to the deductible costs can be made based on the number of occupants using the premises as a home each month. This adjustment is subtracted from actual expenses so that personal costs are excluded (*FB 2013, cl 94*).

(2)    *National rates* – This flat rate expense replaces all locally agreed rates of private use disallowance from 6 April 2013.

(3)    *Further information* – Guidance on the simplified expenses for small businesses is given here: www.hmrc.gov.uk/budget-updates/march2013/simpler-income-tax-tech-note.pdf.

## FARMERS, MARKET GARDENERS AND CREATIVE ARTISTS – RELIEF FOR FLUCTUATING PROFITS

(*ITTOIA 2005, Pt 2, Ch 16*))

## General

(1)    *Who can use it* – Individuals and partnerships engaged in farming, market gardening, the intensive rearing in the UK of livestock or fish on a commercial basis for human food production, or individuals who personally create literary or artistic works, can elect to average profits and losses to take account of fluctuating profits. The averaging rules do not apply to farming activities carried on by a company.

(2)    *Authors and artists* – Profit averaging is available to a taxpayer carrying on a trade or profession on profits wholly or mainly derived from qualifying creative works, ie literary, dramatic, musical or artistic works or designs created by the taxpayer, or one or more of the partners personally where the business is carried on in partnership. This relief is not available to companies, but a special relief for companies in the creative industries has been introduced from April 2013, see **Chapter 7**.

(3)    *How to claim* – Claims are made in the self assessment return for the later year. An averaging claim must normally be made not later than 12 months after 31 January following the later of the two years to be averaged. However, the time limit may be extended if profits are adjusted for some other reason (*ITTOIA 2005, s 222(6)*; see BIM73155).

(4)    *Further information* – Detailed technical guidance is given in the HMRC Business Income Manual at paras BIM73000–73190. Guidance for taxpayers is found in HMRC Help Sheets HS224, HS234.

## Full averaging

(5)  *Less than 70% of profits* – If relevant profits for two consecutive years of assessment are such that one year's profits do not exceed 70% of the profits of the other year, or if relevant profits for one of the tax years is nil, the effect of a claim is broadly to aggregate the profits for the two years and treat one half of the total as the assessable profit for each year.

(6)  *Less than 75% of profits* – An averaging claim requires relevant profits of one of two consecutive tax years to be less than 75% of the profits of the other, or the profits for one of the years to be nil. If the lower profit figure is between 70% and 75% of the higher profit figure, marginal relief may apply.

## Marginal relief

(7)  *Between 70% and 75%* – If the profits for one year exceed 70% of the profits for the other, but are less than 75% of those profits, marginal relief is available. Marginal relief is calculated as follows (*ITTOIA 2005, s 223(4)*):

*Step 1* – Calculate the adjustment, using the following formula:

$$(D \times 3) - (P \times 0.75)$$

where:  D is the difference between the relevant profits for the two years; and

P is the higher relevant profits of the two years

*Step 2* – Add the adjustment to the relevant profits of the tax year of which those profits are lower.

*Step 3* – Deduct the adjustment from the relevant profits of the tax year of which those profits are higher.

(8)  A trading loss is treated as a nil profit for averaging purposes.

## CAR HIRE COSTS

*(ITTOIA 2005 s 48; CTA 2009, ss 56, 1251(2);* BIM47714 *et seq)*

(1)  *Deduction for lease costs* – For leases commencing on or after 1 April 2013 (for corporation tax) or 6 April 2013 (for income tax), the amount of deduction which would otherwise be allowable is reduced by 15% if $CO_2$ emissions exceed 130g/km (160g/km for leases commencing between 1/6 April 2009 and 31 March/5 April 2013).

(2)  *No restriction* – The above restriction does not apply to:

- cars first registered before 1 March 2001;
- cars with low $CO_2$ emissions;
- electrically propelled cars; and
- qualifying hire cars.

(3)  *Prior to 1 or 6 April 2009* – Before April 2009 the restricted deduction for hire charges of motor cars with a retail price of more than £12,000 was calculated as follows:

$$\frac{£12,000 + \frac{1}{2}(\text{retail price} - £12,000)}{\text{retail price}} \times \text{hire charge}$$

## FURNISHED HOLIDAY LETTINGS (FHL)

*(ITTOIA 2005, ss 323–326A; CTA 2009, ss 265–268A)*

### 'Qualifying holiday accommodation' periods

*(ITTOIA 2005, s 325; CTA 2009, s 267)*

| Condition | During the relevant period |
| --- | --- |
| Available for commercial letting | 210 days (140 days for 2011–12 and earlier years) |
| Actually let commercially | 105 days ( 70 days in 2011–12 and earlier years) |
| | A period of longer-term occupation is not a letting as holiday accommodation (see below). |
| Pattern of occupation | No more than 155 days of longer-term occupation |

**Notes**

(1)   *'Qualifying holiday accommodation'* – Accommodation which is let during the tax year (or accounting period, for companies) is 'qualifying holiday accommodation' for that year or accounting period if the 'available for letting', 'actual letting' and 'pattern of occupation' conditions are all satisfied.

(2)   *Period of longer-term occupation* – This is a continuous period of more than 31 days during which the accommodation is in the same occupation, other than under circumstances that are not normal.

(3)   *'Relevant period'* – The 'relevant period' is determined as follows (*ITTOA 2005, s 324; CTA 2009, s 266*):

   •   Accommodation not let by the individual or company as furnished accommodation in the previous tax year (or in the 12 months immediately before the accounting period, for companies) – 12 months beginning with the first day in the tax year or accounting period on which it is so let.

   •   Accommodation let by the individual or company as furnished accommodation in the previous tax year (or in the 12 months immediately before the accounting period, for companies) but not in the following tax year (or not in the 12 months immediately after the accounting period, for companies) – 12 months ending with the last day in the tax year or accounting period on which it was so let.

   •   Any other case – The tax year (or 12 months ending with the last day of the accounting period, for companies).

(4)   *'Averaging' election* – An individual or company who lets several properties as furnished holiday accommodation can elect for the number of days actually let to be averaged over one or more of the properties, such that all the properties reach the minimum threshold of 105 days actually let for the relevant tax year (or accounting period, for companies) (see *ITTOIA 2005, s 326; CTA 2009, s 268*).

(5)   *'Period of grace' election* – This can be used from 2011–12 where a property has qualified as FHL either on the actual days let or because of the use of an averaging election in the previous tax year (or accounting period, for companies). The owner

can elect to treat the property as continuing to qualify for up to two later years or accounting periods, even though it does not satisfy the 'letting condition' of 105 days in those years or accounting periods. The election must be made in the first tax year or accounting period in which the letting condition is not met (see *ITTOIA 2005, s 326A; CTA 2009, s 268A*).

(6)     *Further information* – See HMRC's Property Income Manual at PIM4113, and also Helpsheet HS253 'Furnished holiday lettings' in respect of individuals, etc (www.hmrc.gov.uk/helpsheets/hs253.pdf).

# TIME LIMITS FOR CLAIMS AND ELECTIONS

*(TMA 1970, s 43(1))*

(1)     Claims must be made on the tax return or by an amendment to the return. Except where another period is expressly prescribed, a claim for relief in respect of income tax must be within four years after the end of the tax year.

(2)     Specific exceptions in respect of business profits and losses include the following:

| Provision | Time limit | |
|---|---|---|
| Averaging of profits of farmers or creative artists<br><br>*(ITTIOA 2005, s 222(5))* | First anniversary of 31 January after end of second tax year | |
| Stock transferred to a connected party on cessation of trade to be valued at higher of cost or sale price<br><br>*(ITTOIA 2005, s 178(4); CTA 2009, s 167(4))* | (a) | Individuals – First anniversary of 31 January following the tax year of cessation |
| | (b) | Companies – Two years after the end of the accounting period of cessation |
| Herd basis<br><br>*(ITTOIA 2005, s 124(2); CTA 2009, s 122(2))* | (a) | Individuals – First anniversary of 31 January following the tax year in which the first relevant period of account ends |
| | (b) | Companies – Two years after the end of the relevant accounting period |
| Change of accounting date<br><br>*(ITTOIA 2005, s 217(2))* | Filing date for the relevant tax return | |
| Post-cessation relief<br><br>*(ITTOIA 2005, s 257(4); ITA 2007, s 96(4))* | First anniversary of 31 January following the tax year | |
| Furnished holiday lettings: averaging of letting periods<br><br>*(ITTOIA 2005, s 326(6))* | First anniversary of 31 January following the tax year | |
| Furnished holiday lettings: grace period election<br><br>*(ITTOIA 2005, s 326A(2))* | First anniversary of 31 January following the tax year | |

*continued*

| Provision | Time limit |
| --- | --- |
| Current and preceding year set-off of trading losses<br><br>*(ITA 2007, s 64(5))* | First anniversary of 31 January following the loss-making year |
| Three year carry back of trading losses in opening years of trade<br><br>*(ITA 2007, s 72(3))* | First anniversary of 31 January following the tax year in which the loss is made |
| Relief for trade etc losses against capital gains of the year in which the loss was made or the previous year<br><br>*(TCGA 1992, s 261B(8))* | First anniversary of 31 January following the tax year in which the loss was made |

# 7

# Taxation of companies

## RATES OF CORPORATION TAX

*(CTA 2010, Pt 2, Ch 2, 3; Pt 3)*

| | **Financial Year commencing 1 April** | | | |
|---|---|---|---|---|
| | **2013** | **2012** | **2011** | **2010** |
| **Small Profits Rate** | 20% | 20% | 20% | 21% |
| Small Profits Rate can be claimed by qualifying companies with profits not exceeding | £300,000 | £300,000 | £300,000 | £300,000 |
| Marginal Relief Lower Limit | £300,000 | £300,000 | £300,000 | £300,000 |
| Marginal Relief Upper Limit | £1,500,000 | £1,500,000 | £1,500,000 | £1,500,000 |
| Standard fraction | 3/400 | 1/100 | 3/200 | 7/400 |
| Main rate of Corporation Tax | 23% | 24% | 26% | 28% |
| | **2009** | **2008** | **2007** | **2006** |
| **Small Profits Rate** | 21% | 21% | 20% | 19% |
| Small Profits Rate can be claimed by qualifying companies with profits not exceeding | £300,000 | £300,000 | £300,000 | £300,000 |
| Marginal Relief Lower Limit | £300,000 | £300,000 | £300,000 | £300,000 |
| Marginal Relief Upper Limit | £1,500,000 | £1,500,000 | £1,500,000 | £1,500,000 |
| Standard fraction | 7/400 | 7/400 | 1/40 | 11/400 |
| Main rate of Corporation Tax | 28% | 28% | 30% | 30% |

**Notes**

(1) *Formerly known as* – Prior to 1 April 2010, the 'Small Profits Rate' was known as the 'Small Companies' Rate', 'Marginal Relief' as 'Marginal Small Companies' Relief', and 'Standard fraction' as 'Marginal Small Companies' Relief fraction'.

(2) *Future rates* – The Government has announced that the main rate of corporation tax will fall by 2% from 23% to 21% in April 2014, then to 20% in April 2015 *(Budget, 20 March 2013)*.

(3) *Patent Box* – For accounting periods beginning on and after 1 April 2013 any company can elect for a 10% rate of corporation tax to be applied to all profits attributable to qualifying intellectual property (see **Patent Box** below).

(4) *Reduction in thresholds* – The lower and upper limits for the Small Profits Rate and marginal relief purposes are reduced proportionately for accounting periods

of less than 12 months. The limits are also divided by the number of associated companies carrying on a trade or business for all or part of the accounting period *(CTA 2010, s 25)*. The Small Profits Rate does not apply to 'Close Investment Holding Companies' *(CTA 2010, s 18(b))*.

(5)   *Unit trusts and OEICs* – These companies are subject to corporation tax set at the basic income tax rate charged for the tax year beginning on 6 April in that financial year *(CTA 2010, ss 614, 618)*. For financial years 2008 to 2013 the applicable tax rate is 20%.

(6)   *Oil and gas* – For companies with ring fenced profits from oil-related activities, the Small Profits Rate for financial years 2007 to 2014 is 19% and the ring fence fraction is 11/400 *(FA 2011, s 6)*. The main rate of tax for ring fence profits for financial years 2008–2014 is 30%.

(7)   *Above the line R&D* – For qualifying expenditure incurred on and after 1 April 2013 companies can claim an above the line research and development credit at the rate of 10% *(FB 2013, Sch 14)*.

## EFFECTIVE MARGINAL RATES FOR SMALL PROFITS

*(CTA 2010, s 19)*

| Financial Year (Commencing 1 April) | Marginal Small Profits Rate % |
|---|---|
| 2013 | 23.75 |
| 2012 | 25.00 |
| 2011 | 27.50 |
| 2010 | 29.75 |
| 2009 | 29.75 |
| 2008 | 29.75 |
| 2007 | 32.50 |

## MARGINAL RELIEF

*(CTA 2010, s 19)*

The corporation tax charged on the company's taxable total profits of the accounting period is reduced by an amount equal to–

$$F \times (U - A) \times \frac{N}{A}$$

Where:

F is the standard fraction,

U is the upper limit,

A is the amount of the augmented profits, and

N is the amount of the taxable total profits.

**Notes**

(1)    *The standard fraction* – This means the fraction set by Parliament (*CTA 2010, s 19(3)*) (3/400 for 2013).

(2)    *Augmented Profits* – This is defined as the company's taxable total profits plus any franked investment income received by the company, excluding any franked investment income received by the company from a company which is a 51% subsidiary of the receiving company or a company of which the receiving company is a 51% subsidiary, or from a trading company or relevant holding company that is a quasi-subsidiary of the receiving company.

(3)    *Quasi-subsidiary* – This is a company owned by a consortium of which the recipient company is a member, which is not a 75% subsidiary of any company, where no arrangements exist for it to become a 75% subsidiary of any company (*CTA 2010, ss 32, 33*).

# PATENT BOX

(*CTA 2010, Part 8A, as inserted by FA 2012, s 19, Sch 2*)

●    Companies may elect for a special corporation tax rate of 10% to apply to profits attributable to qualifying patents and certain other intellectual property (IP).

●    The patent box provisions ('Profits arising from the exploitation of patents etc') apply with effect in relation to accounting periods beginning on or after 1 April 2013, subject to transitional rules.

**Notes**

(1)    *General* – An election is required for the special rate of corporation tax to apply, which is given effect by granting a deduction from trading profits of an amount that gives the same result as reducing the main rate of corporation tax on eligible profits to the lower IP rate of 10%. The legislation provides a formula to calculate the deduction (*CTA 2010, s 357A*).

(2)    *Time limit* – The above election must be made (or revoked) by giving notice to HMRC specifying the first accounting period to which it relates, no later than the date by which an amended corporation tax return could be made under *FA 1998, Sch 18, para 15* (*CTA 2010, ss 357G, 357GA*).

(3)    *Qualifying companies* – The above election is available to 'qualifying companies' as defined, ie broadly in terms of satisfying a specified ownership requirement in relation to a 'qualifying IP right,' or an 'exclusive licence' in respect of a qualifying IP right (*CTA 2010, Pt 8A, Ch 2*).

(4)    *Relevant IP profits* – The 'relevant IP profits' of the trade are those used in the formula mentioned above. The steps necessary to determine the relevant IP profits are set out in the legislation. The legislation also provides for an election (ie a 'streaming' election) to apply an alternative basis for calculating relevant IP profits of the trade (*CTA 2010, Pt 8A, Chs 3, 4*).

(5)    *Miscellaneous* – The 'patent box' regime includes provisions dealing with the set-off of amounts in respect of 'relevant IP losses' (eg by matching with relevant IP profits of another trade of the company, or of a later accounting period) for

which *CTA 2010, s 357A* would be entitled to a deduction from profits of the trade, subject to transitional rules for the financial years 2013 to 2016. The regime is also subject to anti-avoidance provisions (*CTA 2010, Pt 8A, Chs 5, 6*).

## LOANS TO PARTICIPATORS

*(CTA 2010, s 455, FB 2013, cl 76, Sch 28)*

- A charge to tax applies under *CTA 2010, s 455* if a close company makes a loan or advances money to an individual (or to a company receiving the loan or advance in a fiduciary or representative capacity) who is a participator or an associate of a participator in the company.

- The charge is 25% of the amount of the loan or advance, which is treated as an amount of corporation tax chargeable for the accounting period in which the loan or advance is made.

- The tax, or a proportionate part of it, need not be paid if the loan or advance or part of it has been repaid, released or written off before the tax becomes payable. Where the loan or advance is subsequently repaid, released or written off, there are provisions for the tax to be repaid (*CTA 2010, s 458*).

- *Finance Bill 2013* includes provisions to amend and extend how the *CTA 2010, s 455* charge is applied with respect to loans or repayments made on and after 20 March 2013. There are four broad changes:

  1   *Thirty-day rule*

  Where a loan of £5,000 or more is repaid to the company, but within 30 days amounts totalling £5,000 or more are borrowed by the same borrower or one of his associates, the first loan is treated as not having been repaid and is treated as continuing for the purposes of calculating the corporation tax charge. However, if the repayment is made by a dividend declared by the company and chargeable to income tax on the participator, it is not brought within this rule (*CTA 2010, s 464C*).

  2   *Intention or arrangements in place*

  Where the loan is £15,000 or more, the thirty day rule is ignored if, at the time of the repayment of the first loan, the borrower intends to borrow again from the company or has arrangements in place to do so. If those later loans are made they are treated as a continuation of the first loan. As above if the repayment is made by a dividend declared by the company it is not brought within this rule (*CTA 2010, s 464C*).

  3   *Using a third party*

  Loans channeled from the company through LLPs or partnerships in which the participator is a member are treated as if the loan was made directly to the participator. This also applies if the loan is advanced to a trust of which a participator in the company is a beneficiary, or potential beneficiary.

  4   *Conferring a benefit*

  This is intended to catch the situation where an arrangement, perhaps a partnership structure between the company and a participator is used to transfer value from the company to the participator (*CTA 2010, s 464A*).

# DISINCORPORATION RELIEF

*(FB 2013, cls 57–60)*

- Disincorporation relief can apply for transfers of a business as a going concern from a company to some or all of its shareholders between 1 April 2013 and 31 March 2018.

- Companies with qualifying assets of up to £100,000 can use disincorporation relief.

- The relief applies to transfers of goodwill and interests in land such that no corporation tax applies on the transfer

- The shareholders who receive the assets must be individuals and not members of an LLP.

- The claim for the relief must be made jointly in writing between the shareholders and the company.

# FILING DATES FOR COMPANY TAX RETURNS

*(FA 1998, Sch 18, para 14)*

The filing date for a company tax return is the later of the following periods:

(a)   12 months from the end of the return period;

(b)   If the company's relevant period of account is less than 18 months, 12 months from the end of that period;

(c)   If the company's relevant period of account is longer than 18 months, 30 months from the beginning of that period; or

(d)   three months from the date of a notice by HMRC to deliver the return.

**Notes**

(1)   *Relevant period of account* – In relation to a return for an accounting period this is defined as the period of account of the company in which the last day of that accounting period falls.

(2)   *Online filing* – For all accounting periods beginning on and after 1 April 2010 corporation tax returns, with a very few exceptions, must be filed online using iXBRL. This requires the majority of the figures in the company accounts and tax return to be 'tagged'. For further information see: www.hmrc.gov.uk/thelibrary/ct-online.htm.

## DUE AND PAYABLE DATES

*(TMA 1970, ss 59D, 59E, 59G–H; SI 1998/3175; ITA 2007, Pt 15, Ch 15; CTA 2010, s 455(3))*

| Liability | Due Date |
|---|---|
| Mainstream corporation tax | 9 months and 1 day following the end of the accounting period |
| Mainstream corporation tax paid in instalments: | See note (1) below |
| Income tax on interest, annual payments etc. | 14 days after end of return period |
| Charge on loans to participators in close companies *(CTA 2010, s 455)* | 9 months and 1 day after the end of the accounting period in which the loan or advance was made. |

**Notes**

(1)  *Instalment payments* – Large companies are liable to pay corporation tax in instalments, in accordance with *TMA 1970, s 59E* and *SI 1998/3175*. A 'large' company is one with annual taxable profits exceeding £1.5m, divided by 1 plus the number of any active associated companies. A company is not large for these purposes if its profits are £10,000 or less (reduced proportionately for accounting periods of less than 12 months). In addition, a company is not large if its profits for the accounting period are £10m or less and it was not a large company in the 12 months preceding that accounting period.

The instalment provisions set out the following formula to calculate the amount of the instalments *(SI 1998/3175, regs 5–8)*:

$$3 \times CTI/n$$

where

*CTI* is broadly the amount of the company's total liability for that accounting period; and

*n* is the number of whole months in the accounting period, plus the 'appropriate decimal' (ie broadly the proportion of a whole 30-day month, rounded to 2 decimal places).

The due dates for the instalment payments are as follows:

*1st instalment* – 6 months and 13 days from the start of the accounting period (or date of final instalment, if earlier);

*2nd instalment* (if applicable) – 3 months after 1st instalment;

*3rd instalment* (if applicable) – 3 months after 2nd instalment; and

*final instalment* – 3 months and 14 days from the end of the accounting period.

(2)  *Income tax on interest, annual payments etc* – Return periods end on 31 March, 30 June, 30 September, 31 December and at the end of an accounting period.

(3)  *Section 455 charge* – Tax is not payable in respect of any loan or advance repaid before the date on which the tax under *CTA 2010, s 455* would otherwise become due.

# INTEREST ON OVERDUE TAX

*(TMA 1970, ss 87, 87A, 109; SI 1998/3175, reg 7)*

| Description | Interest runs from |
|---|---|
| Corporation tax | Due and payable date |
| Corporation tax payable in instalments | Date instalment is due to be paid |
| Overdue income tax deducted from certain payments | 14 days after end of return period |
| Overdue tax on loans to participators of close companies | Due and payable date |

**Notes**

(1) *Historical interest rates* – The rates of interest charged on underpaid quarterly instalments are found here: www.hmrc.gov.uk/rates/interest-ctsa.htm. Repayment interest rates are found here: www.hmrc.gov.uk/rates/interest-repayments.htm

(2) *Surrender of tax refund within a group (CTA 2010, ss 963, 964)* – A group company which is due a tax refund for an accounting period may surrender it to another group member, if both companies give notice to HMRC. The effect is that the recipient company is generally treated as having paid the tax when the surrendering company paid it (or on the due and payable date for the surrendering company, if paid earlier).

# INTEREST ON OVERDUE CORPORATION TAX

## CTSA (accounting periods ending from 1 July 1999)

*Unpaid corporation tax (not underpaid instalments)*

| From | % |
|---|---|
| 29 September 2009 | 3.0 |
| 24 March 2009 to 28 September 2009 | 2.5 |
| 27 January 2009 to 23 March 2009 | 3.5 |
| 6 January 2009 to 26 January 2009 | 4.5 |
| 6 December 2008 to 5 January 2009 | 5.5 |
| 6 November 2008 to 5 December 2008 | 6.5 |
| 6 January 2008 to 5 November 2008 | 7.5 |
| 6 August 2007 to 5 January 2008 | 8.5 |
| 6 September 2006 to 5 August 2007 | 7.5 |

*Underpaid instalments (Accounting periods ending from 1 July 1999)*

| From | % |
|---|---|
| 16 March 2009 | 1.50 |
| 16 February 2009 to 15 March 2009 | 2.00 |

*continued*

83

| From | % |
|---|---|
| 19 January 2009 to 15 February 2009 | 2.50 |
| 15 December 2008 to 18 January 2009 | 3.00 |
| 17 November 2008 to 14 December 2008 | 4.00 |
| 20 October 2008 to 16 November 2008 | 5.50 |
| 21 April 2008 to 19 October 2008 | 6.00 |
| 18 February 2008 to 20 April 2008 | 6.25 |
| 17 December 2007 to 17 February 2008 | 6.50 |
| 16 July 2007 to 16 December 2007 | 6.75 |
| 21 May 2007 to 15 July 2007 | 6.50 |
| 22 January 2007 to 20 May 2007 | 6.25 |
| 20 November 2006 to 21 January 2007 | 6.00 |
| 14 August 2006 to 19 November 2006 | 5.75 |
| 15 August 2005 to 13 August 2006 | 5.50 |

*Corporation tax pay and file*

| From | % |
|---|---|
| 29 September 2009 | 3.00% |
| 24 March 2009 to 29 September 2009 | 1.75% |
| 27 January 2009 to 23 March 2009 | 2.75% |
| 6 January 2009 to 26 January 2009 | 3.50% |
| 6 December 2008 to 25 January 2009 | 4.25% |
| 6 November 2008 to 5 December 2008 | 5.00% |
| 6 January 2008 to 5 November 2008 | 6.00% |
| 6 August 2007 to 5 January 2008 | 6.75% |
| 6 September 2006 to 5 August 2007 | 6.00% |

*Corporation tax pre pay and file*

| From | % |
|---|---|
| 29 September 2009 | 3.00% |
| 24 March 2009 to 28 September 2009 | 2.00% |
| 27 January 2009 to 23 March 2009 | 2.75% |
| 6 January 2009 to 26 January 2009 | 3.50% |
| 6 December 2008 to 5 January 2009 | 4.25% |
| 6 November 2008 to 5 December 2008 | 5.00% |
| 6 January 2008 to 5 November 2008 | 5.75% |
| 6 August 2007 to 5 January 2008 | 6.50% |
| 6 September 2006 to 5 August 2007 | 5.75% |

# INTEREST ON TAX REPAYMENTS

*(TA 1988, s 826; SI 1998/3175, reg 8)*

## CTSA (accounting periods ending from 1 July 1999)

*Overpaid corporation tax*

| From | % |
|---|---|
| 29 September 2009 | 0.50 |
| 27 January 2009 to 28 September 2009 | 0.00 |
| 6 January 2009 to 26 January 2009 | 1.00 |
| 6 December 2008 to 5 January 2009 | 2.00 |
| 6 November 2008 to 5 December 2008 | 3.00 |
| 6 January 2008 to 5 November 2008 | 4.00 |
| 6 August 2007 to 5 January 2008 | 5.00 |
| 6 September 2006 to 5 August 2007 | 4.00 |

*Overpaid instalments and early payments not due by instalments*

| From | % |
|---|---|
| 21 September 2009 | 0.50 |
| 16 March 2009 to 20 September 2009 | 0.25 |
| 16 February 2009 to 15 March 2009 | 0.75 |
| 19 January 2009 to 15 February 2009 | 1.25 |
| 15 December 2008 to 18 January 2009 | 1.75 |
| 17 November 2008 to 14 December 2008 | 2.75 |
| 20 October 2008 to 16 November 2008 | 4.25 |
| 21 April 2008 to 19 October 2008 | 4.75 |
| 18 February 2008 to 20 April 2008 | 5.00 |
| 17 December 2007 to 17 February 2008 | 5.25 |
| 16 July 2007 to 16 December 2007 | 5.50 |
| 21 May 2007 to 15 July 2007 | 5.25 |
| 22 January 2007 to 20 May 2007 | 5.00 |
| 20 November 2006 to 21 January 2007 | 4.75 |

*Pay and file*

| From | % |
|---|---|
| 29 September 2009 | 0.50 |
| 27 January 2009 to 28 September 2009 | 0.00 |
| 6 January 2009 to 26 January 2009 | 0.50 |
| 6 December 2008 to 5 January 2009 | 1.25 |
| 6 November 2008 to 5 December 2008 | 2.00 |
| 6 January 2008 to 5 November 2008 | 2.75 |

*continued*

| From | % |
|------|---|
| 6 August 2007 to 5 January 2008 | 3.50 |
| 6 September 2006 to 5 August 2007 | 2.75 |
| 6 September 2005 to 5 September 2006 | 2.00 |

*Pre-pay and file*

| From | % |
|------|---|
| 29 September 2009 | 0.50 |
| 24 March 2009 to 28 September 2009 | 2.00 |
| 27 January 2009 to 23 March 2009 | 2.75 |
| 6 January 2009 to 26 January 2009 | 3.50 |
| 6 December 2008 to 5 January 2009 | 4.25 |
| 6 November 2008 to 5 December 2008 | 5.00 |
| 6 January 2008 to 5 November 2008 | 5.75 |
| 6 August 2007 to 5 January 2008 | 6.50 |
| 6 September 2006 to 5 August 2007 | 5.75 |

## TIME LIMITS FOR CLAIMS AND ELECTIONS

With effect from 1 April 2010 a claim or election for corporation tax purposes must generally be made in writing within four years of the end of the accounting period to which it relates, ie in the absence of any provisions to the contrary (*FA 1998, Sch 18, para 55*, as amended by *FA 2008, s 118, Sch 39*; see also *SI 2009/403*). Previously, the general time limit was six years from the end of the accounting period.

| Provision | Time limit |
|-----------|------------|
| Appropriation of asset to trading stock: election to adjust trading profit by the amount of the gain or loss on the deemed disposal at market value (*TCGA 1992, s 161(3)*). | 2 years from the end of the accounting period in which the asset is appropriated as trading stock. |
| Reallocation of chargeable gain or an allowable loss within a group (*TCGA 1992, s 171A(5)*). | 2 years from the end of the transferring company's accounting period in which the gain or loss accrues. |
| Stock transferred to a connected person on the cessation of trade to be valued at higher of cost or selling price (*CTA 2009, s 167(4)*). | 2 years from the end of the accounting period of cessation. Election must be made by both parties. |
| Relief for trading losses against total profits of the same, or an earlier, accounting period (*CTA 2010, s 37(7)*). | 2 years from the end of the loss making accounting period. |
| Terminal loss relief on the cessation of trade (*CTA 2010, s 39*). | 2 years from the end of the loss making accounting period. |
| Carry-forward of trading losses (*CTA 2010, s 45*). | No formal claim necessary. |

| Provision | Time limit |
|---|---|
| Group relief (*FA 1998, Sch 18, para 74*). | Group relief claims must be made or withdrawn by the later of the following:<br><br>(1)  12 months from the filing date for the claimant company's tax return for the accounting period of the claim;<br><br>(2)  30 days after the completion of an enquiry into that return;<br><br>(3)  30 days after the issue of a notice of amendment by HMRC following the completion of an enquiry; or<br><br>(4)  30 days after the determination of any appeal against an HMRC amendment (in (3) above). |
| Capital allowances (*FA 1988, Sch 18, para 82*). | As for group relief (see above). |
| Surrender of company tax refund within group (*CTA 2010, s 963(3)*). | Before the refund is made to the surrendering company. |
| Intangible fixed assets: election to write down cost for tax purposes at a fixed rate (*CTA 2009, s 730*). | 2 years from the end of the accounting period in which the company creates or acquires the asset. |
| Set-off of loss on disposal of shares in unquoted trading company against income of investment company (*CTA 2010, s 70(4)*). | 2 years from the end of the accounting period in which the loss was incurred. |
| Company distributions – election that distribution should not be treated as exempt (*CTA 2009, s 931R*). | Second anniversary of the end of the accounting period in which the distribution is received. |
| Relief for a non-trading deficit on loan relationships (including any non-trading exchange losses) (*CTA 2009, ss 458(2), 460(1)*). | • Claim to carry forward the deficit to later accounting periods – 2 years from the end of the accounting period following the deficit period.<br><br>• Claim to set off deficit against profits of the deficit period or earlier periods – 2 years from end of period in which deficit arises. |

**Notes**

(1)  *Extended time limits* – In some cases, HMRC may allow a longer claim period at its discretion.

(2)  *Temporary extension of loss relief carry back provisions* – the loss relief carry back period is extended from 12 months to 3 years, in respect of a trading loss incurred in an accounting period ending after 23 November 2008 and ending before 24 November 2010 (*FA 2009, Sch 6, para 3*).

(3)   *Group relief* – The above references to an enquiry do not include a restricted enquiry into an amendment of a return (ie where the restriction arises because the time limit for enquiring into that return has expired), where the amendment consists of a group relief claim or the withdrawal of such a claim (*FA 1998, Sch 18, para 74(4)*).

## DISCOVERY ASSESSMENTS

(*FA 1998, Sch 18, para 46*)

### Time limits

| Circumstances | Time Limit |
|---|---|
| Loss of tax not due to careless or deliberate behaviour | 4 years from the end of the accounting period |
| *(FA 1998, Sch 18, para 46(1))* | |
| Loss of tax due to careless behaviour of the company or agent etc | 6 years from the end of the accounting period |
| *(FA 1998, Sch 18, para 46(2), 46(2B))* | |
| Loss of tax due to deliberate behaviour by the company or agent etc | 20 years from the end of the accounting period |
| *(FA 1998, Sch 18, para 46(2A)(a), (2B))* | |

### Notes

(1)   *General* – The above time limits were introduced by *FA 2008, Sch 39* ('Time limits for assessments, claims etc). For periods prior to the introduction of the above time limits (in *SI 2009/403*), the normal time limit for assessments is 6 years after the end of the accounting period to which it relates. For 'fraud or negligence' the time limit is 21 years after the end of the accounting period.

(2)   *Scope* – Separate 'discovery' assessment provisions and time limits apply to the failure to notify chargeability to tax, and the failure to provide information about an avoidance scheme (*TMA 1970, s 118(2); FA 1998, Sch 18, paras 46(1), 46(2A) (b), (c)*). A table of assessment time limits for corporation tax purposes is included in HMRC's Compliance Handbook (at CH56200).

## INDEXATION ALLOWANCE

*(TCGA 1992, Ch IV)*

## (a) Retail Prices Index (RPI) Table

|      | Jan   | Feb   | Mar   | Apr   | May   | Jun   | Jul   | Aug   | Sep   | Oct   | Nov   | Dec   |
|------|-------|-------|-------|-------|-------|-------|-------|-------|-------|-------|-------|-------|
| 1982 |       |       | 79.44 | 81.04 | 81.62 | 81.85 | 81.88 | 81.90 | 81.85 | 82.26 | 82.66 | 82.51 |
| 1983 | 82.61 | 82.97 | 83.12 | 84.28 | 84.64 | 84.84 | 85.30 | 85.68 | 86.06 | 86.36 | 86.67 | 86.89 |
| 1984 | 86.84 | 87.20 | 87.48 | 88.64 | 88.97 | 89.20 | 89.10 | 89.94 | 90.11 | 90.67 | 90.95 | 90.87 |
| 1985 | 91.20 | 91.94 | 92.80 | 94.78 | 95.21 | 95.41 | 95.23 | 95.49 | 95.44 | 95.59 | 95.92 | 96.05 |
| 1986 | 96.25 | 96.60 | 96.73 | 97.67 | 97.85 | 97.79 | 97.52 | 97.82 | 98.30 | 98.45 | 99.29 | 99.62 |
| 1987 | 100.0 | 100.4 | 100.6 | 101.8 | 101.9 | 101.9 | 101.8 | 102.1 | 102.4 | 102.9 | 103.4 | 103.3 |
| 1988 | 103.3 | 103.7 | 104.1 | 105.8 | 106.2 | 106.6 | 106.7 | 107.9 | 108.4 | 109.5 | 110.0 | 110.3 |
| 1989 | 111.0 | 111.8 | 112.3 | 114.3 | 115.0 | 115.4 | 115.5 | 115.8 | 116.6 | 117.5 | 118.5 | 118.8 |
| 1990 | 119.5 | 120.2 | 121.4 | 125.1 | 126.2 | 126.7 | 126.8 | 128.1 | 129.3 | 130.3 | 130.0 | 129.9 |
| 1991 | 130.2 | 130.9 | 131.4 | 133.1 | 133.5 | 134.1 | 133.8 | 134.1 | 134.6 | 135.1 | 135.6 | 135.7 |
| 1992 | 135.6 | 136.3 | 136.7 | 138.8 | 139.3 | 139.3 | 138.8 | 138.9 | 139.4 | 139.9 | 139.7 | 139.2 |
| 1993 | 137.9 | 138.8 | 139.3 | 140.6 | 141.1 | 141.0 | 140.7 | 141.3 | 141.9 | 141.8 | 141.6 | 141.9 |
| 1994 | 141.3 | 142.1 | 142.5 | 144.2 | 144.7 | 144.7 | 144.0 | 144.7 | 145.0 | 145.2 | 145.3 | 146.0 |
| 1995 | 146.0 | 146.9 | 147.5 | 149.0 | 149.6 | 149.8 | 149.1 | 149.9 | 150.6 | 149.8 | 149.8 | 150.7 |
| 1996 | 150.2 | 150.9 | 151.5 | 152.6 | 152.9 | 153.0 | 152.4 | 153.1 | 153.8 | 153.8 | 153.9 | 154.4 |
| 1997 | 154.4 | 155.0 | 155.4 | 156.3 | 156.9 | 157.5 | 157.5 | 158.5 | 159.3 | 159.5 | 159.6 | 160.0 |
| 1998 | 159.5 | 160.3 | 160.8 | 162.6 | 163.5 | 163.4 | 163.0 | 163.7 | 164.4 | 164.5 | 164.4 | 164.4 |
| 1999 | 163.4 | 163.7 | 164.1 | 165.2 | 165.6 | 165.6 | 165.1 | 165.5 | 166.2 | 166.5 | 166.7 | 167.3 |
| 2000 | 166.6 | 167.5 | 168.4 | 170.1 | 170.7 | 171.1 | 170.5 | 170.5 | 171.7 | 171.6 | 172.1 | 172.2 |
| 2001 | 171.1 | 172.0 | 172.2 | 173.1 | 174.2 | 174.4 | 173.3 | 174.0 | 174.6 | 174.3 | 173.6 | 173.4 |
| 2002 | 173.3 | 173.8 | 174.5 | 175.7 | 176.2 | 176.2 | 175.9 | 176.4 | 177.6 | 177.9 | 178.2 | 178.5 |
| 2003 | 178.4 | 179.3 | 179.9 | 181.2 | 181.5 | 181.3 | 181.3 | 181.6 | 182.5 | 182.6 | 182.7 | 183.5 |
| 2004 | 183.1 | 183.8 | 184.6 | 185.7 | 186.5 | 186.8 | 186.8 | 187.4 | 188.1 | 188.6 | 189.0 | 189.9 |
| 2005 | 188.9 | 189.6 | 190.5 | 191.6 | 192.0 | 192.2 | 192.2 | 192.6 | 193.1 | 193.3 | 193.6 | 194.1 |
| 2006 | 193.4 | 194.2 | 195.0 | 196.5 | 197.7 | 198.5 | 198.5 | 199.2 | 200.1 | 200.4 | 201.1 | 202.7 |
| 2007 | 201.6 | 203.1 | 204.4 | 205.4 | 206.2 | 207.3 | 206.1 | 207.3 | 208.0 | 208.9 | 209.7 | 210.9 |
| 2008 | 209.8 | 211.4 | 212.1 | 214.0 | 215.1 | 216.8 | 216.5 | 217.2 | 218.4 | 217.7 | 216.0 | 212.9 |
| 2009 | 210.1 | 211.4 | 211.3 | 211.5 | 212.8 | 213.4 | 213.4 | 214.4 | 215.3 | 216.0 | 216.6 | 218.0 |
| 2010 | 217.9 | 219.2 | 220.7 | 222.8 | 223.6 | 224.1 | 223.6 | 224.5 | 225.3 | 225.8 | 226.8 | 228.4 |
| 2011 | 229.0 | 231.3 | 232.5 | 234.4 | 235.2 | 235.2 | 234.7 | 236.1 | 237.9 | 238.0 | 238.5 | 239.4 |
| 2012 | 238.0 | 239.9 | 240.8 | 242.5 | 241.8 | 242.8 | 242.1 | 243.0 | 244.2 | 245.6 | 245.6 | 246.8 |
| 2013 | 245.8 | 247.6 |       |       |       |       |       |       |       |       |       |       |

**Acknowledgement**: Office for National Statistics website: www.ons.gov.uk

## (b) Indexation formula

The formula for calculating indexation factors is as follows *(TCGA 1992, s 54(1))*:

$$\frac{(RD - RI)}{RI}$$

Where:

RD is the RPI for the month of disposal; and

RI is the RPI for March 1982 (or the month in which the expenditure was incurred, if later).

The resulting figure is applied to each item of qualifying expenditure in the computation, by multiplying the expenditure by the relevant indexation factor as calculated.

**Notes**

(1)   *Which periods* – Indexation allowance applies to periods from March 1982 onwards. It is broadly an allowance for inflation, based on the indexed rise in allowable expenditure for capital gains purposes.

(2)   *Who can use it* – Indexation allowance can be used by companies within the charge to corporation tax (*TCGA 1992, s 52A*). The allowance is the aggregate of the indexed rise in each item of such expenditure. It can reduce an unindexed gain to nil, but cannot generally be applied to create or increase a loss (*s 53(1)*).

(3)   *Publication* – Indexation allowance tables showing the indexed rise in respect of disposals taking place in particular months are published on the HMRC website:

www.hmrc.gov.uk/rates/cg-indexation-allowance/index.htm

(4)   *Other taxpayers* – Indexation allowance was abolished for individuals, trustees and personal representatives in respect of disposals from 6 April 2008, and frozen for disposals between 6 April 1998 and 5 April 2008 (*TCGA 1992, s 54(1)*), see **Chapter 8: Capital gains tax: Indexation allowance**.

*8*

# Capital Gains Tax

## RATES AND ANNUAL EXEMPTIONS
*(TCGA 1992, ss 3, 4, Sch 1)*

| Tax Year | Annual exempt amount | | Tax rate paid by | | |
| --- | --- | --- | --- | --- | --- |
| | **Individuals, personal representatives (PR's) and trusts for disabled** | **General trusts** | **Individuals within:** | | **Trustees and PR's** |
| | | | **Basic rate band** | **Higher tax bands** | |
| | **£** | **£** | **%** | **%** | **%** |
| 2013–14 | 10,900 | 5,450 | 18 | 28 | 28 |
| 2012–13 | 10,600 | 5,300 | 18 | 28 | 28 |
| 2011–12 | 10,600 | 5,300 | 18 | 28 | 28 |
| 2010–11 (23 June 2010 to 5 April 2011) | 10,100 | 5,050 | 18 | 28 | 28 |
| 2010–11 (6 April to 22 June 2010) | 10,100 | 5,050 | 18 | 18 | 18 |
| 2009–10 | 10,100 | 5,050 | 18 | 18 | 18 |
| 2008–09 | 9,600 | 4,800 | 18 | 18 | 18 |

**Notes**

(1)  *Remittance basis users* – From 2008–09, an individual who claims to use the remittance basis for a tax year is not entitled to the annual capital gains exemption for that year (*ITA 2007, s 809G*). However the annual exempt amount remains available where the remittance basis applies without a claim – eg where the individual's unremitted foreign income and gains are less than £2,000 for the year (*ITA 2007, s 809D*).

(2)  *Personal representatives* – The annual exemption is available to personal representatives in the tax year of death and the following two years (*TCGA 1992, s 3(7)*).

(3)  *Trustees* – The annual exemption for trustees is divided by the number of qualifying settlements created by one settlor, subject to a lower limit of 10% of the annual exemption for individuals for that tax year (*TCGA 1992, Sch 1, para 2*).

(4)  *2010–11* – In this year the CGT rates changed with effect from 23 June 2010, but the annual exempt amounts were not changed and applied for the whole tax year.

(5)   *Entrepreneurs' relief rate* – A 10% rate of capital gains tax applies from 23 June 2010, in respect of gains qualifying for entrepreneurs' relief (*TCGA 1992, s 169N(3)*; see **Entrepreneurs' relief** below).

(6)   *Earlier years* – For 2007–08 and earlier tax years, capital gains were taxed as the top slice of income at income tax rates.

## CHATTEL EXEMPTION

(*TCGA 1992, s 262*)

|  | Exemption (max sale proceeds) | Marginal relief ( max chargeable gain) |
|---|---|---|
| From 1989–90 onwards | £6,000 | 5/3 of the excess over £6,000 |

## OTHER EXEMPTIONS AND RELIEFS

### Entrepreneurs' relief

(*TCGA 1992 ss 169H–169S*)

| Date of qualifying business disposal | Lifetime limit |
|---|---|
| From 6 April 2011 | £10 million |
| 23 June 2010–5 April 2011 | £5 million |
| 6 April 2010–22 June 2010 | £2 million |
| 6 April 2008–5 April 2010 | £1 million |

*Conditions*

(1)   The relief broadly applies to qualifying disposals by an individual or certain trustees on or after 6 April 2008 of:

● all or part of a trade carried on alone or in partnership;

● assets of such a trade following cessation; or

● shares or securities in the individual's 'personal company', where the company is a trading company (or the holding company of a trading group) and the individual is an officer or employee of the company (or of a trading group member) (see *TCGA 1992, ss 169H, 169I*); and

● the relevant conditions are met throughout a period of at least one year ending with the date of disposal or cessation of trade (see *TCGA 1992, s 169I*).

(2)   A personal company is one in which the taxpayer holds at least 5% of the ordinary share capital and control at least 5% of the voting rights of the company.

(3)   Trustees can claim relief on the disposal of settlement business assets if a qualifying beneficiary has an interest in possession in the whole or a relevant part of the settled property, where all the conditions for the relief are satisfied by the beneficiary (see *TCGA 1992, s 169J*).

(4)   Transitional rules apply to allow relief to be claimed in some circumstances where a gain made before 6 April 2008 is deferred using QCBs, EIS or VCT and becomes chargeable on or after that date (*FA 2008, Sch 3, paras 7, 8*).

(5)   From 6 April 2013 gains made on shares acquired through exercising EMI options on or after 6 April 2012 can qualify for entrepreneurs' relief, even if the taxpayer holds less than 5% of the ordinary share capital of the company.

*Calculation of relief*

- For disposals arising on and after 23 June 2010 the net gains qualifying for entrepreneurs' relief are charged at the rate of 10%.

- For disposals made from 6 April 2008 to 22 June 2010, the qualifying net gains are reduced by 4/9ths before being charged to tax at the flat rate of 18%.

## ROLLOVER RELIEF FOR BUSINESS ASSETS

(*TCGA 1992, Pt 5, Ch 1*)

Qualifying assets (*TCGA 1992, s 155*):

| Class of asset | Description |
| --- | --- |
| 1A | Land and buildings occupied (and used) only for the purposes of a trade; |
| 1B | Fixed plant or machinery (not forming part of a building); |
| 2 | Ships, aircraft and hovercraft; |
| 3 | Satellites, space stations and spacecraft (including launch vehicles); |
| 4 | Goodwill; |
| 5 | Milk quotas (and formerly potato quotas); |
| 6 | Ewe and suckler cow premium quotas; |
| 7 | Fish quotas; |
| 7A | Payment entitlements under the single payment scheme for farmers; |
| 8A | Lloyd's underwriters' syndicate capacity |
| 8B | Lloyd's members agent pooling arrangements. |

**Note**

*Corporate claims* – For the purposes of corporation tax, assets in categories 4 to 7A listed above, if owned by a company at any time on or after 1 April 2002, would fall within the intangible assets regime and are therefore excluded from business asset rollover relief (see *TCGA 1992, s 156ZB*).

## MAIN RESIDENCE RELIEF

(*TCGA 1992, ss 222–226B*)

(1)   Also known as principal private residence relief (PPR). Relief from CGT is given on the disposal of (or of an interest in) a dwelling house which has been the individual's only or main residence, and on land enjoyed with that residence as its garden or grounds up to the permitted area of half a hectare, or more if the additional land is required for the reasonable enjoyment of the property.

(2)   The relief is time apportioned for periods of occupation, and for certain periods of deemed occupation. The last 36 months of ownership are allowed in any event,

if the property was at some time the individual's only or main residence (*TCGA 1992, s 223(1)*).

(3)   Where an individual has two or more residences, they may elect within 2 years of the second property becoming a residence, which property is to be treated as the main residence (*TCGA 1992 s 222(5)*).

(4)   A married couple or civil partnership may have only one main residence at any time (*TCGA 1992 s 222(6)*).

(5)   If the main residence has been wholly or partly let as residential accommodation at any time in the period of ownership, lettings relief can provide an exemption for gains limited to the lower of:

- the gain attributable to the let period;

- £40,000 per owner; and

- the gain exempt as main residence relief.

## HIGH VALUE RESIDENTIAL PROPERTY

Residential properties worth £2 million or more are classified as 'high value' and are subject to the following tax charges when owned by non-natural persons:

- Stamp duty land tax at 15% (see **Chapter 11: Stamp Taxes**)

- Annual tax on enveloped dwellings (ATED) (see **Chapter 13: Other taxes and duties**)

- CGT on gains in value from 6 April 2013 onwards when the disposed of by a non-natural person.

## ENTERPRISE INVESTMENT SCHEME (EIS)

*(TCGA 1992, s 150A, Sch 5B)*

(1)   *Disposal relief* – A gain on the disposal of EIS shares after the relevant three-year period is exempt from capital gains tax to the extent that full income tax relief has been given on the shares.

(2)   *Reinvestment relief* – This is available for gains on assets where the disposal proceeds are reinvested in new EIS shares upon making a claim. All or part of the original gain can be deferred, and is brought back into charge on the occurrence of a·chargeable event.

For further details, see **Chapter 5: Pensions, Investment Income etc: Enterprise Investment Scheme (EIS).**

## SEED ENTERPRISE INVESTMENT SCHEME (SEIS)

*(TCGA1992, ss150E–150G & ITA 2007, Pt 5A)*

(1)   *Disposal relief* – A gain on the disposal of SEIS shares after the relevant three-year period is exempt from capital gains tax to the extent that full income tax relief has been given, and not withdrawn, on the shares.

(2)    *Reinvestment relief* – This is available for gains arising from disposals in 2012–13 or 2013–14 where the disposal proceeds are reinvested in new SEIS shares in those tax years.

For further details, see **Chapter 5: Pensions, Investment Income etc: Seed Enterprise Investment Scheme (SEIS).**

## CHARITIES AND CASCs

(*TCGA 1992, ss 256, 257*)

(1)    Gains accruing to charities which are both applicable and applied for charitable purposes are generally exempt for capital gains tax purposes.

(2)    Relief from capital gains tax generally applies to gifts to charities and certain other bodies. The relief was extended from 6 April 2002 to asset disposals to Community Amateur Sports Clubs (CASCs).

## LEASES WHICH ARE WASTING ASSETS

(*TCGA 1992, Sch 8, para 1*)

### Depreciation table

| Years | % | Monthly increment* | Years | % | Monthly increment* |
|---|---|---|---|---|---|
| 50 or more | 100 | – | 30 | 87.330 | 0.087 |
| 49 | 99.657 | 0.029 | 29 | 86.226 | 0.092 |
| 48 | 99.289 | 0.031 | 28 | 85.053 | 0.098 |
| 47 | 98.902 | 0.032 | 27 | 83.816 | 0.103 |
| 46 | 98.490 | 0.034 | 26 | 82.496 | 0.110 |
| 45 | 98.059 | 0.036 | 25 | 81.100 | 0.116 |
| 44 | 97.595 | 0.039 | 24 | 79.622 | 0.123 |
| 43 | 97.107 | 0.041 | 23 | 78.055 | 0.131 |
| 42 | 96.593 | 0.043 | 22 | 76.399 | 0.138 |
| 41 | 96.041 | 0.046 | 21 | 74.635 | 0.147 |
| 40 | 95.457 | 0.049 | 20 | 72.770 | 0.155 |
| 39 | 94.842 | 0.051 | 19 | 70.791 | 0.165 |
| 38 | 94.189 | 0.054 | 18 | 68.697 | 0.175 |
| 37 | 93.497 | 0.058 | 17 | 66.470 | 0.186 |
| 36 | 92.761 | 0.061 | 16 | 64.116 | 0.196 |
| 35 | 91.981 | 0.065 | 15 | 61.617 | 0.208 |
| 34 | 91.156 | 0.069 | 14 | 58.971 | 0.221 |
| 33 | 90.280 | 0.073 | 13 | 56.167 | 0.234 |
| 32 | 89.354 | 0.077 | 12 | 53.191 | 0.248 |
| 31 | 88.371 | 0.082 | 11 | 50.038 | 0.263 |

*continued*

| Years | % | Monthly increment* | Years | % | Monthly increment* |
|---|---|---|---|---|---|
| 10 | 46.695 | 0.279 | 4 | 21.983 | 0.395 |
| 9 | 43.154 | 0.295 | 3 | 16.959 | 0.419 |
| 8 | 39.399 | 0.313 | 2 | 11.629 | 0.444 |
| 7 | 35.414 | 0.332 | 1 | 5.983 | 0.470 |
| 6 | 31.195 | 0.352 | 0 | 0 | 0.499 |
| 5 | 26.722 | 0.373 | | | |

**Notes**

(1)  **Formula:** Fraction of expenditure disallowed:

$$\frac{A - B}{A}$$

Where:

A is the percentage for duration of lease at acquisition or expenditure; and

B is the percentage for the duration of the lease at disposal.

(2)  **\* Fraction of years:** Add one-twelfth of the difference between the percentage for the whole year and the next higher percentage for each additional month. For a period of less that one month, odd days under 14 are not counted; 14 or more odd days are rounded up and treated as a month.

## SHORT LEASE PREMIUMS

(*ITTOIA 2005, s 277*)

See **Chapter 5: Pensions, Investment Income etc** as to the calculation of the proportion of any premium received in respect of a lease of less than 50 years which is partly chargeable to capital gains tax, and that part which is chargeable to income tax as property business profits.

## EXEMPT GILT-EDGED SECURITIES

(*TCGA 1992, ss 16(2), 115, Sch 9*)

Gains on the following securities are not chargeable gains and any losses are not allowable losses.

| | |
|---|---|
| 2.50% | Annuities 1905 or after |
| 2.75% | Annuities 1905 or after |
| 2.50% | Consolidated Stock 1923 or after |
| 3.50% | War Loan 1952 or after |
| 4.00% | Consolidated Loan 1957 or after |
| 3.50% | Conversion Loan 1961 or after |
| 3.00% | Treasury Stock 1966 or after |

| | |
|---|---|
| 2.50% | Treasury Stock 1975 or after |
| 12.75% | Treasury Loan 1992 |
| 8.00% | Treasury Loan 1992 |
| 10.00% | Treasury Stock 1992 |
| 3.00% | Treasury Stock 1992 |
| 12.25% | Exchequer Stock 1992 |
| 13.50% | Exchequer Stock 1992 |
| 10.50% | Treasury Convertible Stock 1992 |
| 2.00% | Index-Linked Treasury Stock 1992 |
| 12.50% | Treasury Loan 1993 |
| 6.00% | Funding Loan 1993 |
| 13.75% | Treasury Loan 1993 |
| 10.00% | Treasury Loan 1993 |
| 8.25% | Treasury Stock 1993 |
| 14.50% | Treasury Loan 1994 |
| 12.50% | Exchequer Stock 1994 |
| 9.00% | Treasury Loan 1994 |
| 10.00% | Treasury Loan 1994 |
| 13.50% | Exchequer Stock 1994 |
| 8.50% | Treasury Stock 1994 |
| 8.50% | Treasury Stock 1994 'A' |
| 2.00% | Index-Linked Treasury Stock 1994 |
| 3.00% | Exchequer Gas Stock 1990–95 |
| 12.00% | Treasury Stock 1995 |
| 10.25% | Exchequer Stock 1995 |
| 12.75% | Treasury Loan 1995 |
| 9.00% | Treasury Loan 1992–96 |
| 15.25% | Treasury Loan 1996 |
| 13.25% | Exchequer Loan 1996 |
| 14.00% | Treasury Stock 1996 |
| 2.00% | Index-Linked Treasury Stock 1996 |
| 10.00% | Conversion Stock 1996 |
| 10.00% | Conversion Stock 1996 'A' |
| 10.00% | Conversion Stock 1996 'B' |
| 13.25% | Treasury Loan 1997 |
| 10.50% | Exchequer Stock 1997 |
| 8.75% | Treasury Loan 1997 |
| 8.75% | Treasury Loan 1997 'B' |
| 8.75% | Treasury Loan 1997 'C' |
| 8.75% | Treasury Loan 1997 'D' |
| 8.75% | Treasury Loan 1997 'E' |
| 15.00% | Exchequer Stock 1997 |

*continued*

97

| 7.00% | Treasury Convertible Stock 1997 |
| 6.75% | Treasury Loan 1995–98 |
| 15.50% | Treasury Loan 1998 |
| 12.00% | Exchequer Stock 1998 |
| 12.00% | Exchequer Stock 1998 'A' |
| 9.75% | Exchequer Stock 1998 |
| 9.75% | Exchequer Stock 1998 'A' |
| 7.25% | Treasury Stock 1998 'A' |
| 7.25% | Treasury Stock 1998 'B' |
| 12.00% | Exchequer Stock 1998 'B' |
| 4.625% | Index-Linked Treasury Stock 1998 |
| 7.25% | Treasury Stock 1998 |
| 9.50% | Treasury Loan 1999 |
| 10.50% | Treasury Stock 1999 |
| 12.25% | Exchequer Stock 1999 |
| 12.25% | Exchequer Stock 1999 'A' |
| 12.25% | Exchequer Stock 1999 'B' |
| 2.50% | Index-Linked Treasury Convertible Stock 1999 |
| 10.25% | Conversion Stock 1999 |
| 6.00% | Treasury Stock 1999 |
|  | Floating Rate Treasury Stock 1999 |
| 9.00% | Conversion Stock 2000 |
| 9.00% | Conversion Stock 2000 'A' |
| 9.00% | Conversion Stock 2000 'B' |
| 9.00% | Conversion Stock 2000 'C' |
| 8.50% | Treasury Loan 2000 |
| 8.00% | Treasury Stock 2000 |
| 8.00% | Treasury Stock 2000 'A' |
| 13.00% | Treasury Stock 2000 |
| 13.00% | Treasury Stock 2000 'A' |
| 7.00% | Treasury Stock 2001 |
| 7.00% | Treasury Stock 2001 'A' |
| 14.00% | Treasury Stock 1998–2001 |
| 2.50% | Index-Linked Treasury Stock 2001 |
| 9.75% | Conversion Stock 2001 |
| 10.00% | Treasury Stock 2001 |
| 9.50% | Conversion Loan 2001 |
| 10.00% | Treasury Stock 2001 'A' |
| 10.00% | Treasury Stock 2001 'B' |
|  | Floating Rate Treasury Stock |
| 12.00% | Exchequer Stock 1999–2002 |
| 12.00% | Exchequer Stock 1999–2002 'A' |
| 9.50% | Conversion Stock 2002 |

| | |
|---|---|
| 10.00% | Conversion Stock 2002 |
| 9.00% | Exchequer Stock 2002 |
| 7.00% | Treasury Stock 2002 |
| 9.75% | Treasury Stock 2002 |
| 9.75% | Treasury Stock 2002 'A' |
| 9.75% | Treasury Stock 2002 'B' |
| 9.75% | Treasury Stock 2002 'C' |
| 13.75% | Treasury Stock 2000–2003 |
| 13.75% | Treasury Stock 2000–2003 'A' |
| 2.50% | Index-Linked Treasury Stock 2003 |
| 9.75% | Conversion Loan 2003 |
| 6.50% | Treasury Stock 2003 |
| 8.00% | Treasury Stock 2003 |
| 8.00% | Treasury Stock 2003 'A' |
| 10.00% | Treasury Stock 2003 |
| 10.00% | Treasury Stock 2003 'A' |
| 10.00% | Treasury Stock 2003 'B' |
| 3.50% | Funding Stock 1999–2004 |
| 11.50% | Treasury Stock 2001–2004 |
| 9.50% | Conversion Stock 2004 |
| 10.00% | Treasury Stock 2004 |
| 6.75% | Treasury Stock 2004 |
| 5.00% | Treasury Stock 2004 |
| 6.75% | Treasury Stock 2004 'A' |
| 4.375% | Index-Linked Treasury Stock 2004 |
| 9.50% | Conversion Stock 2004 'A' |
| 12.50% | Treasury Stock 2003–2005 |
| 12.50% | Treasury Stock 2003–2005 'A' |
| 10.50% | Exchequer Stock 2005 |
| 9.50% | Conversion Stock 2005 |
| 9.50% | Conversion Stock 2005 'A' |
| 8.50% | Treasury Stock 2005 |
| 8.00% | Treasury Loan 2002–2006 |
| 8.00% | Treasury Loan 2002–2006 'A' |
| 2.00% | Index-Linked Treasury Stock 2006 |
| 9.75% | Conversion Stock 2006 |
| 7.50% | Treasury Stock 2006 |
| 7.75% | Treasury Stock 2006 |
| 11.75% | Treasury Stock 2003–2007 |
| 11.75% | Treasury Stock 2003–2007 'A' |
| 7.25% | Treasury Stock 2007 |
| 4.50% | Treasury Stock 2007 |

*continued*

| | |
|---|---|
| 8.50% | Treasury Loan 2007 |
| 8.50% | Treasury Loan 2007 'A' |
| 8.50% | Treasury Loan 2007 'B' |
| 8.50% | Treasury Loan 2007 'C' |
| 13.50% | Treasury Stock 2004–2008 |
| 9.00% | Treasury Loan 2008 |
| 9.00% | Treasury Loan 2008 'A' |
| 9.00% | Treasury Loan 2008 'B' |
| 9.00% | Treasury Loan 2008 'C' |
| 9.00% | Treasury Loan 2008 'D' |
| 5.00% | Treasury Stock 2008 |
| 2.50% | Index-Linked Treasury Stock 2009 |
| 5.75% | Treasury Stock 2009 |
| 8.00% | Treasury Stock 2009 |
| 4.00% | Treasury Stock 2009 |
| 8.00% | Treasury Stock 2009 'A' |
| 4.75% | Treasury Stock 2010 |
| 6.25% | Treasury Stock 2010 |
| 2.25% | Indexed-Linked Treasury Stock 2011 |
| 4.25% | Treasury Gilt 2011 |
| 9.00% | Conversion Loan 2011 |
| 9.00% | Conversion Loan 2011 'A' |
| 9.00% | Conversion Loan 2011 'B' |
| 9.00% | Conversion Loan 2011 'C' |
| 9.00% | Conversion Loan 2011 'D' |
| 3.25% | Treasury Gilt 2011 |
| 5.50% | Treasury Stock 2008–2012 |
| 9.00% | Treasury Stock 2012 |
| 9.00% | Treasury Stock 2012 'A' |
| 5.00% | Treasury Stock 2012 |
| 5.25% | Treasury Gilt 2012 |
| 2.50% | Index-Linked Treasury Stock 2013 |
| 8.00% | Treasury Stock 2013 |
| 4.50% | Treasury Gilt 2013 |
| 2.25% | Treasury Gilt 2014 |
| 5.00% | Treasury Stock 2014 |
| 7.75% | Treasury Loan 2012–2015 |
| 2.75% | Treasury Gilt 2015 |
| 4.75% | Treasury Stock 2015 |
| 8.00% | Treasury Stock 2015 |
| 8.00% | Treasury Stock 2015 'A' |
| 2.50% | Treasury Stock 1986–2016 |
| 2.50% | Index-Linked Treasury Stock 2016 |

| | |
|---|---|
| 2.50% | Index-Linked Treasury Stock 2016 'A' |
| 4.00% | Treasury Gilt 2016 |
| 2.00% | Treasury Gilt 2016 |
| 12.00% | Exchequer Stock 2013–2017 |
| 1.00% | Treasury Gilt 2017 |
| 1.25% | Index-Linked Treasury Gilt 2017 |
| 1.75% | Treasury Gilt 2017 |
| 8.75% | Treasury Stock 2017 |
| 8.75% | Treasury Stock 2017 'A' |
| 5.00% | Treasury Gilt 2018 |
| 3.75% | Treasury Gilt 2019 |
| 4.50% | Treasury Gilt 2019 |
| 2.50% | Index-Linked Treasury Stock 2020 |
| 4.75% | Treasury Stock 2020 |
| 3.75% | Treasury Gilt 2020 |
| 8.00% | Treasury Stock 2021 |
| 3.75% | Treasury Gilt 2021 |
| 1.75% | Treasury Gilt 2022 |
| 1.875% | Index-Linked Treasury Gilt 2022 |
| 4.00% | Treasury Gilt 2022 |
| 0.125% | Index-linked Treasury Gilt 2024 |
| 2.50% | Index-Linked Treasury Stock 2024 |
| 5.00% | Treasury Stock 2025 |
| 1.25% | Index-Linked Treasury Gilt 2027 |
| 4.25% | Treasury Gilt 2027 |
| 6.00% | Treasury Stock 2028 |
| 0.125% | Index-linked Treasury Gilt 2029 |
| 4.125% | Index-Linked Treasury Stock 2030 |
| 4.75% | Treasury Gilt 2030 |
| 1.25% | Index-linked Treasury Gilt 2032 |
| 4.25% | Treasury Stock 2032 |
| 0.75% | Index-linked Treasury Gilt |
| 4.50% | Treasury Gilt 2034 |
| 2.00% | Index-Linked Treasury Stock 2035 |
| 4.25% | Treasury Stock 2036 |
| 1.125% | Index-Linked Treasury Gilt 2037 |
| 4.75% | Treasury Stock 2038 |
| 4.25% | Treasury Gilt 2039 |
| 0.625% | Index-linked Treasury Gilt 2040 |
| 4.25% | Treasury Gilt 2040 |
| 0.625% | Index-linked Treasury Gilt 2042 |
| 4.50% | Treasury Stock 2042 |

*continued*

| | |
|---|---|
| 0.125% | Index-linked Treasury Gilt 2044 |
| 3.25% | Treasury Gilt 2044 |
| 4.25% | Treasury Gilt 2046 |
| 0.75% | Index-Linked Treasury Gilt 2047 |
| 4.25% | Treasury Gilt 2049 |
| 0.50% | Index-linked Treasury Gilt 2050 |
| 0.25% | Index-linked Treasury Gilt 2052 |
| 3.75% | Treasury Gilt 2052 |
| 1.25% | Indexed-linked Treasury Gilt 2055 |
| 4.25% | Treasury Gilt 2055 |
| 4.00% | Treasury Gilt 2060 |
| 0.375% | Index-linked Treasury Gilt 2062 |

**Securities issued by certain public corporations and guaranteed by the Treasury**

| | |
|---|---|
| 3.00% | North of Scotland Electricity Stock 1989–92 |

## IDENTIFICATION OF SECURITIES

(*TCGA 1992, ss 104–109*)

### Disposals by individuals and trustees

Disposals on or after 6 April 2008 are to be identified with acquisitions in the following order:

(1)   Same day acquisitions (*TCGA 1992, s 105(1)(b)*) (subject to an election under *s 105A* (see below));

(2)   Acquisitions within the following 30 days on the basis of earlier acquisitions in that period, rather than later ones (a FIFO basis) (*s 106A(5)*); and

(3)   Securities within the expanded *s 104* holding, which specifically does not include acquisitions under (1) and (2) above, on the basis of later acquisitions before earlier ones (a LIFO basis) (*s 106A*).

Where the number of securities which comprise the disposal exceed those identified under the above rules, that excess is identified with subsequent acquisitions beyond the 30-day period referred to above, taking the earliest one first.

### Disposals by companies

Order of identification:

(1)   Any acquisition on the same day (*TCGA, s 105(1)(b)*);

(2)   Acquisitions within the previous 10 days (*s 107(3)*) (on a 'first in, first out' (FIFO) basis);

(3)   Acquisitions since 1 April 1982 ('the *s 104* holding', previously termed 'the new holding') (*s 107(7), (8)*);

(4)   Acquisitions in the period 6 April 1965 to 31 March 1982 ('the 1982 holding') (*s 107(7), (9)*); and

(5)   Those held on 6 April 1965, in respect of which no election has been made to include them in the pre-1982 pool; these will be identified on a last-in, first-out (LIFO) basis (*s 107(7), (9)*).

For disposals before 5 December 2005, where a company or group of companies held at least 2% of the shares or securities of that class, acquisitions and disposals within one month (for most quoted shares or securities) or six months (for other disposals) could be matched.

## Personal representatives' allowable expenses in respect of deaths after 5 April 2004

(*SP 2/04*)

| Gross value of estate | Allowable expenditure |
| --- | --- |
| Not exceeding £50,000 | 1.8% of the probate value of assets sold by the personal representatives. |
| Over £50,000 but not exceeding £90,000 | £900, divided among all assets of the estate in proportion to their probate values and allowed in those proportions on assets sold by the personal representatives. |
| Over £90,000 but not exceeding £400,000 | 1% of the probate value of assets sold. |
| Over £400,000 but not exceeding £500,000 | £4,000, divided among all assets of the estate in proportion to their probate values and allowed in those proportions on assets sold by the personal representatives. |
| Over £500,000 but not exceeding £1,000,000 | 0.8% of the probate value of assets sold. |
| Over £1,000,000 but not exceeding £5,000,000 | £8,000, divided among all assets of the estate in proportion to their probate values and allowed in those proportions on assets sold by the personal representatives. |
| Over £5,000,000 | 0.16% of the probate value of the assets sold, subject to a maximum of £10,000. |

## TIME LIMITS FOR ELECTIONS AND CLAIMS

The general time limit for claims and elections is four years from the end of the tax year or accounting period (*TMA 1970, s 43(1)*). HMRC may allow an extension of the normal time limit for certain elections and claims.

For elections made up to 31 March 2010 the normal rule was that claims by individuals and trustees had to be made within five years from 31 January next following the year to which they relate, for companies the limit was six years from the end of the relevant chargeable period.

| Provision | Time limit | References |
|---|---|---|
| Asset of negligible value | 2 years from end of tax year (or accounting period, if a company) in which deemed disposal/reacquisition takes place | *TCGA 1992, s 24(2)* |
| Re-basing of all assets to 31 March 1982 values | For companies only: 2 years from end of accounting period of disposal | *TCGA 1992, s 35(6)* |
| 50% relief if deferred charge on gains before 31 March 1982 (pre 06/04/08 disposals) | 2 years from end of accounting period of disposal (if a company) | *TCGA 1992, s 36, Sch 4 para 9(1)* |
| Variation within 2 years of death not to constitute a disposal for CGT purposes | 6 months from date of variation (nb election not necessary for variations from 1 August 2002; instrument of variation must contain a statement relying on *TCGA 1992, s 62(6)* (see *TCGA 1992, s 62(7)*) | *TCGA 1992, s 62(6)* |
| Employee share schemes – identifying disposals with acquisitions on "same day" transactions | Within 12 months from 31 January next following the tax year of the first disposal | *TCGA 1992, s 105B(2)* |
| Earn-out right to be treated as a security | Within 12 months from 31 January next following the tax year in which the right is conferred (or 2 years from end of accounting period, if a company) | *TCGA 1992, s 138A(5)* |
| Replacement of business assets (roll-over relief) | 4 years from the end of the tax year (or accounting period) Note: Replacement asset to be purchased between 12 months before and 3 years after disposal of old asset (see *TCGA 1992, s 152(3)*) | *TCGA 1992, s 152(1)* |
| Asset appropriated to trading stock: trading profits to be adjusted by gain or loss on the deemed disposal at market value | Within 12 months from 31 January next following the year of assessment in which ends the period of account in which the asset is appropriated to trading stock (or 2 years from the end of the accounting period in which the asset is appropriated to trading stock, if a company) | *TCGA 1992, s 161(3A)* |
| Disapplication of incorporation relief under TCGA 1992, s 162 | 2 years from 31 January following the end of the year of assessment in which the business is transferred If all the new assets have been disposed of by the end of the year of assessment following the one in which the business transfer took place, the time limit is 12 months from 31 January next following the tax year of the business transfer | *TCGA 1992, s 162A(3), (4)* |
| Hold-over of relief for gifts of business assets | 4 years from the end of the tax year. | *TCGA 1992, s 165(1)* |

| Provision | Time limit | References |
|---|---|---|
| Entrepreneurs' relief | Within 12 months from 31 January following the tax year in which the qualifying business disposal is made | *TCGA 1992, s 169M(3)* |
| Deemed disposal/ reacquisition on expiry of mineral lease | 4 years from the relevant date | *TCGA 1992, s 203(2)* |
| Main residence notification | 2 years from the beginning of a period for which it is necessary to determine which of 2 or more residences is an individual's main residence (eg acquisition of a second private residence) | *TCGA 1992, s 222(5)* |
| Small part disposals of land: consideration to be deducted from allowable expenditure on a subsequent disposal | Within 12 months from 31 January next following the tax year of disposal (or 2 years from end of accounting period of disposal, if a company) | *TCGA 1992, s 242(2A)* |
| Irrecoverable loan to a trader | 4 years from the end of the tax year (or accounting period) | *TCGA 1992, s 253(3)* |
| Hold-over relief for gifts on which IHT is immediately chargeable etc | 4 years from the end of the tax year. | *TCGA 1992, s 260(1)* |
| Trading losses relieved against gains | 12 months from 31 January next following the tax year in which loss arose | *TCGA 1992, s 261B(8)* |
| Post-cessation expenses relieved against gains | 12 months from 31 January next following the tax year in which expenses paid | *TCGA 1992, s 261D(6)* |
| Delayed remittances of foreign gains | 4 years from the end of the tax year (or accounting period) | *TCGA 1992, s 279(5)* |
| Loss on disposal of right to deferred unascertainable consideration to be treated as accruing in an earlier year | Within 12 months from 31 January next following the year of the loss | *TCGA 1992, s 279D(8)* |

# INDEXATION ALLOWANCE

(*TCGA 1992, ss 53, 54*)

Indexation allowance was introduced in 1982. It is broadly an allowance for inflation, based on the indexed rise in allowable expenditure for capital gains purposes. The allowance is the aggregate of the indexed rise in each item of such expenditure.

The formula for calculating indexation factors is as follows (*TCGA 1992, s 54(1)*):

$$\frac{(RD - RI)}{RI}$$

105

Where:   RD is the Retail Prices Index (RPI) for the month of disposal; and

RI is the RPI for March 1982 or the month in which the expenditure was incurred, if later).

The resulting figure is applied to each item of qualifying expenditure in the computation, by multiplying the expenditure by the relevant indexation factor.

Indexation allowance was abolished for disposals from 6 April 2008, except for disposals made by companies within the charge to corporation tax (*TCGA 1992, s 52A*).

For individuals, trustees and personal representatives, indexation allowance was frozen for disposals between 6 April 1998 and 5 April 2008. The table below shows the indexation factors up to April 1998, which can be applied to disposals up to 5 April 2008 in order to reduce gains, but not to create or increase a loss.

## Indexation: March 1982–April 1998

| Date cost incurred | 1982 | 1983 | 1984 | 1985 | 1986 | 1987 |
|---|---|---|---|---|---|---|
| Jan |  | 0.968 | 0.872 | 0.783 | 0.689 | 0.626 |
| Feb |  | 0.960 | 0.865 | 0.769 | 0.683 | 0.620 |
| Mar | 1.047 | 0.956 | 0.859 | 0.752 | 0.681 | 0.616 |
| Apr | 1.006 | 0.929 | 0.834 | 0.716 | 0.665 | 0.597 |
| May | 0.992 | 0.921 | 0.828 | 0.708 | 0.662 | 0.596 |
| Jun | 0.987 | 0.917 | 0.823 | 0.704 | 0.663 | 0.596 |
| Jul | 0.986 | 0.906 | 0.825 | 0.707 | 0.667 | 0.597 |
| Aug | 0.985 | 0.898 | 0.808 | 0.703 | 0.662 | 0.593 |
| Sep | 0.987 | 0.889 | 0.804 | 0.704 | 0.654 | 0.588 |
| Oct | 0.977 | 0.883 | 0.793 | 0.701 | 0.652 | 0.580 |
| Nov | 0.967 | 0.876 | 0.788 | 0.695 | 0.638 | 0.573 |
| Dec | 0.971 | 0.871 | 0.789 | 0.693 | 0.632 | 0.574 |

| Date cost incurred | 1988 | 1989 | 1990 | 1991 | 1992 | 1993 |
|---|---|---|---|---|---|---|
| Jan | 0.574 | 0.465 | 0.361 | 0.249 | 0.199 | 0.179 |
| Feb | 0.568 | 0.454 | 0.353 | 0.242 | 0.193 | 0.171 |
| Mar | 0.562 | 0.448 | 0.339 | 0.237 | 0.189 | 0.167 |
| Apr | 0.537 | 0.423 | 0.300 | 0.222 | 0.171 | 0.156 |
| May | 0.531 | 0.414 | 0.288 | 0.218 | 0.167 | 0.152 |
| Jun | 0.525 | 0.409 | 0.283 | 0.213 | 0.167 | 0.153 |
| Jul | 0.524 | 0.408 | 0.282 | 0.215 | 0.171 | 0.156 |
| Aug | 0.507 | 0.404 | 0.269 | 0.213 | 0.171 | 0.151 |
| Sep | 0.500 | 0.395 | 0.258 | 0.208 | 0.166 | 0.146 |
| Oct | 0.485 | 0.384 | 0.248 | 0.204 | 0.162 | 0.147 |
| Nov | 0.478 | 0.372 | 0.251 | 0.199 | 0.164 | 0.148 |
| Dec | 0.474 | 0.369 | 0.252 | 0.198 | 0.168 | 0.146 |

| Date cost incurred | 1994 | 1995 | 1996 | 1997 | 1998 |
|---|---|---|---|---|---|
| Jan | 0.151 | 0.114 | 0.083 | 0.053 | 0.019 |
| Feb | 0.144 | 0.107 | 0.078 | 0.049 | 0.014 |
| Mar | 0.141 | 0.102 | 0.073 | 0.046 | 0.011 |
| Apr | 0.128 | 0.091 | 0.066 | 0.040 | |
| May | 0.124 | 0.087 | 0.063 | 0.036 | |
| Jun | 0.124 | 0.085 | 0.063 | 0.032 | |
| Jul | 0.129 | 0.091 | 0.067 | 0.032 | |
| Aug | 0.124 | 0.085 | 0.062 | 0.026 | |
| Sep | 0.121 | 0.080 | 0.057 | 0.021 | |
| Oct | 0.120 | 0.085 | 0.057 | 0.019 | |
| Nov | 0.119 | 0.085 | 0.057 | 0.019 | |
| Dec | 0.114 | 0.079 | 0.053 | 0.016 | |

## COMPANIES

(1) Indexation allowance continues to be available for corporation tax purposes after April 2008, see **Chapter 7: Taxation of Companies**.

(2) Various measures of RPI are published by the Office for National Statistics. The RPI series used for tax purposes is the 'all items RPI' rebased at Jan 1987 = 100 (code CHAW). This can be viewed here: www.ons.gov.uk/ons/datasets-and-tables/data-selector.html?cdid=CHAW&dataset=mm23&table-id=2.1

(3) Monthly RPI figures used for indexation allowance are also published by HMRC. Tables showing the indexed rise to be used in calculating the indexation allowance in respect of assets disposed of in a particular month can be found here: www.hmrc.gov.uk/rates/cg-indexation-allowance/index.htm.

## ASSETS OF NEGLIGIBLE VALUE

*(TCGA 1992, s 24(2))*

*General* – Individual or corporate owners can make a 'negligible value' claim in respect of specified assets or shares if the asset has become of negligible value during the period of ownership. The effect of a negligible value claim is that the claimant is treated as having sold and immediately reacquired the asset at the time of the claim or (subject to certain conditions) at any earlier time specified in the claim, for consideration equal to the value specified in the claim.

*Claims* – The negligible value legislation does not specify the form in which a negligible value claim should be made. Nor does HMRC provide a specific claim form. Claims by individuals etc should be made in accordance with *TMA 1970, s 42*. Claims by companies should be made in accordance with *FA 1998, Sch 18, Pt VII* (CG13128).

In practice, negligible value claims are generally made with the claimant's tax return (eg in the 'Additional information' section of the self-assessment return for individuals), or by a later amendment to a return. Otherwise, the claim is made by written notice or letter

107

to HMRC. Form CG34 ('Post-transaction checks for capital gains') may accompany a negligible value claim made to HMRC prior to the submission of the claimant's tax return, to enable HMRC to check asset valuations.

*Negligible value list* – HMRC publishes a list of shares or securities formerly quoted on the London Stock Exchange, which have been officially declared of negligible value for the purposes of a claim under TCGA 1992, s 24(2) by HMRC Shares and Assets Valuation (SAV). The list of negligible value agreements is available here: www.hmrc. gov.uk/cgt/negvalist.htm.

*Time limit* – See **Time limits for elections and claims** (above) as to the time limit for making negligible value claims.

*Further information* – HMRC guidance on negligible value claims and procedures is contained in Help Sheet HS286 ('Negligible value claims and Income Tax losses on disposals of shares you have subscribed for in qualifying trading companies') (www. hmrc.gov.uk/helpsheets/hs286.pdf), in HMRC's Capital Gains Manual at CG13128, and in HMRC's Shares and Assets Valuation Manual at SVM107150.

# 9

# Inheritance tax and gifts

*(IHTA 1984, s 7, Sch 1)*

## INHERITANCE TAX (IHT) THRESHOLDS AND RATES

| Period | Upper limit | Rate of tax | Grossing up rate for each £ over the upper limit |
|---|---|---|---|
| | £ | | |
| 6 April 2009–5 April 2018 | 325,000 | | |
| 2008–09 | 312,000 | | |
| 2007–08 | 300,000 | 20% on gross | |
| 2006–07 | 285,000 | lifetime | ¼ for net |
| 2005–06 | 275,000 | transfers over | lifetime |
| 2004–05 | 263,000 | the cumulative | transfers |
| 2003–04 | 255,000 | upper limit | |
| 2002–03 | 250,000 | | |
| 2001–02 | 242,000 | | |
| 2000–01 | 234,000 | | |
| 1999–2000 | 231,000 | | |
| 1989–99 | 223,000 | | |
| 1997–98 | 215,000 | | |
| 1996–97 | 200,000 | | |
| 1995–96 | 154,000 | 40% on | 2/3 for net |
| 10 March 1992 to 5 April 1995 | 150,000 | transfers on | transfers on |
| 6 April 1991 to 9 March 1992 | 140,000 | death over the | death (not |
| 1990–91 | 128,000 | cumulative | bearing own |
| 1989–90 | 118,000 | upper limit | tax) |
| 15 March 1988 to 5 April 1989 | 110,000 | | |
| 17 March 1987 to 14 March 1988 | 90,000 | | |
| 18 March 1986 to 16 March 1987 | 71,000 | | |

**Notes**

(1) *What is covered* – the above rates and thresholds apply to lifetime transfers and transfers on death or within seven years before death.

(2) *Nil rate band* – The IHT threshold (or 'nil rate band') is set at £325,000 for the tax years 2010–11 to 2014–15 inclusive (*FA 2010, s 8*).

(3)   *Frozen nil rate band* – Legislation will be introduced in *Finance Bill 2014* to freeze the nil rate band until 2017–18 (*Budget, 20 March 2013*).

(4)   *Charity discount* – A lower IHT rate of 36% can apply to a deceased person's estate, where 10% or more of the net estate has been left to charities and/or registered community amateur sports clubs, with effect for deaths on or after 6 April 2012 (*IHTA 1984, Sch 1A*) (see **Gifts to charities** below).

## Capital transfer tax (inheritance tax thresholds) – 13 March 1975 to 17 March 1986

| From | To | Limit |
|---|---|---|
| 06.04.1985 | 17.03.1986 | £67,000 |
| 13.03.1984 | 05.04.1985 | £64,000 |
| 15.03.1983 | 12.03.1984 | £60,000 |
| 09.03.1982 | 14.03.1983 | £55,000 |
| 26.03.1980 | 08.03.1982 | £50,000 |
| 27.10.1977 | 25.03.1980 | £25,000 |
| 13.03.1975 | 26.10.1977 | £15,000 |

## Estate duty (Inheritance tax thresholds) – 16 August 1914 to 12 March 1975

*England, Wales and Scotland*

| From | To | Limit |
|---|---|---|
| 22.03.1972 | 12.03.1975 | £15,000 |
| 31.03.1971 | 21.03.1972 | £12,500 |
| 16.04.1969 | 30.03.1971 | £10,000 |
| 04.04.1963 | 15.04.1969 | £5,000 |
| 09.04.1962 | 03.04.1963 | £4,000 |
| 30.07.1954 | 08.04.1962 | £3,000 |
| 10.04.1946 | 29.07.1954 | £2,000 |
| 16.08.1914 | 09.04.1946 | £100 |

*Northern Ireland*

| From | To | Limit |
|---|---|---|
| 22.03.1972 | 12.03.1975 | £15,000 |
| 05.05.1971 | 21.03.1972 | £12,500 |
| 04.06.1969 | 04.05.1971 | £10,000 |
| 22.05.1963 | 03.06.1969 | £5,000 |
| 04.07.1962 | 21.05.1963 | £4,000 |
| 01.11.1954 | 03.07.1962 | £3,000 |
| 29.08.1946 | 31.10.1954 | £2,000 |
| 16.08.1914 | 28.08.1946 | £100 |

## ANNUAL AND SMALL GIFT EXEMPTION

*(IHTA 1984, ss 19, 20)*

| Period | Annual exemption | Small Gift exemption (to the same person) |
|--------|------------------|-------------------------------------------|
| From 6 April 1981 | £3,000 | £250 |
| 6 April 1980 to 5 April 1981 | £2,000 | £250 |
| 6 April 1976 to 5 April 1980 | £2,000 | £100 |

**Note**

To the extent that the annual exemption is unused for a particular tax year, it can be carried forward to the next year but not beyond *(IHTA 1984, s 19(2))*.

## GIFTS IN CONSIDERATION OF MARRIAGE/CIVIL PARTNERSHIP

*(IHTA 1984, s 22)*

| Donor | Limit |
|-------|-------|
| Parent of party to the marriage/civil partnership | £5,000 |
| Remoter ancestor than parent of party to the marriage/civil partnership | £2,500 |
| Party to the marriage/civil partnership | £2,500 |
| Any other person | £1,000 |

**Note**

If the value transferred by the gift is greater than the amount of the available exemption, it is an exempt transfer up to the amount of the available exemption, and the excess is chargeable.

## NON-UK DOMICILED SPOUSE / CIVIL PARTNER GIFT EXEMPTION

*(IHTA 1984, s 18)*

| Transfers: | Limit |
|------------|-------|
| From 6 April 2013 | £325,000 |
| From 9 March 1982 | £55,000 |

**Notes**

(1)  *Civil partners* – The exemption was extended to civil partners with effect from 5 December 2005 *(SI 2005/3229)*.

(2)  *Nil rate band alignment* – With effect for gifts made on and after 6 April 2013 the IHT-exempt amount that a UK-domiciled individual can transfer to their non-UK domiciled spouse or civil partner is increased to the nil rate band level and will be linked to the level of the nil rate band in future years *(FB 2013, cl 176)*.

(3)  *Election* – Individuals who are domiciled outside the UK and who have a UK-domiciled spouse or civil partner can elect to be treated as domiciled in the UK for the purposes of IHT. This election can be made at any time after marriage or civil partnership and within two years of the death where that occurs on or after 6 April 2013 (*FB 2013, cl 175*).

## AGRICULTURAL AND BUSINESS PROPERTY RELIEF

(*IHTA 1984, Pt V, Chs 1, 2*)

| Agricultural property (notes (1), (2)) | | Business Property | |
|---|---|---|---|
| Nature of property | Disposals from 6 April 1996 % | Nature of property | Disposals from 6 April 1996 % |
| Vacant possession or right to obtain it within 12 months | 100 | Business or interest in a business (note (4)) | 100 |
| Tenanted land with vacant possession value (note (3)) | 100 | Quoted company: controlling shareholding | 50 |
| Agricultural land let on or after 1 September 1995 | 100 | Unquoted company: controlling shareholding (note (4)) | 100 |
| Any other circumstances | 50 | Unquoted company: shareholding more than 25% (note (4)) | 100 |
| | | Unquoted company: shareholding 25% or less (note (5)) | 100 |
| | | Unquoted securities: control holding | 100 |
| | | Settled property used in life tenant's business (note (6)) | 100/50 |
| | | Land, buildings, machinery or plant used by transferor's company or partnership | 50 |

**Notes**

(1)  *EEA states* – IHT due or paid from 23 April 2003 in respect of agricultural property located in a qualifying EEA state at the time of the chargeable event is eligible for relief (*FA 2009, s 122*).

(2)  *Grazing land* – If land is let to graze animals or take grass from land for a season, and vacant possession reverts to the landowner within a year, any agricultural property relief due will be at the 100% rate (IHTM24142).

(3)  *Old tenancies* – Land let on a tenancy commencing before 10 March 1981 may qualify for relief at 100% in certain circumstances, ie broadly if the transferor owned the land before 10 March 1981, the land would have qualified for relief

(under *FA 1975, Sch 8*) had it been transferred before that date, and the transferor did not have vacant possession (or entitlement to it) from then until the date of death/transfer (*IHTA 1984, s 116(2), (3)*).

(4)   *Majority shareholdings* – The rate of relief was increased from 50% with effect from 10 March 1992.

(5)   *Minority shareholdings* – The rate of relief was increased from 50% with effect from 6 April 1996.

(6)   *Settled property* – The higher rate applies if the settled property is transferred with the business on death (see *IHTM25243*).

(7)   *Deductions for debts* – Provisions in *Finance Bill 2013* will require any debt incurred to acquire an asset on which relief is due under APR, BPR or woodlands relief to be first deducted from the value of that asset before any excess is deducted from the value of the total estate (*FB 2013, cl 174, Sch 34*).

## QUICK SUCCESSION RELIEF

(*IHTA 1984, s 141*)

| Years between transfers | | Percentage (applied to formula – see below) % |
|---|---|---|
| **More than** | **Not more than** | |
| 0 | 1 | 100 |
| 1 | 2 | 80 |
| 2 | 3 | 60 |
| 3 | 4 | 40 |
| 4 | 5 | 20 |

**Note**

Formula:

$$\text{Percentage} \times \text{Tax charge on earlier transfer} \times \frac{\text{Increase in value of transferee's estate}}{\text{Value of earlier chargeable transfer}}$$

## TAPER RELIEF

(*IHTA 1984, s 7(4)*)

| Period between gift and death | % of full charge at death rates |
|---|---|
| 3 years or less | 100 |
| Over 3 years but not more than 4 years | 80 |
| Over 4 years but not more than 5 years | 60 |
| Over 5 years but not more than 6 years | 40 |
| Over 6 years but not more than 7 years | 20 |

**Notes**

(1)  *Lifetime gifts* – The relief provides for a reduced tax charge on gifts made within seven years before death. The amount of relief depends on the length of time the deceased survived following the transfer. The tax otherwise due at the death rates is reduced by applying the percentages in the preceding table.

(2)  *Doesn't apply* – Taper relief does not apply where the tapered tax would otherwise have been less than the tax which would have been chargeable on the original transfer using half death rates (*IHTA 1984, s 7(5)*).

## PRE-OWNED ASSETS

(*FA 2004, s 84, Sch 15*)

### General

An income tax charge arises where an individual continues to benefit from property previously owned by them. The charge arises in respect of the following:

- land;

- chattels; and

- intangible property (in a settlement where the settlor retains an interest).

No tax is payable if the aggregate amount attributable to a chargeable person does not exceed £5,000. However, if benefits exceed £5,000, the charge is on the full amount.

### Land

The chargeable amount is the 'appropriate rental value' less any amount paid under a legal obligation in respect of the occupation of the land. The 'appropriate rental value' is calculated using the following formula:

$$R \times \frac{DV}{V}$$

Where:  R is the rental value of the relevant land for the taxable period;

DV is the value at the valuation date of the interest in the relevant land that was disposed of by the chargeable person or, where the disposal was a non-exempt sale, the appropriate proportion of that value; and

V is the value of the relevant land at the valuation date.

The 'taxable period' is the year of assessment, or part of a year of assessment, during which the relevant conditions are met.

The 'rental value' is based on the assumption of a letting from year to year where the tenant pays the taxes, rates and charges and the landlord is responsible for repairs and insurance. Land may be valued on a five-yearly rather than an annual valuation (*SI 2005/724, reg 4*).

### Chattels

The chargeable amount is the 'appropriate amount' less any amount paid under a legal obligation to the owner of the chattel. The 'appropriate amount' is:

$$N \times \frac{DV}{V}$$

Where:    N is the notional interest for the taxable period, at the prescribed rate, on the value of the chattel at the valuation date;

DV is the value at the valuation date of the interest in the relevant chattel that was disposed of by the chargeable person or, where the disposal was a non-exempt sale, the appropriate proportion of that asset; and

V is the value of the chattel at the valuation date.

## Intangible property in settlor-interested settlements

The chargeable amount in relation to the relevant property is:

$$N - T$$

Where:    N is the notional amount of interest for the taxable period, at the prescribed rate, on the value of the property at the valuation date; and

T is the amount of income tax or capital gains tax payable by the chargeable person in the taxable period by virtue of gains from contracts of life assurance, income from settlements where the settlor retains an interest, transfer of assets abroad, the charge on settlors with an interest in settlements and the attribution of gains to settlors with an interest in non-resident or dual resident settlements for capital gains tax purposes.

### Notes

(1)    *Prescribed rate* – This rate is the official rate of interest on first day of each taxable period (usually 6 April), which must be applied to the values of chattels and intangibles when quantifying the cash value of the benefit enjoyed, (*SI 2005/724, regs 2, 3*).

(2)    *Further information* – HMRC's guidance on pre-owned assets can be found at www.hmrc.gov.uk/manuals/ihtmanual/IHTM44000.htm.

## DELIVERY OF IHT ACCOUNTS: DUE DATES

*(IHTA 1984, s 216)*

| Type of transfer | Due Date |
|---|---|
| Chargeable lifetime transfer | Later of:<br>– 12 months after end of month in which transfer occurred<br>– 3 months after person became liable |

*continued*

| Type of transfer | Due Date |
|---|---|
| Transfers on death | Later of:<br>– 12 months after end of month in which death occurred<br>– 3 months after personal representatives first act in that capacity |
| Potentially exempt transfers which have become chargeable | 12 months after end of month in which the transferor died |
| Gifts subject to reservation included in donor's estate at death | 12 months after end of month in which death occurred |
| National heritage property or woodlands (on disposal) | 6 months after end of month in which chargeable event occurred |

## DELIVERY OF ACCOUNTS: EXCEPTED TRANSFERS, ESTATES AND SETTLEMENTS

*(IHTA 1984, ss 216, 256; SI 2008/605; SI 2004/2543 (as amended); SI 2008/606)*

### Excepted transfers

*From 6 April 2007*

*(SI 2008/605, reg 4)*

For chargeable transfers from 6 April 2007, no account is necessary where:

- the transfer is in cash or quoted shares or securities and the value of the transfer and other chargeable transfers made in the preceding seven years does not exceed the IHT threshold; or

- the value of the transfer (ignoring business and agricultural property relief) and other chargeable transfers made in the preceding seven years does not exceed 80% of the IHT threshold, and the value of the transfer does not exceed the net amount of the threshold available to the transferor at the time of the transfer.

Similar rules apply in determining whether the termination of an interest in possession in settled property is excepted from the requirement to deliver an account (*SI 2008/605, reg 5*).

*Before 6 April 2007*

*(SI 2002/1731)*

Certain small lifetime transfers and terminations of interests in possession were (from 6 April 1981) excused from delivering an IHT account. The excepted transfer limits for periods to 5 April 2007 are as follows:

(a)   Total chargeable transfers in the tax year – £10,000; and

(b)   Total transferred by that and all previous chargeable transfers in the last ten years – £40,000.

## Excepted estates

| Deaths from | Before | Excepted estate limit | Assets held outside UK – limit | Total value of settled property | Specified transfers – limit | Specified exempt transfers – limit |
|---|---|---|---|---|---|---|
| 6/4/2011 | 5/4/2014 | 325,000 | 100,000 | 150,000 | 150,000 | 1,000,000 |
| 6/4/2010 | 5/4/2011 | 325,000 | 100,000 | 150,000 | 150,000 | 1,000,000 |
| 6/4/2009 | 5/4/2010 | 325,000 | 100,000 | 150,000 | 150,000 | 1,000,000 |
| 6/4/2008 | 5/4/2009 | 312,000 | 100,000 | 150,000 | 150,000 | 1,000,000 |
| 6/4/2007 | 5/4/2008 | 300,000 | 100,000 | 150,000 | 150,000 | 1,000,000 |
| 1/9/2006 | 5/4/2007 | 285,000 | 100,000 | 150,000 | 150,000 | 1,000,000 |
| 6/4/2006 | 31/8/2006 | 285,000 | 75,000 | 100,000 | 100,000 | 1,000,000 |

**Notes**

(1)   *General* – The current excepted estate provisions are contained in *SI 2004/2543*. The regulations essentially provide for three categories of excepted estate:

(a)   The 'low value' estate;

(b)   The 'exempt estate'; and

(c)   The 'foreign domiciliaries' estate.

(2)   *Transferable nil rate band* – For deaths on and after 6 April 2010, the low value and exempt estate categories are expanded to twice the nil rate band. This only applies if a claim is made for 100% of the nil rate band to be transferred from an earlier deceased spouse or civil partner, subject to other conditions being satisfied. The excepted estate return form IHT205, or C5 in Scotland, must be used (*SI 2011/214*).

(3)   *Alternatively secured pension funds* – For deaths occurring from 6 April 2011 the conditions relating to the alternatively secured pension fund do not have effect (*SI 2004/2543, reg 4(10)*).

(4)   *Earlier years* – For the rules for estates where the death was before 1 September 2006 see: www.hmrc.gov.uk/inheritancetax/iht-probate-forms/excepted-estates. htm#4

(5)   *Further guidance* – A list of what is not an excepted estate is found here: www. hmrc.gov.uk/inheritancetax/iht-probate-forms/excepted-estates.htm. For technical guidance see HMRC Inheritance Tax Manual IHTM06011 et seq.

## Excepted settlements

*(IHTA 1984, ss 216, 256; SI 2008/606)*

*From 6 April 2007*

No account is necessary of settled property in which no qualifying interest in possession subsists for chargeable events from 6 April 2007, broadly where:

*Either*:

- Cash has always been the only property comprised in the settlement;

- The settlor has added no further property to the settlement;

- The trustees have been UK resident since the settlement commenced;

- The gross value of settled property has not exceeded £1,000 since the settlement commenced; and

- There are no related settlements.

*or*

- The settlor was UK domiciled when the settlement was made, and remained so until the chargeable event, or until death (whichever is earlier);

- The trustees have been UK resident since the settlement commenced; and

- There are no related settlements; and *either*

- For ten-year anniversary IHT charge purposes, the value of the notional aggregate chargeable transfer (in *IHTA 1984, s 66(3)*) does not exceed 80% of the nil rate band; *or*

- On a chargeable event before the settlement's first ten-year anniversary, the value of the notional aggregate chargeable transfer (in *IHTA 1984, s 68(4)*) does not exceed 80% of the nil rate band; *or*

- On a chargeable event between ten-year anniversaries, the value of the notional aggregate chargeable transfer (in *IHTA 1984, s 66(3)*, taking account of *s 69*) does not exceed 80% of the nil rate band; *or*

- Where an IHT charge arises in respect of an 'age 18 to 25' trust (under *IHTA 1984, s 71E*), the value of the notional aggregate chargeable transfer (as adjusted in accordance with *IHTA 1984, s 71F(8)*) does not exceed 80% of the nil rate band.

### Before 6 April 2007

For chargeable events occurring between 6 April 2002 and 5 April 2007, no account is necessary of settled property in which no qualifying interest in possession subsists broadly in the following circumstances (*SI 2002/1732*):

- Cash is the only asset in the settlement;

- The settlor added no further assets since making the settlement;

- The trustees have been UK resident since the settlement commenced;

- The gross value of settled assets at the time of the chargeable event does not exceed £1,000; and

- There are no related settlements.

### Note

Further guidance – For HMRC guidance on excepted settlements, see HMRC Inheritance Tax Manual, IHTM06120 et seq.

# DUE DATES FOR PAYMENT OF IHT

*(IHTA 1984, s 226)*

| Transfer | Due Date |
|---|---|
| Chargeable transfers other than death made between: | |
| 6 April and 30 September | 30 April in following year |
| 1 October and 5 April | 6 months after end of month in which transfer was made |
| Chargeable transfers which have conditional exemptions for heritage | 6 months after end of month in which chargeable event occurred |
| Charge to tax on disposals of trees or underwood | |
| Transfers on death | Earlier of : |
| | – 6 months after of month in which death occurs; or |
| | – delivery of account by personal representatives |
| Chargeable transfers and potentially exempt transfers within 7 years of death | 6 months after end of month in which death occurs |

# PENALTIES

See **Chapter 17**

# INTEREST RATES

*(IHTA 1984, s 233)*

| Interest period | Interest rate (%) | Interest rate repaid (%) | Days |
|---|---|---|---|
| From 29 Sept 2009 | 3% | 0.5% | – |
| 24 March 2009 to 28 Sept 2009 | 0% | 0% | 189 |
| 27 Jan 2009 to 23 March 2009 | 1% | 1% | 56 |
| 6 Jan 2009 to 26 Jan 2009 | 2% | 2% | 21 |
| 6 Nov 2008 to 5 Jan 2009 | 3% | 3% | 61 |
| 6 Jan 2008 to 5 Nov 2008 | 4% | 4% | 304 |
| 6 August 2007 to 5 Jan 2008 | 5% | 5% | 153 |
| 6 Sept 2006 to 5 August 2007 | 4% | 4% | 334 |

**Note**

Interest rates for earlier years can be found here: www.hmrc.gov.uk/rates/iht-interest-rates.htm

## INTEREST ON IHT PAID IN YEARLY INSTALMENTS

*(IHTA 1984, ss 227, 234)*

| Month of death | Due date | Interest starts from |
|---|---|---|
| January | 31 July | 1 August |
| February | 31 August | 1 September |
| March | 30 September | 1 October |
| April | 31 October | 1 November |
| May | 30 November | 1 December |
| June | 31 December | 1 January |
| July | 31 January | 1 February |
| August | 28/29 February | 1 March |
| September | 31 March | 1 April |
| October | 30 April | 1 May |
| November | 31 May | 1 June |
| December | 30 June | 1 July |

**Note**

For IHT payable by ten equal yearly instalments, the first instalment is due six months from the end of the month in which the individual died. The second instalment is due on the same day 12 months after the first payment, and subsequent instalments are due on the same day each year. The preceding table shows how to work out the due date. Interest commences from the following day.

## DISTRIBUTION OF INTESTATE ESTATES

### The following provisions relate to England and Wales only

*(Administration of Estates Act 1925, s 46)*

| **(1)   Spouse or civil partner and issue survive** | |
|---|---|
| *Spouse or civil partner receives* | *Issue receives* |
| • All personal chattels; <br>• £250,000 absolutely (or the entire interest where this is less); and <br>• Life interest in one-half of residue (if any). | • One half of residue (if any) on statutory trusts (plus the other half of residue on statutory trusts upon the death of the spouse). |
| **(2)   Spouse or civil partner survives without issue, but a surviving parent or brother or sister or issue of a brother or sister** | |
| *Spouse or civil partner receives* | *Residuary estate to* |
| • All personal chattels; <br>• £450,000 absolutely (or entire estate where this is less); and <br>• One half of residue (if any) absolutely. | • The deceased's parent(s). <br>• If no parent survives: on trust for the deceased's brothers and sisters of the whole blood (and the issue of any such deceased brother or sister). |

**(3) Spouse or civil partner survives but no issue, parents, brothers or sisters or their issue**

Whole estate to surviving spouse or civil partner.

**(4) No spouse or civil partner survives**

Estate held in the following order with no class beneficiaries participating unless all those in a prior class have predeceased. Statutory trusts may apply except under (b), (e) and (h):

(a)   Issue of deceased.

(b)   Parent(s).

(c)   Brothers and sisters (or issue).

(d)   Half-brothers and half-sisters (or issue).

(e)   Grandparent(s).

(f)   Uncles and aunts (or issue).

(g)   Half-brothers and half-sisters of deceased's parents (or issue).

(h)   The Crown, the Duchy of Lancaster or the Duke of Cornwall.

**Notes**

(1)   *General* – The distribution of a deceased individual's estate, and the IHT liability in respect of the estate, can be affected if the individual died without having made a valid will. The above fixed sums of £250,000 and £450,000 apply for deaths on or after 1 February 2009 (*SI 2009/135*). Previously, the fixed sums were £125,000 and £200,000 respectively.

(2)   *Civil partners* – The *Administration of Estates Act 1925* was extended (by the *Civil Partnership Act 2004, Sch 4, paras 7–12*) to include a surviving civil partner, who effectively acquires the same rights as a surviving spouse in cases of intestacy.

(3)   *Survivorship* – The above provisions in favour of the deceased's spouse or civil partner are subject to a 28 day survival period (*AEA 1925, s 46(2A)*).

(4)   *Further information* – The above is an outline of the intestacy provisions affective for deaths in England and Wales. Further information is available in HMRC's IHT manual (at IHTM12101 onwards), and from the Justice website:

www.justice.gov.uk/guidance/courts-and-tribunals/courts/probate/why-make-a-will.htm

For deaths in Scotland refer to: www.scotland.gov.uk/Publications/2006/04/12094440/20

# GIFTS TO CHARITIES ETC

*(IHTA 1984, s 7(2), Sch 1A)*

- A lower rate of IHT of 36% (as opposed to the 40% rate normally charged on death on the net value of the estate above the available nil rate band) is chargeable on a deceased person's estate broadly where 10% or more of the net estate has been left to charities and/or registered community amateur sports clubs.

- The lower rate is available in relation to deaths occurring on or after 6 April 2012.

**Notes**

(1)   *General* – The reduced IHT rate is subject to a 'charitable giving' condition that the 'donated amount' is at least 10% of the 'baseline amount' (as defined) for one or more components of the estate.

(2)   *Components* – The three components of the estate as defined for these purposes are the survivorship or a special destination (or corresponding provisions in a non-UK jurisdiction), settled property and general components. The general component excludes gifts with reservation.

(3)   *Election* – An election is available to merge estate components in appropriate circumstances. The election must be made by all of the 'appropriate persons' (as defined) in respect of the components concerned. Alternatively, an election is available to 'opt out' of the lower rate for one or more components of the estate. In both cases, the election must be made by written notice within two years after the deceased's death (and may be withdrawn within two years and one month after death, or such longer period as HMRC may allow).

(4)   *Variations* – Whether or not an estate qualifies for the reduced rate of IHT, where on or after 6 April 2012 an Instrument of Variation is executed, leaving or increasing a legacy to charity, the variation will only be treated as being made by the deceased where it is shown that the charity has been notified of the variation (*IHTA 1984, s 142(3A)*).

(5)   *HMRC guidance* – Guidance for taxpayers on the reduced rate of IHT is found here: www.hmrc.gov.uk/inheritancetax/pass-money-property/charity-reduce.htm. Technical guidance is found in the HMRC inheritance tax manual at paras IHTM11101-11178.

## GIFTS OF PRE-EMINENT PROPERTY (CULTURAL GIFTS SCHEME)

*(FA 2012, s 49, Sch 14)*

|  | Tax reduction |
| --- | --- |
| **Individuals** | |
| Income tax and capital gains tax* | 30% |
| **Companies** | |
| Corporation tax | 20% |

* If the individual does not express a preference, the tax reduction is first applied to the individual's income tax liability, then to any capital gains tax liability.

**Notes**

(1)   *General* – A reduction in income tax and/or capital gains tax (individuals), or corporation tax (companies), is available where an individual or corporate donor makes a 'qualifying gift' of 'pre-eminent property' (as defined) to be held for the

benefit of the public or the nation. The gift offer must be registered and accepted under a scheme set up by the Secretary of State. The relief provisions apply from a date to be appointed by Treasury order.

(2)  *Individuals* – An individual can spread the tax reduction over a period of up to five tax years, ie the tax year in which the offer is registered or any of the following four tax years. The total tax reduction figure is 30% of the qualifying gift's agreed value. The relief applies to individuals, but not those acting as trustees or personal representatives.

(3)  *Companies* – If a company makes a qualifying gift, a tax reduction (for the accounting period in which an offer to make the gift is registered) is treated as arising when the company's corporation tax liability became due (or the registration date, if later). The tax reduction is 20% of the qualifying gift's agreed value, although the company may choose to accept a lower percentage if it so wishes.

(4)  *Capital gains* – A gain on the gift of an object under the scheme is exempt from capital gains tax or corporation tax on chargeable gains (*TCGA 1992, s 258(1A)*).

(5)  *Inheritance tax* – Gifts of property under the scheme are exempt from inheritance tax under *IHTA 1984, s 25* ('Gifts for national purposes, etc') (*IHTA 1984, s 25(3)*).

(6)  *Further information* – The scheme is to be administered by the Department for Culture Media and Sport and the Arts Council. Guidance can be found here: www.artscouncil.org.uk/what-we-do/supporting-museums/cultural-property/tax-incentives/cultural-gifts-scheme/.

*10*

# Capital Allowances

## PLANT AND MACHINERY

*(CAA 2001, Pt 2)*

### Writing down allowances (WDAs)

*(CAA 2001, s 56)*

|  | Main rate (%) | Special rate (%) |
|---|---|---|
| From April 2012 | 18 | 8 |
| April 2008 to April 2012 | 20 | 10 |
| Before April 2008 | 25 | – |

**Notes**

(1)  *Changes* – The changes in WDA rates from 1 April 2012 (corporation tax) or 6 April 2012 (for income tax) were made by *FA 2011, s 10*.

(2)  *Straddling periods* – For chargeable periods which straddle the above relevant dates, the rate of WDA is a hybrid of the rates before and after the changes.

(3)  *Further information* – guidance for taxpayers is found here: www.hmrc.gov.uk/ capital-allowances/plant.htm. Technical guidance is found in the HMRC Capital Allowances manual at para CA23220.

### Annual investment allowance (AIA)

*(CAA 2001, s 51A)*

| Expenditure incurred in period: | Maximum annual allowance £ |
|---|---|
| From 1 January 2015 | 25,000 |
| From 1 January 2013 to 31 December 2014 | 250,000 |
| From April 2012 | 25,000 |
| April 2010 to April 2012 | 100,000 |
| April 2008 to April 2010 | 50,000 |

**Notes**

(1)  *Temporary increase* – The temporary increase in the AIA for two years from 1 January 2013 applies to all businesses whether within the charge to corporation tax

or income tax. The rules for calculating the maximum allowance due for periods that straddle the dates of change are particularly complex (*FB 2013, cl 7, Sch 1*).

(2)    *Chargeable periods* – The AIA is given for a chargeable period. As a general rule, the annual limit is proportionately increased or decreased for chargeable periods longer or shorter than 12 months.

(3)    *Reduction in AIA* – The reduction from 1 April 2012 (for corporation tax) or 6 April 2012 (for income tax) was made by *FA 2011, s 11*.

(4)    *Straddling periods* – For chargeable periods which straddle the above relevant dates, the maximum AIA entitlement is calculated by splitting the chargeable period into two chargeable periods, the first ending with the date before the relevant date, and the second commencing from the relevant date. The maximum AIA available is then calculated according to the transitional rules.

(5)    *Not qualifying* – The AIA cannot be claimed by a trust or by a partnership where one or more members is a company (*CAA 2001, s 38A, ss 51A–51N*).

(6)    *Exclusions* – The AIA is not due in respect of the purchase of cars, and it also cannot be claimed for the period when the trade ceases (*CAA 2001, s 38B*).

## First year allowances (FYAs)

(*CAA 2001, s 52*)

FYAs at a rate of 100%, are available for the following types of expenditure incurred by businesses of any size, subject to general exclusions listed below (see **First year allowances: general exclusions**).

| Expenditure on | Section in CAA 2001 |
|---|---|
| Certain energy–saving plant or machinery (see note 1 below) | *s 45A* |
| Cars with low $CO_2$ emissions | *s 45D* |
| Goods vehicles with zero emissions (see note 2 below) | *s 45DA* |
| Plant or machinery for gas refuelling stations (see note 3 below) | *s 45E* |
| Plant or machinery for use by a company wholly in a ring fence trade | *s 45F* |
| Environmentally beneficial plant or machinery | *s 45H* |
| Certain new investment by companies in new plant or machinery in designated assisted areas in Enterprise Zones (for further details, see **Enterprise Zones** below) | *s 45K* |

**Notes**

(1)    For energy-saving plant or machinery also known as enhanced capital allowances (ECAs):

- The items that qualify under the ECA scheme are lists on the Energy Technology list: https://etl.decc.gov.uk/etl/site.html. Changes are made frequently to this list by regulations (eg: *SI 2012/1831; SI 2012/1838*).

- From April 2012 ECAs do not apply to plant or machinery which generates electricity or heat (or produces biogas or biofuels) attracting tariff payments under the Feed-in Tariff (FiT) or Renewable Heat Incentive (RHI) schemes (*CAA 2001, s 45AA*).

(2)   Zero-emission goods vehicles:

- 100% FYAs are generally available for business expenditure on registered new and unused (not second hand) zero-emission goods vehicles, for a period of five years from 1 April 2010 (corporation tax) and 6 April 2010 (income tax) (*CAA 2001, s 45DA*).

- Expenditure on zero-emissions goods vehicles does not qualify for 100% FYAs broadly if the person who incurred it is (or forms part of) an undertaking that is a 'firm in difficulty' and/or is subject to an outstanding recovery order. In addition, expenditure is excluded if incurred for a qualifying activity in the fishery or aquacultural sectors, or which manages the waste of undertakings. Expenditure is also excluded if taken into account for the purposes of a 'relevant grant' or 'relevant payment' made towards it (*CAA 2001, s 45DB*).

  There is a cap on the amount of expenditure on zero-emission goods vehicles that qualifies for FYAs, of €85 million per undertaking over the five-year life of the allowances (*CAA 2001, s 212T*).

(3)   *Gas refuelling equipment* – The 100% FYA for plant and machinery used in gas, biogas and hydrogen refuelling stations is extended to 31 March 2015 (*FB 2013, cl 68*).

## Temporary first year allowances (FYAs)

(*FA 2009, s 24*)

A temporary FYA at 40% was available for expenditure on plant and machinery in the 12 months ended 31 March 2010 (for corporation tax) or 5 April 2010 (for income tax).

## First year allowances: general exclusions

(*CAA 2001, s 46(2)*)

No first year allowances are available for the following types of expenditure:

- expenditure incurred in the chargeable period in which the qualifying activity is permanently discontinued;

- cars (other than those with low $CO_2$ emissions);

- certain ships (within *CAA 2001, s 94*, but see *FB 2013, cl 69*);

- certain railway assets (exclusion removed by *FB 2013, cl 69*);

- expenditure that would be long–life asset expenditure but for transitional provisions (in *CAA 2001, Sch 3, para 20*);

- expenditure on the provision of plant or machinery for leasing (whether in the course of a trade or otherwise) (subject to exceptions in *CAA 2001, s 46(5)*);

- certain anti–avoidance cases where the obtaining of a FYA is linked to a change in the nature or conduct of a trade;

- plant and machinery that was initially acquired for purposes other than those of the qualifying activity;

- plant or machinery that was provided for long funding leasing but later starts to be used for other purposes; and

- plant and machinery that was acquired by way of gift.

## CARS

*(CAA 2001, ss 45D, 52, Pt 2, Ch 10A)*

The rate of capital allowances is based on the car's carbon dioxide emissions, as summarised below:

| CO₂ emissions | | Capital allowances |
|---|---|---|
| **From 2009–2010 to 2012–13** | **From 2013–2014 to 2014–15** | |
| Up to 110g/km | Up to 95g/km | FYAs at 100% available |
| Up to 160g/km | Up to 130g/km | Main rate pool applies |
| Over 160g/km | Over 130g/km | 'Special rate' pool applies |

**Notes**

(1)  The 100% FYA for business cars with $CO_2$ emissions up to 110g/km applies only for expenditure up to 31 March 2013 on cars which are new and unused (not second hand) *(CAA 2001, s 45D)*.

(2)  *Cars with private use* – The main or special rates apply as above (depending on $CO_2$ emissions) but the car is retained in a single asset pool (see HMRC Capital Allowances Manual, *CA23535*). Allowances are restricted for private use.

(3)  *Leased cars* – See **Chapter 6: Taxation of business profits: car hire costs**.

(4)  *Prior to April 2009* – A standard rate of WDA applied, and allowances were restricted to £3,000 for cars costing £12,000 or more. A proportion of the hire cost of cars was disallowed for tax purposes where the retail price when new exceeded £12,000 *(CAA 2001, Pt 2, Ch 8)*.

(5)  *Capital allowances rates* – For WDA rates in respect of the main rate pool and special rate pool, see **Writing down allowances** (WDAs) above.

## Integral features

*(CAA 2001, ss 33A–B, 104A(1), 104D)*

Expenditure on integral features is excluded from the main capital allowances pool, but can qualify for the AIA. WDAs are given at the special rate (see above) on the reducing balance of the pool. The following fall within the definition of integral features:

- electrical systems (including lighting systems);

- cold water systems;

- space or water heating systems, powered systems of ventilation, air cooling or air purification, and any floor or ceiling comprised in such systems;

- lifts, escalators and moving walkways; and

- external solar shading.

**Notes**

(1)  *Insulation* – The above items do not include any asset whose principal purpose is to insulate or enclose the interior of a building, or to provide an interior wall, floor or ceiling intended to remain permanently in place (*CAA 2001, 33(A)(6)*).

(2)  *Repairs* – Expenditure on integral features (eg repairs) is treated as being on the replacement of the integral feature, if the expenditure exceeds 50% of the item's replacement cost (*s 33B*).

(3)  *Solar panels* – Expenditure incurred on or after 1 April 2012 (for corporation tax) or 6 April 2012 (for income tax) on solar panels (whether integral or not) must be included in the special rate pool (*s 45AA*).

## Fixtures

*(CAA 2001, Pt 2, Ch 14)*

The availability of capital allowances to a purchaser of fixtures on or after 1 April 2012 (for corporation tax) or 6 April 2012 (for income tax) is conditional on either:

(a)  the seller and purchaser using one of two pre-existing procedures (a joint election under *CAA 2001, ss 198–199* or determination by the First Tier Tribunal) to fix the value of the fixtures transferred within two years of the transfer, or

(b)  the past owner providing a written statement of the amount of the disposal value of fixtures which he had some time earlier been required to bring into account.

After a transitional period of two years, from 1 or 6 April 2014 it will also be necessary to show that previous business expenditure on qualifying fixtures had been pooled before a subsequent transfer on to another person (*CAA 2001, s 187A*).

## SHORT-LIFE ASSETS

| Expenditure incurred | Period of short life |
|---|---|
| From April 2011 | 8 years |
| Before April 2011 | 4 years |

**Notes**

(1)  *Why* – Where an asset is expected to have a short useful life the business can elect for the asset to be allocated to a single asset pool, so its value is not pooled with other assets. This ensures the full value of the asset is relieved for tax purposes over its useful life certain assets are excluded from being short-life assets (*CAA 2001, s 83, s 84*).

(2)  *Change* – with effect from 1 April 2011 for companies and 6 April 2011 for income tax, the period for which an asset can be held in the single asset pool and treated as a short-life asset is extended to eight years (*CAA 2001, s 86*).

## INDUSTRIAL AND AGRICULTURAL BUILDINGS ALLOWANCES

*(CAA 2001, Pt 3; FA 2008, ss 84–85)*

| Period commencing | Percentage of allowance given % | Effective rate of allowance % |
|---|---|---|
| 1 to 6 April 2011 and later | 0 (abolished) | 0 |
| 1 to 6 April 2010 | 25% | 1% |
| 1 to 6 April 2009 | 50% | 2% |
| 1 to 6 April 2008 | 75% | 3% |
| 1 to 6 April 2007 and earlier | 100% | 4% |

**Notes**

(1)  *Abolished* – Industrial buildings allowances (including those for qualifying hotels) and agricultural buildings allowances were abolished in *Finance Act 2008* with effect from 1 April 2011 (for corporation tax) and 6 April 2011 (for income tax).

(2)  *Transitional period* – For the purposes of reducing allowance entitlement from April 2008 to April 2011, the above percentages are applied to the allowances that would otherwise be available in respect of the qualifying expenditure.

## OTHER ALLOWANCES

*(CAA 2001, ss 298–306; Pts 3A, 4A, 5–10)*

| Allowances | Date of expenditure | Initial allowance | Writing down allowance |
|---|---|---|---|
| Assured tenancy | 10 March 1982 to 31 March 1992 | – | 4% (Note 1) |
| Business premises renovation | From 11 April 2007 | 100% | 25% (Notes 1, 2) |
| Dredging | From 1 April 1986 | – | 4% (Note 1) |
| Enterprise zones | Expenditure on industrial or commercial buildings if:<br><br>(a) incurred within 10 years of site being included within the enterprise zone; or<br><br>(b) contracted within that 10-year period and incurred within 20 years after site being included in the zone. | 100% | 25% (Notes 1, 3) |
| Flat conversion | From 11 May 2001 to 31 March or 5 April 2013 | 100% | 25% (Notes 1, 4) |
| Know–how | From 1 April 1986 | – | 25% (Note 5) |

*continued*

| Allowances | Date of expenditure | Initial allowance | Writing down allowance |
|---|---|---|---|
| Mineral extraction | From 1 April 1986 | – | 10% (acquisition of mineral asset); or 25% (other expenditure) |
| Patents | From 1 April 1986 | – | 25% (Note 5) |
| Research and development | From 5 November 1962 | 100% | |

**Notes**

(1)   *WDAs on straight line* – These WDAs are given on a 'straight line' basis rather than a 'reducing balance' basis.

(2)   *BPRA* – The business premises renovation allowance has been extended to 2017 and a number of changes have been made to ensure that it continues to comply with the rules for EU State Aid (*SI 2012/868*).

(3)   *Enterprise Zones* – Allowances for industrial and commercial buildings in 'old' ten-year enterprise zones were abolished with effect from 1 April 2011 (corporation tax) and 6 April 2011 (income tax) (*FA 2008, s 84*). The last such enterprise zone to be designated was Tyne Riverside (North Tyneside and South Tyneside) on 21 October 1996.

(4)   *Flats over shops* – This allowance is withdrawn for expenditure after 31 March 2013 (for corporation tax) and 5 April 2013 (for income tax) (*FA 2012, s 227, Sch 39*).

(5)   *Patents and Know-how* – Capital allowances for know-how and patents still apply for income tax, but were replaced for most corporation tax purposes by the Intangible Assets regime with effect from 1 April 2002.

## TIME LIMITS FOR ELECTIONS AND CLAIMS

*(FA 1998, Sch 18, Part IX; CAA 2001, s 3; s 85(2); ss 198, 201, 260(6), 266, 569–570)*

| Claim | Time Limit |
|---|---|
| Capital allowances: general <br><br> (*CAA 2001, s 3; FA 1998, Sch 18, Part IX*) | Later of: <br><br> (1) 12 months after the filing date for the return in respect of the tax year or accounting period to which the claim relates; <br><br> (2) 30 days after a closure notice issued on completion of an enquiry; <br><br> (3) 30 days after notice of amendment to a return issued following completion of an enquiry; or <br><br> (4) 30 days after the determination of any appeal against an HMRC amendment. |

| Claim | Time Limit |
|---|---|
| 'Short life' asset election (income tax)<br><br>*(CAA 2001, s 85(2))* | 12 months from 31 January next following the tax year in which the relevant chargeable period ends (ie generally the chargeable period in which the qualifying expenditure was incurred) |
| 'Short life' asset election (corporation tax)<br><br>*(CAA 2001, s 85(2))* | 2 years from the end of the relevant chargeable period (ie generally the chargeable period in which the qualifying expenditure was incurred) |
| Purchase of interest in land that includes a fixture – election to fix apportionment of disposal proceeds<br><br>*(CAA 2001, ss 198, 201)* | 2 years from the date of purchase |
| Lease of interest in land that includes a fixture – election to fix apportionment of disposal proceeds<br><br>(CAA 2001, ss 199, 201) | 2 years from the date the lease is granted |
| Set–off of capital allowances on special leasing (corporation tax)<br><br>*(CAA 2001, s 260(6))* | 2 years from end of accounting period |
| Business successions – transfers between connected parties of plant and machinery at tax–written down value<br><br>*(CAA 2001, s 266)* | 2 years from the date on which the succession took place |
| Connected parties and controlled sales treated as being at market value: election for sale to be treated as being for an alternative amount<br><br>*(CAA 2001, s 570(5))* | 2 years from the date of sale |

**Note**

*Capital allowances claims: general* – Capital allowances must be claimed. Most capital allowances are claimed in the tax return (*CAA 2001, s 3*). However, the claims rules for income tax (*TMA 1970, s 42*) and corporation tax (*FA 1998, Sch 18, paras 54–60*) apply in certain instances (*CAA 2001, s 3(4), (5)*):

● Special leasing plant and machinery allowances claims;

● Claims to carry back balancing allowances in respect of mining concerns (these cease to have effect with the abolition of industrial buildings allowances from 1 or 6 April 2011); and

● Claims for patent allowances on non–trading expenditure (in income tax cases).

## ENTERPRISE ZONES

*(CA 2001, ss 45K–45N as inserted by FA 2012, s 44, Sch 11)*

Enhanced Capital Allowances (ECAs) are available to trading companies investing in new plant and machinery in certain designated areas in Enterprise Zones with effect from 1 April 2012.

**Notes**

(1)    *General* – First-year allowances (FYAs) of 100% are available for a limited period to companies (but not unincorporated businesses) investing in new and unused plant or machinery for use primarily in designated assisted areas within Enterprise Zones. To qualify for 100% FYAs under these provisions, the expenditure must be incurred for the purposes of a qualifying activity. The expenditure must be new investment rather than replacement, and must not be on a means of transport or transport equipment for the purposes of a business in the road freight or air transport sectors. There is a cap on the amount of expenditure on new plant or machinery in designated assisted areas that qualifies for FYAs, of €125 million for each 'investment project' (as defined).

(2)    *Scope* – The FYAs apply to expenditure incurred in the 5-year period from 1 April 2012 to 31 March 2017 inclusive. The expenditure must be incurred at a time when the designated area is in an assisted area (as defined by the *Assisted Areas Order, SI 2007/107*), and certain defined conditions must be met.

(3)    *Assisted areas* – The following Enterprise Zones will qualify for 100% FYAs (Autumn Statement, 29 November 2011):

- Black Country

- Humber Renewable Energy Super Cluster

- Liverpool

- North Eastern

- Sheffield

- Tees Valley

The following additional designated area will qualify for 100% FYAs (Speech by Chief Secretary to the Treasury, 9 March 2012):

- the designated Paull site with Humber Green Port Corridor

The following additional designated areas will qualify for 100% FYAs (Budget, 21 March 2012):

- a designated site in the London Royal Docks Enterprise Zone

- designated sites in enterprise areas in Scotland, including Irvine, Nigg and Dundee

- a designated site at Deeside in North Wales

A full list of current zones and maps is to be published on the Treasury website *(Budget, 21 March 2012)*.

(4)    *Exclusions* – Expenditure in such designated assisted areas does not qualify for 100% FYAs broadly if the company that incurred it is (or forms part of) an undertaking that is a 'firm in difficulty' and/or is subject to an outstanding recovery order. In addition, expenditure is excluded if incurred for a qualifying activity in the fishery or aquacultural sectors, managing the waste of undertakings, or engaged in any of the coal, steel, shipbuilding or synthetic fibres sectors or in the primary production of agricultural products. Expenditure is also excluded if taken into account for the purposes of a 'relevant grant' or 'relevant payment' made towards it.

*11*

# Stamp Taxes

## STAMP DUTY LAND TAX (SDLT)

### SDLT on land or property

*(FA 2003, s 55; FA 2010, s 7)*

| Effective Date | Residential property | Non-residential or mixed property | Rate % |
|---|---|---|---|
| From 22 March 2012 | Up to £125,000 | Up to £150,000 | 0 |
| | £125,001–£250,000* | £150,001–£250,000 | 1 |
| | £250,001–£500,000 | £250,001–£500,000 | 3 |
| | £500,001–£1,000,000 | £500,001 and over | 4 |
| | £1,000,001–£2,000,000 | n/a | 5 |
| | £2,000,001 and over (see note 3) | n/a | 7 |
| From 6 April 2011 to 21 March 2012 | Up to £125,000 | Up to £150,000 | 0 |
| | £125,001–£250,000 (note 5) | £150,001–£250,000 | 1 |
| | £250,001–£500,000 | £250,001–£500,000 | 3 |
| | £500,001–£1,000,000 | £500,001 and over | 4 |
| | £1,000,001 and over | n/a | 5 |
| 1 January 2010 to 5 April 2011 | Up to £125,000 | Up to £150,000 | 0 |
| | £125,001–£250,000 (note 2) | £150,001–£250,000 | 1 |
| | £250,001–£500,000 | £250,001–£500,000 | 3 |
| | £500,001 and over | £500,001 and over | 4 |
| 3 September 2008 to 31 December 2009 | Up to £175,000 | Up to £150,000 | 0 |
| | £175,001–£250,000 | £150,001–£250,000 | 1 |
| | £250,001–£500,000 | £250,001–£500,000 | 3 |
| | £500,001 and over | £500,001 and over | 4 |
| 23 March 2006 to 2 September 2008 | Up to £125,000 | Up to £150,000 | 0 |
| | £125,001–£250,000 | £150,001–£250,000 | 1 |
| | £250,001–£500,000 | £250,001–£500,000 | 3 |
| | £500,001 and over | £500,001 and over | 4 |

**Notes**

(1)  *Calculation of SDLT* – SDLT on chargeable transactions is calculated as a percentage of the amount of relevant consideration for the land or property (*FA 2001, s 55(1)*).

(2)  *Acquisitions of multiple dwellings* – On or after 19 July 2011, relief can be claimed for transactions which include the acquisition of interests in more than one dwelling. The rate of SDLT is determined by reference to the consideration divided by the number of dwellings, but subject to a minimum rate of 1% (*FA 2003, s 58D, Sch 6B*).

(3)  *Anti-avoidance* – The following measures are designed to combat avoidance of SDLT by the 'enveloping' of high value properties into companies:

- With effect from 21 March 2012, residential properties over £2,000,000 purchased by non-natural persons are liable to SDLT at 15% (*FA 2012, s 214, Sch 35*).

- An annual charge on enveloped dwellings valued at over £2 million owned by non-natural persons, is introduced with effect from 1 April 2013, See **Chapter 13: Other Taxes and Duties**.

- Capital gains tax applies to gains accruing from 6 April 2013 on disposals of UK residential property by non-natural persons (*FB 2013 cl 64, Sch 24*).

(4)  *Avoidance schemes* – The Government indicated that anti-avoidance measures would be introduced, with effect from 21 March 2012, to put beyond doubt that an SDLT avoidance scheme that relies on the sub-sales rules does not work. The change makes it explicit that the grant or assignment of an option cannot be a 'transfer of rights' (*FA 2012, s 212; FB 2013, cl 192*).

(5)  *First time buyers* – For purchases of residential property in the period 25 March 2010 to 25 March 2012 valued at under £250,000, an SDLT exemption applied where the purchaser was a first time buyer. The relief applied irrespective of whether or not the property is in a disadvantaged area (*FA 2003, s 57AA*).

(6)  *Earlier years* – The rates and thresholds of SDLT for purchases in earlier years can be found here: www.hmrc.gov.uk/so/rates/rates-mar10-apr11.htm#4.

## Land in disadvantaged areas

(*FA 2003, s 57, Sch 6*)

| Effective Date | Residential property | Non-residential or mixed property | Rate % |
|---|---|---|---|
| From 22 March 2012 to 5 April 2013 | Up to £150,000 | up to £150,000 | 0 |
| | £150,001–£250,000* | | 1 |
| | £250,001–£500,000 | | 3 |
| | £500,001–£1,000,000 | | 4 |
| | £1,00,001–£2,000,000 | | 5 |
| | £2,000,001 and over | | 7 |

*continued*

| Effective Date | Residential property | Non-residential or mixed property | Rate % |
|---|---|---|---|
| From 6 April 2011 to 21 March 2012 | £150,000 | up to £150,000 | 0 |
| | £150,001–£250,000* | £150,001–£250,000 | 1 |
| | £250,001–£500,000 | £250,001–£500,000 | 3 |
| | £500,000–£1,000,000 | £500,001 and over | 4 |
| | £1,000,001 and over | n/a | 5 |
| 17 March 2005 to 5 April 2011 | £150,000 | up to £150,000 | 0 |
| | £150,001–£250,000* | £150,001–£250,000 | 1 |
| | £250,001–£500,000 | £250,001–£500,000 | 3 |
| | £500,001 and over | £500,001 and over | 4 |

**Notes**

(1)   *General* – Disadvantaged area relief is not available for non-residential land transactions with an effective date on or after 17 March 2005. However, the relief remains available for the completion of contracts entered into and substantially performed on or before 16 March 2005, or for the completion or substantial performance of other contracts entered into on or before 16 March 2005, where certain conditions are satisfied (see *SDLTM20110*).

(2)   *Abolition of the relief* – This relief is abolished with effect from 6 April 2013, and claims must be made before 6 May 2014 (*FA 2012, Sch 39, paras 8, 13*).

## Lease rentals

*(FA 2003, s 56, Sch 5)*

| Effective Date | Residential property | Non-residential or mixed property | Rate % |
|---|---|---|---|
| From 1 January 2010 | £125,000 | £150,000 | 0 |
| | over £125,000 | over £150,000 | 1 |
| 3 September 2008 to 31 December 2009 | £175,000 | £150,000 | 0 |
| | over £175,000 | over £150,000 | 1 |
| 23 March 2006 to 2 September 2008 | £125,000 | £150,000 | 0 |
| | over £125,000 | over £150,000 | 1 |
| 17 March 2005 to 22 March 2006 | £120,000 | £150,000 | 0 |
| | over £120,000 | over £150,000 | 1 |
| 1 December 2003 to 16 March 2005 | £60,000 | £150,000 | 0 |
| | over £60,000 | over £150,000 | 1 |

**Notes**

(1)   *General* – Where the chargeable consideration includes rent, SDLT is payable on the lease premium and on the 'net present value' (NPV) of the rent payable. Online SDLT calculators are available on the HMRC website in respect of both new leases and freehold transactions: (www.hmrc.gov.uk/sdlt/calculate/calculators.htm).

(2)   *Annual rent* – Where the annual rent for the lease of non-residential property amounts to £1,000 or more, the 0% SDLT band is unavailable in respect of any

lease premium (*FA 2003, Sch 5, para 9A*). Prior to 12 March 2008, this rule also applied to residential properties, if the annual rent exceeded £600.

(3)   *First time buyers* – SDLT exemption applies to the acquisition of residential property on a freehold property or lease premium where the chargeable consideration (excluding rent) is more than £125,000 but not more than £150,000, the purchaser is a first time buyer, and the effective date of the transaction is on or after 25 March 2010 but before 25 March 2012 (*FA 2003, s 57AA*). SDLT on rent is as above.

## Stamp duty on land transactions before 1 December 2003

SDLT was introduced from 1 December 2003. Stamp duty rates and tables in respect of freehold property and leasehold property transactions prior to SDLT taking effect are available on the HMRC website: www.hmrc.gov.uk/sd/land/landtransfers-rates.htm.

## STAMP DUTY

(*FA 1986, s 67; FA 1999, s 112, Schs 13, 15*)

Stamp duty in respect of land transactions was replaced by SDLT with effect from 1 December 2003, subject to transitional provisions for land transactions effected in pursuance of a contract entered into on or before 10 July 2003 (see **SDLT** above). However:

- Stamp duty remains chargeable in respect of certain transfers on sale, including the conveyance or transfer of stock or marketable securities (0.5%). However, stamp duty is not payable on transfers of stock or marketable securities on or after 13 March 2008 if the consideration is £1,000 or less, and the instrument is certified at £1,000 (*FA 1999, Sch 13, paras 1(3A), 3*).

- A special stamp duty rate of 1.5% applies to depositary receipts in certain circumstances (*FA 1986, s 67*). A stamp duty rate of 1.5% also applies in respect of bearer instruments in certain circumstances (*FA 1999, Sch 15*).

- Fixed stamp duty is charged without reference to the value of transactions. For instruments executed from 1 October 1999, the amount of every fixed duty is £5 (*FA 1999, s 112(2)*). Fixed duties were generally abolished for most instruments executed from 13 March 2008. However, fixed duty has been retained for certain instruments effecting land transactions (*FA 2008, Sch 32, para 22*).

Stamp duty which is not fixed ('ad valorem' stamp duty) is rounded up to the nearest multiple of £5 (*FA 1999, s 112(1)(b)*).

## EXEMPT INSTRUMENTS

(*FA 1985, s 87; SI 1987/516*)

A   The vesting of property subject to a trust in the trustees of the trust on the appointment of a new trustee, or in the continuing trustees on the retirement of a trustee.

B   The conveyance or transfer of property the subject of a specific devise or legacy to the beneficiary named in the will (or his nominee).

C       The conveyance or transfer of property which forms part of an intestate's estate to the person entitled on intestacy (or his nominee).

D       The appropriation of property within *section 84(4)* of the *Finance Act 1985* (death: appropriation in satisfaction of a general legacy of money) or *section 84(5)* or *(7)* of that Act (death: appropriation in satisfaction of any interest of surviving spouse or civil partner and in Scotland also of any interest of issue).

E       The conveyance or transfer of property which forms part of the residuary estate of a testator to a beneficiary (or his nominee) entitled solely by virtue of his entitlement under the will.

F       The conveyance or transfer of property out of a settlement in or towards satisfaction of a beneficiary's interest, not being an interest acquired for money or money's worth, being a conveyance or transfer constituting a distribution of property in accordance with the provisions of the settlement.

G       The conveyance or transfer of property on and in consideration only of marriage to a party to the marriage (or his nominee) or to trustees to be held on the terms of a settlement made in consideration only of the marriage.

GG      The conveyance or transfer of property on and in consideration only of the formation of a civil partnership to a party to the civil partnership (or his nominee) or to trustees to be held on the terms of a settlement made in consideration only of the civil partnership.

H       The conveyance or transfer of property within *section 83(1)* or *(1A)* of the *Finance Act 1985* (transfers in connection with divorce or dissolution of civil partnership etc).

I       The conveyance or transfer by the liquidator of property which formed part of the assets of the company in liquidation to a shareholder of that company (or his nominee) in or towards satisfaction of the shareholder's rights on a winding-up.

J       The grant in fee simple of an easement in or over land for no consideration in money or money's worth.

K       The grant of a servitude for no consideration in money or money's worth.

L       The conveyance or transfer of property operating as a voluntary disposition *inter vivos* for no consideration in money or money's worth nor any consideration referred to in *section 57* of the *Stamp Act 1891* (conveyance in consideration of a debt etc).

M       The conveyance or transfer of property by an instrument within *section 84(1)* of the *Finance Act 1985* (death: varying disposition).

N       The declaration of any use or trust of or concerning a life policy, or property representing, or benefits arising under, a life policy.

**Notes**

(1)     *Exemptions* – Instruments of transfer executed from 1 May 1987 which effect one or more of the transactions specified above and which are properly certified (eg a gift of ordinary shares between family members) are exempt from fixed stamp duty, and do not need to be presented to HMRC for the payment of duty, or for adjudication.

(2)  *Category N* – This was inserted by the *Stamp Duty (Exempt Instruments) (Amendment) Regulations, SI 1999/2539, reg 5* with effect from 1 October 1999.

(3)  *Category GG* – This was inserted by *Tax and Civil Partnership (No 2) Regulations, SI 2005/3230 reg 2*, with effect from 5 December 2005.

(4)  *No more than £1,000* – The above are in addition to various other stamp duty exemptions, including an exemption from ad valorem duty for transfers of stock or marketable securities where the consideration is certified as not exceeding £1,000 *(FA 1999, Sch 13, para 1(3A))*.

(5)  *Further information* – For further information on stamp duty exemptions see *Stamp Taxes* by Kevin Griffin (Bloomsbury Professional).

## STAMP DUTY RESERVE TAX (SDRT)

*(FA 1986, Pt IV; FA 1999, Sch 19, Pt II)*

| Charge | Rate |
| --- | --- |
| General share transactions *(FA 1986, s 87)* | 0.5% |
| Transfer of securities into depository receipt schemes and clearance services *(FA 1986, ss 93, 96)* | 1.5% |
| Charge in respect of units in unit trusts and shares in open–ended investment companies *(FA 1999, Sch 19, para 3)* | 0.5% |

**Notes**

(1)  *Reason why* – Stamp duty reserve tax (SDRT) was introduced in 1986 to cater for paperless share transactions. SDRT operates alongside the stamp duty charge on share transfers.

(2)  *Rounding* – The above charges are rounded to the nearest penny, taking any ½p as nearest to the next whole penny above *(FA 1986, s 99(13))*.

## ADMINISTRATION

## SDLT penalties

See **Chapter 17**

## STAMP TAXES – INTEREST ON LATE PAYMENTS AND OVERPAYMENTS

*(SA 1891, s 15A; FA 1999, s 110; FA 2003, ss 87, 89; SI 1986/1711, regs 13, 14)*

| Period | Late payment Rate % | Overpayments Rate % |
|---|---|---|
| From 29 September 2009 | 3.00 | 0.50 |
| 24 March 2009 to 28 September 2009 | 2.50 | 0.00 |
| 27 January 2009 to 23 March 2009 | 3.50 | 0.00 |
| 6 January 2009 to 26 January 2009 | 4.50 | 0.75 |
| 6 December 2008 to 5 January 2009 | 5.50 | 1.50 |
| 6 November 2008 to 5 December 2008 | 6.50 | 2.25 |
| 6 January 2008 to 5 November 2008 | 7.50 | 3.00 |
| 6 August 2007 to 5 January 2008 | 8.50 | 4.00 |
| 6 September 2006 to 5 August 2007 | 7.50 | 3.00 |

**Notes**

(1)  *General* – Interest on unpaid stamp duty applies from the end of 30 days after the date on which the document was executed until the duty is paid, with effect for instruments executed from 1 October 1999. The interest is rounded down to the nearest multiple of £5, and no interest is payable (or repayable) on amounts of less than £25. Interest on repayment of overpaid duty applies in relation to documents executed from 1 October 1999.

(2)  *SDLT* – Interest on unpaid SDLT runs from the end of 30 days after the 'relevant date' (generally the effective date of the transaction) until the tax is paid. The relevant dates for repayment of overpaid SDLT are from the date on which the payment is lodged with HMRC until the date when the repayment order is issued.

(3)  *SDRT* – Interest on SDRT is charged from the 'accountable date' to the date of payment. If SDRT is overpaid then any repayment of SDRT will be made with interest from the date that it was paid, However, no interest is added to SDRT repayments under £25.

(4)  *Earlier years* – Interest rates on late payments for earlier years can be found here: www.hmrc.gov.uk/rates/interest-late.htm#itnic. Interest paid on repayments is found here: www.hmrc.gov.uk/rates/interest-repayments.htm#itnic.

*12*

# VAT

## RATES

*(VATA 1994, s 2(1))*

| Effective date | Standard rate |
|---|---|
| | % |
| 04/01/11 | 20.0 |
| 01/01/10 | 17.5 |
| 01/12/08 | 15.0 |
| 01/04/91 | 17.5 |

**Notes**

(1)  *Reduced rate* – Set at 5% for certain supplies made, and acquisitions taking place, after 31 October 2001 (*VATA 1994, s 29A, Sch 7A*), see page 150.

(2)  *Standard rate* – This rate of VAT was increased from 17.5% to 20% in relation to any supply made from 4 January 2011, and any acquisition or importation taking place from that date (*F(No 2)A 2010, s 3*). Anti-avoidance provisions introduce a supplementary VAT charge of 2.5% on certain supplies that span the date of the change in VAT rate (*F(No 2)A 2010, Sch 2*).

## VAT fraction

| VAT percentage (%) | VAT fraction |
|---|---|
| 20.0 | 1/6 |
| 17.5 | 7/47 |
| 15.0 | 3/23 |
| 5.0 | 1/21 |

**Note**

The VAT fraction is used to calculate the VAT element of VAT-inclusive goods and services at the appropriate rate.

## ZERO-RATED SUPPLIES

*(VATA 1994, Sch 8)*

| Group Number | Subject matter |
|:---:|:---|
| 1 | Food (see note 6) |
| 2 | Sewerage services and water |
| 3 | Books, etc (see note 4) |
| 4 | Talking books for the blind and handicapped and wireless sets for the blind |
| 5 | Construction of buildings, etc |
| 6 | Protected buildings |
| 7 | International services |
| 8 | Transport (see note 3) |
| 9 | Caravans and houseboats (see note 5) |
| 10 | Gold |
| 11 | Bank notes |
| 12 | Drugs, medicines, aids for the handicapped, etc |
| 13 | Imports, exports etc |
| 15 | Charities etc |
| 16 | Clothing and footwear for children and babies |
| 17 | Emissions allowances – repealed for supplies made after 31 October 2010 (see note 1) |

### Notes

(1)  *Emissions allowances (Group 17)* – Added by *SI 2009/2093, art 4*, with effect from 31 July 2009 but repealed for supplies made after 31 October 2010 and replaced by the reverse charge (*SI 2010/2549*).

(2)  *Group 14* – Deleted by *SI 1999/1642*, with effect from 1 July 2009.

(3)  *'Qualifying aircraft'* – The definition of aircraft which may be supplied at the zero rate was amended (by *F(No 3)A 2010, s 21*) with effect in relation to supplies made from 1 January 2011. Zero-rating applies from that date to supplies of aircraft 'used by an airline operating for reward chiefly on international routes' (*VATA 1994, Sch 8, Group 8, Note A1(b)*). This change removes aircraft weight and design/adaptation criteria for all supplies other than to state institutions, to bring UK legislation into line with EU legislation.

(4)  *Group 3* – From 19 July 2011, zero-rating is withdrawn from printed matter where the printed matter is ancillary to a differently rated service, and where, if the service and printed matter had been supplied by a single company, the two supplies would have been treated as a single standard-rated, reduced-rated or exempt supply (*FA 2011, s 74*).

(5)  *Caravans* – From 6 April 2013 the rate of VAT applied to supplies of holiday caravans depends on the size of the caravan (over/under 7 meters) and whether it complies with standard BS 3632. See VAT information sheet 11/12.

(6)  *Hot food and sports drinks* – From 1 October 2012 standard rate VAT is imposed, where it didn't already apply, to hot food and sports drinks. However, pre-baked hot

products which are allowed to cool naturally are zero rated, see VAT information sheets 12/12 and 15/12.

## REDUCED RATE SUPPLIES

*(VATA 1994, Sch 7A)*

| Group Number | Subject matter |
| --- | --- |
| 1 | Supplies of domestic fuel or power |
| 2 | Installation of energy-saving materials (see note 2) |
| 3 | Grant-funded installation of heating equipment or security goods or connection of gas supply. |
| 4 | Women's sanitary products |
| 5 | Children's car seats (see note 3) |
| 6 | Residential conversions |
| 7 | Residential renovations and alterations |
| 8 | Contraceptive products (from 1 July 2006: *SI 2006/1472*) |
| 9 | Welfare advice or information (from 1 July 2006: *SI 2006/1472*) |
| 10 | Installation of mobility aids for the elderly (from 1 July 2007: *SI 2007/1601*) |
| 11 | Smoking cessation products (1 year from 1 July 2007: *SI 2007/1601*; permanently from 1 July 2008: *SI 2008/1410*) |

**Notes**

(1) *Effective from* – The current reduced VAT rate (5%) applies with effect for certain supplies made, and acquisitions taking place, after 31 October 2001 (*VATA 1994, s 29A*).

(2) *Installation of energy-saving materials* – with effect for supplies made on or after 1 August 2013 buildings used for charitable or non-business purposes are removed from the scope of the reduced rate of VAT for the supply and installation of energy-saving materials (*VATA 1994, Sch 7A, Pt 2, group 2*). See VAT Notice 708/6.

(3) *Children's car seats (Group 5)* – Extended to related base units from 1 July 2009 (*SI 2009/1359*).

## EXEMPT SUPPLIES

*(VATA 1994, Sch 9)*

| Group Number | Subject matter |
| --- | --- |
| 1 | Land (see note 5) |
| 2 | Insurance |
| 3 | Postal services |
| 4 | Betting, gaming and lotteries |

*continued*

| Group Number | Subject matter |
|:---:|---|
| 5 | Finance |
| 6 | Education |
| 7 | Health and welfare |
| 8 | Burial and cremation |
| 9 | Subscriptions to trade unions, professional and other public interest bodies |
| 10 | Sport, sports competitions and physical education |
| 11 | Works of art etc |
| 12 | Fund-raising events by charities and other qualifying bodies |
| 13 | Cultural services etc (from 1 June 1996: *SI 1996/1256*) |
| 14 | Supplies of goods where input tax cannot be recovered (from 1 March 2000: *SI 1999/2833*) |
| 15 | Investment gold (from 1 January 2000: *SI 1999/3116*) |
| 16 | Supplies of services by groups involving cost sharing |

**Notes**

(1)   *Postal services* – The definition of postal service was restricted from 31 January 2011 to supplies of public postal services and incidental goods made by a universal service provider (ie the Royal Mail) (*F(No 3)A 2010, s 22*).

(2)   *Cost sharing* – Exempts from VAT the supply of services by a group which consists of persons engaged in exempt or non-taxable activities so long as the services are supplied to group members at cost and for the purposes of those activities. The exemption aims to reduce a barrier that might otherwise prevent businesses and organisations that have exempt and/or non-business activities for VAT purposes from joining with others to share costs.

(3)   *Supplies by public bodies* – Government departments, local authorities and analogous institutions are not generally subject to VAT when making supplies of goods or services (*VATA 1994, s 41A*).

(4)   *Low Value Consignment Relief* – This relief from VAT for mail order goods imported into the UK from the Channel Islands has been withdrawn with effect from 1 April 2012 (*FA 2012, s 199*).

(5)   *Land* – There are many exceptions to this exemption, so VAT on the supply of land or buildings can apply at any rate of VAT (see VAT notice 742). For example the hire of hairdressers' chairs are standard rated, as are self-storage facilities (see VAT information sheets 13/12 & 14/12). Approved alterations to listed buildings are standard rated from 1 October 2012, subject to transitional arangements (see VAT information sheet 10/12).

# REGISTRATION LIMITS

## UK taxable supplies

(*VATA 1994, Sch 1 para 1*; Supplement to VAT Notices 700/1 and 700/11)

| Effective date | Turnover:<br>(a) Past year exceeded; or<br>(b) Next 30 days will exceed: | Exception: Turnover for next year will not exceed: |
|---|---|---|
| | £ | £ |
| 01/04/13 | 79,000 | 77,000 |
| 01/04/12 | 77,000 | 75,000 |
| 01/04/11 | 73,000 | 71,000 |
| 01/04/10 | 70,000 | 68,000 |
| 01/05/09 | 68,000 | 66,000 |
| 01/04/08 | 67,000 | 65,000 |
| 01/04/07 | 64,000 | 62,000 |

### Notes

(1) *Taxable supplies* – Turnover includes zero-rated sales, but not exempt, non-business or outside the scope supplies. Supplies of capital assets (excluding any supplies of land on which the option to tax has been exercised) do not count towards the turnover limit. The same applies to any taxable supplies which would not be taxable supplies apart from *VATA 1994, s 7(4)* (ie in connection with 'distance selling'). Any supplies or acquisitions to which *VATA 1994, s 18B(4)* (last acquisition or supply of goods before removal from fiscal warehousing) applies, and supplies treated as made by him under *s 18C(3)* (self-supply of services on removal of goods from warehousing), are also disregarded (*VATA 1994, Sch 1, para 1(7)–(9)*).

(2) *Compulsory registration* – A person who makes taxable supplies but is not registered under *VATA 1994* becomes liable to be registered if: (a) the one year; or (b) 30 day turnover limits above are exceeded (*Sch 1, para 1*). However, the one-year turnover test in (a) above is subject to an exception (see note 4 below).

(3) *Going concern* – If all or part of a business carried on by a taxable person is transferred to another person as a going concern, and the transferee is not registered under *VATA 1994* at the time of transfer, the transferee becomes liable to be registered if: (a) the one-year; or (b) 30-day limits above are exceeded (*Sch 1, para 2*). However, the one-year turnover test in (a) above is subject to an exception (see note 4 below).

(4) *Exception* – A person does not become liable to be registered under the mandatory (see note 2) or going concern (see note 3) provisions under the one-year turnover test in (a) above if HMRC are satisfied that the value of his taxable supplies in the one year period beginning when he would otherwise become liable to be registered does not exceed the exception limits in the table above (*Sch 1, para 3*).

(5) *Non-UK established businesses* – From 1 December 2012, businesses without a UK establishment (non-established businesses) who make any UK taxable supplies must register for UK VAT regardless of the value of taxable supplies they make in the UK (*Sch 1A*).

145

## Supplies from other EU member states ('distance selling')

(*VATA 1994, Sch 2*; VAT Notice 700/1, Section 5)

(1)   A taxable person in another EU state which supplies and delivers goods to non-VAT registered customers in the UK broadly becomes liable to register here on any day if, in the period beginning with 1 January of the year in which that day falls, the value of its relevant supplies exceeds £70,000.

(2)   This limit has not changed since it was introduced on 1 January 1993.

(3)   Special rules apply to the sale of excise goods (eg alcohol and tobacco) (see VAT Notice 700/1, section 5.6).

## Acquisitions from other EU member states

(*VATA 1994, Sch 3;* VAT Notice 700/1, Section 6)

| Effective date | Registration threshold |
|----------------|------------------------|
|                | £                      |
| 1/4/13         | 79,000                 |
| 1/4/12         | 77,000                 |
| 1/4/11         | 73,000                 |
| 1/4/10         | 70,000                 |
| 1/5/09         | 68,000                 |
| 1/4/08         | 67,000                 |
| 1/4/07         | 64,000                 |

**Notes**

(1)   *No intended supply* – Where an unregistered business or organisation, which does not make or intend to make any taxable supplies in the UK, buys goods from a VAT registered supplier in another EU state to bring to the UK, these are known as relevant acquisitions. This would typically apply to a business making exempt supplies only or using the goods to make non-business supplies only.

(2)   *Annual measure* – The business must register for VAT where the value of relevant acquisitions exceeds the registration limit in the calendar year to 31 December, or if there are reasonable grounds for believing that the value of relevant acquisitions will exceed the registration limit in the next 30 days.

## DEREGISTRATION LIMITS

## De-registration: UK taxable supplies

(*VATA 1994, Sch 1, para 4*)

| Effective date | Turnover threshold |
|----------------|--------------------|
|                | £                  |
| 1/4/13         | 77,000             |
| 1/4/12         | 75,000             |

| Effective date | Turnover threshold £ |
|---|---|
| 1/4/11 | 71,000 |
| 1/4/10 | 68,000 |
| 1/5/09 | 66,000 |
| 1/4/08 | 65,000 |
| 1/4/07 | 62,000 |

**Notes**

(1) *General* – The turnover threshold applies to the value of taxable supplies in the next 12 months.

(2) *Voluntary deregistration* – A business can ask HMRC to cancel its VAT registration if its annual VAT taxable turnover falls, or is expected to fall in the next 12 months, below the threshold for deregistration. Registration cannot be cancelled if the reduction in turnover is due to the intention of the business to stop trading or suspend making taxable supplies for 30 days or more in the next 12 months. (VAT Notice 700/11, para 2.2).

(3) *Compulsory deregistration* – A business which is registered due to making taxable supplies in the UK must cancel the registration in certain circumstances, eg ceasing to make taxable supplies, or if the business intended to make taxable supplies but no longer intends doing so (VAT Notice 700/11, para 2.1).

## Deregistration: Supplies from other EU member states

(*VATA 1994, Sch 2, para 2*; VAT Notice 700/11, para 3)

(1) *General* – If the business was registered because it exceeded the distance sales threshold (currently £70,000), then it may apply to cancel its registration where:

   (a) the value of its distance sales in the year ending 31 December did not exceed the threshold; and

   (b) the value of its distance sales in the year following, beginning 1 January, will not exceed the threshold.

(2) *Compulsory deregistration* – If the business was registered due to making distance sales from other EC member states, the registration must be cancelled if either the business ceases to make distance sales, or if the business intended to make distance sales but no longer intends to do so and is not eligible or liable for registration as a result of any taxable supplies, acquisitions or relevant supplies (VAT Notice 700/11, para 3.1).

(3) *Voluntary deregistration* – If the business is applying for voluntary deregistration, was registered because the UK was the place of supply for its distance sales, and had opted and made supplies, the business remains registered in the UK for at least two calendar years from the date of first supply following registration. However, if the business opted but did not start to make supplies, the business may apply for cancellation of registration (VAT Notice 700/11, para 3.2).

147

## Acquisitions from other EU member states

(*VATA 1994, Sch 3, para 2*; VAT Notice 700/11, para 4.2)

| Effective date | Relevant acquisitions threshold £ |
|---|---|
| 1/4/13 | 79,000 |
| 1/4/12 | 77,000 |
| 1/4/11 | 73,000 |
| 1/4/10 | 70,000 |
| 1/5/09 | 68,000 |
| 1/4/08 | 67,000 |
| 1/4/07 | 64,000 |

**Notes**

(1)  *General* – If the business was registered because it had previously exceeded the relevant acquisitions threshold, then it may apply to cancel its registration where:

(a)  the value of its relevant acquisitions in the year ending 31 December did not exceed the threshold; and

(b)  the value of its relevant acquisitions in the year following, beginning 1 January, will not exceed the threshold.

(2)  *Compulsory deregistration* – If the business was registered due to making relevant acquisitions from other EC member states, the registration must be cancelled if the business ceases to make relevant acquisitions, or if the business intended to make relevant acquisitions but no longer intends doing so and is not eligible or liable for registration as a result of any taxable supplies, distance sales or relevant supplies (VAT Notice 700/11, para 4.1).

(3)  *Voluntary deregistration* – An application for voluntary registration may be made if the business was registered because the acquisition threshold was previously exceeded, the value of relevant acquisitions in the year ending 31 December did not exceed the threshold, and the value of relevant acquisitions in the following year will not exceed the threshold. However, a business which voluntarily registered for relevant acquisitions will remain registered in the UK for at least two calendar years unless entitlement to be registered has ceased (VAT Notice 700/11, para 4.2).

## ANNUAL ACCOUNTING SCHEME

(*VAT Regulations 1995 (SI 1995/2518), regs 52, 53*; VAT Notice 732)

| Effective date | Joining threshold £ | Leaving threshold £ |
|---|---|---|
| 1/4/06 | 1,350,000 | 1,600,000 |
| 1/4/04 | 660,000 | 825,000 |
| 1/4/01 | 600,000 | 750,000 |

**Notes**

(1)    *Joining threshold* – A business can use the scheme if estimated taxable supplies for the coming year are not expected to exceed the above joining threshold, subject to certain other criteria (see *SI 1995/2518, reg 52*, and VAT Notice 732, paras 2.1 and 2.6).

(2)    *Leaving threshold* – A business must leave the scheme if at the end of the current accounting year (or transitional accounting period) the value of taxable supplies in that year (or period) exceeds the leaving threshold (*SI 1995/2518, reg 53*).

## CASH ACCOUNTING SCHEME

(*VAT Regulations 1995 (SI 1995/2518), regs 58, 60*; VAT Notice 731)

| Effective date | Joining threshold (Column 1) £ | Leaving threshold (Column 2) £ |
|---|---|---|
| 1/4/07 | 1,350,000 | 1,600,000 |
| 1/4/04 | 660,000 | 825,000 |
| 1/4/01 | 600,000 | 750,000 |

**Notes**

(1)    *Joining threshold* – A business can use the scheme if estimated taxable supplies in the next year is not expected to exceed the above joining threshold, and subject to certain other criteria (see *SI 1995/2518, reg 58*, and VAT Notice 731, para 2.1).

(2)    *Leaving threshold* – A business must leave the scheme if the value of taxable supplies for a 12 month period (ending at the end of a tax period) has exceeded the above leaving threshold (*SI 1995/2518, reg 60*; see also VAT Notice 731, para 6.2).

(3)    *'One-off' sales increases* – A business may remain on cash accounting where it exceeds the amount in column 2 above because of a one-off increase in sales resulting from a genuine commercial activity, provided there are reasonable grounds for believing that the value of its taxable supplies in the next 12 months will be below the amount in column 1 (see VAT Notice 731, para 2.6).

## FLAT-RATE SCHEME FOR SMALL BUSINESSES

(*VAT Regulations 1995 (SI 1995/2518), regs 55K, 55L, 55M; SI 2010/2940, regs 2, 4*; VAT Notice 733)

| Category of business | From 4 January 2011 % | 1 January 2010 to 3 January 2011 % | 1 December 2008 to 31 December 2009 % |
|---|---|---|---|
| Accountancy or book-keeping | 14.5 | 13.0 | 11.5 |
| Advertising | 11.0 | 10.0 | 8.5 |
| Agricultural services | 11.0 | 10.0 | 7.0 |

*continued*

| Category of business | From 4 January 2011 | 1 January 2010 to 3 January 2011 | 1 December 2008 to 31 December 2009 |
|---|---|---|---|
| | % | % | % |
| Any other activity not listed elsewhere | 12.0 | 10.5 | 9.0 |
| Architect, civil and structural engineer or surveyor | 14.5 | 13.0 | 11.0 |
| Boarding or care of animals | 12.0 | 10.5 | 9.5 |
| Business services that are not listed elsewhere | 12.0 | 10.5 | 9.5 |
| Catering services including restaurants and takeaways | 12.5 | 11.0 | 10.5 |
| Computer and IT consultancy or data processing | 14.5 | 13.0 | 11.5 |
| Computer repair services | 10.5 | 9.5 | 10.0 |
| Dealing in waste or scrap | 10.5 | 9.5 | 8.5 |
| Entertainment or journalism | 12.5 | 11.0 | 9.5 |
| Estate agency or property management services | 12.0 | 10.5 | 9.5 |
| Farming or agriculture that is not listed elsewhere | 6.5 | 6.0 | 5.5 |
| Film, radio, television or video production | 13.0 | 11.5 | 9.5 |
| Financial services | 13.5 | 12.0 | 10.5 |
| Forestry or fishing | 10.5 | 9.5 | 8.0 |
| General building or construction services* | 9.5 | 8.5 | 7.5 |
| Hairdressing or other beauty treatment services | 13.0 | 11.5 | 10.5 |
| Hiring or renting goods | 9.5 | 8.5 | 7.5 |
| Hotel or accommodation | 10.5 | 9.5 | 8.5 |
| Investigation or security | 12.0 | 10.5 | 9.0 |
| Labour-only building or construction services* | 14.5 | 13.0 | 11.5 |
| Laundry or dry-cleaning services | 12.0 | 10.5 | 9.5 |
| Lawyer or legal services | 14.5 | 13.0 | 12.0 |
| Library, archive, museum or other cultural activity | 9.5 | 8.5 | 7.5 |
| Management consultancy | 14.0 | 12.5 | 11.0 |
| Manufacturing fabricated metal products | 10.5 | 9.5 | 8.5 |
| Manufacturing food | 9.0 | 8.0 | 7.0 |
| Manufacturing that is not listed elsewhere | 9.5 | 8.5 | 7.5 |

| Category of business | From 4 January 2011 | 1 January 2010 to 3 January 2011 | 1 December 2008 to 31 December 2009 |
|---|---|---|---|
| | % | % | % |
| Manufacturing yarn, textiles or clothing | 9.0 | 8.0 | 7.5 |
| Membership organisation | 8.0 | 7.0 | 5.5 |
| Mining or quarrying | 10.0 | 9.0 | 8.0 |
| Packaging | 9.0 | 8.0 | 7.5 |
| Photography | 11.0 | 10.0 | 8.5 |
| Post offices | 5.0 | 4.5 | 2.0 |
| Printing | 8.5 | 7.5 | 6.5 |
| Publishing | 11.0 | 10.0 | 8.5 |
| Pubs | 6.5 | 6.0 | 5.5 |
| Real estate activity not listed elsewhere | 14.0 | 12.5 | 11.0 |
| Repairing personal or household goods | 10.0 | 9.0 | 7.5 |
| Repairing vehicles | 8.5 | 7.5 | 6.5 |
| Retailing food, confectionery, tobacco, newspapers or children's clothing | 4.0 | 3.5 | 2.0 |
| Retailing pharmaceuticals, medical goods, cosmetics or toiletries | 8.0 | 7.0 | 6.0 |
| Retailing that is not listed elsewhere | 7.5 | 6.5 | 5.5 |
| Retailing vehicles or fuel | 6.5 | 6.0 | 5.5 |
| Secretarial services | 13.0 | 11.5 | 9.5 |
| Social work | 11.0 | 10.0 | 8.0 |
| Sport or recreation | 8.5 | 7.5 | 6.0 |
| Transport or storage, including couriers, freight, removals and taxis | 10.0 | 9.0 | 8.0 |
| Travel agency | 10.5 | 9.5 | 8.0 |
| Veterinary medicine | 11.0 | 10.0 | 8.0 |
| Wholesaling agricultural products | 8.0 | 7.0 | 5.5 |
| Wholesaling food | 7.5 | 6.5 | 5.0 |
| Wholesaling that is not listed elsewhere | 8.5 | 7.5 | 6.0 |

* 'Labour-only building or construction services' means building or construction services where the value of materials supplied is less than 10% of relevant turnover from such services; any other building or construction services are 'general building or construction services'.

**Notes**

(1) *Eligibility* – The flat-rate scheme is open to businesses who expect taxable supplies in the next year to be no more than £150,000 excluding VAT (from 10 April 2003) (VAT Notice 733, para 3.1). In addition, up to 1 April 2009 when this requirement was removed, total business income in that next year must not exceed £187,500 including VAT. Admission to the scheme is also subject to certain other criteria (see *SI 1995/2518, reg 55L* and VAT Notice 733, para 3.6).

(2) *Withdrawal* – From 4 January 2011 a business must leave the scheme if either its tax inclusive annual flat rate turnover (excluding sales of capital assets) exceeds £230,000 at any anniversary of the start date, or if its tax inclusive turnover in the next 30 days alone can reasonably be expected to exceed £230,000. Prior to 4 January 2011, both exit thresholds were £225,000. A business may leave the scheme voluntarily at any time on giving notice (see *SI 1995/2518, reg 55M*).

(3) *Discount* – A newly registered business is generally entitled to a 1% discount on the normal percentage until the day before its first anniversary of becoming VAT registered (see *SI 1995/2518, reg 55JB*; VAT Notice 733, para 4.5).

## PARTIAL EXEMPTION DE MINIMIS LIMITS

(*VAT Regulations, SI 1995/2518, regs 106, 107*; VAT Notice 706)

| **Exempt input tax not exceeding:** |
|---|
| ● £625 per month on average; and |
| ● 50% of total input tax for the period concerned |

**Notes**

(1) *De-minimis threshold* – Businesses which have both taxable and exempt income can treat all their exempt input tax as taxable input tax and recover it all, provided the exempt input tax is below the *de minimis* limit. The input tax claimed in each tax period is provisional until any under or over recovery of input tax is accounted for in an annual adjustment.

(2) *New tests* – For VAT periods starting on or after 1 April 2010, two optional simplified *de minimis* tests are available, and also the opportunity for a business to treat itself as *de minimis* throughout a tax year if it was *de minimis* in the previous tax year – but still subject to an annual adjustment at the end of the tax year, which could make the business partly exempt and subject to an input tax payback (see *SI 1995/2518, reg 107*; VAT Information Sheet 04/10).

## CAPITAL GOODS SCHEME (CGS)

(*VAT Regulations 1995, SI 1995/2518, Part XV*; VAT Notice 706/2)

### Assets included in the scheme

● Land and buildings – costing £250,000 or more (excluding VAT)

● Computers and computer equipment and from 1 January 2011 this was extended to include ships, boats and aircraft – costing £50,000 or more (excluding VAT)

The CGS requires the adjustment of input tax recovered by partially exempt traders and from 1 January 2011, businesses that have business/non-business use on property, computers, aircraft, ships and boats.

## Adjustment periods

(*SI 1995/2518, reg 114*)

| Asset | No of intervals in adjustment period |
|---|---|
| Computers | 5 |
| An interest in land, buildings or civil engineering works acquired when the interest (eg a lease) had less than 10 years to run | 5 |
| All other assets | 10 |

**Notes**

(1) *Land and buildings* – In addition to the purchase or construction of a building, the capital goods scheme can apply to alterations, constructions of extensions or annexes, refurbishments and civil engineering works (*SI 1995/2518, reg 113*). Prior to 1 January 2011 building alterations and constructions of extensions or annexes were only included where additional floor space of 10% or more was created by the works.

(2) *Adjustments* – Input tax is initially recovered under the normal partial exemption rules. Section 6 of VAT Notice 706/2 ('Capital goods scheme') explains how to make subsequent adjustments under the scheme.

## VAT INVOICES

(*SI 1995/2518, reg 14*)

A VAT invoice must show the following:

- A sequential number based on one or more series which uniquely identifies the document

- The time of the supply

- The date of the issue of the document

- The name, address and registration number of the supplier

- The name and address of the person to whom the goods or services are supplied

- A description sufficient to identify the goods or services supplied

- For each description, the quantity of the goods or the extent of the services, and the rate of VAT and the amount payable, excluding VAT, expressed in any currency.

- The gross total amount payable, excluding VAT, expressed in any currency

- The rate of any cash discount offered

- The total amount of VAT chargeable, expressed in sterling

- The unit price

- Where the VAT invoice includes zero-rated or exempt goods or services, the total of those values separately showing clearly that there is no VAT payable on them

- Where a margin scheme is applied under *VATA 1994, s 50A* (see Note 3 below) or *s 53* (certain supplies made by a tour operator), a relevant reference or any indication that a margin scheme has been applied

- Where a VAT invoice relates in whole or part to a supply where the person supplied is liable to pay the tax (ie a reverse charge), a relevant reference or any indication that the supply is one where the customer is liable to pay the tax.

**Notes**

(1) *Retailers' invoices* – A retailer who makes a sale of goods or services for £250 or less (including VAT) can issue a simplified invoice (where the customer asks for a VAT invoice), if the supply is other than to a person in another member state. The VAT invoice need only contain the following particulars (*SI 1995/2518, reg 16*):

- The name, address and registration number of the retailer;

- The time of the supply;

- A description sufficient to identify the goods or services supplied;

- The total amount payable including VAT; and

- For each rate of VAT chargeable, the gross amount payable including VAT, and the VAT rate applicable.

(2) *Invoices to persons in other EU member states* – Where a VAT invoice is provided for a person in another EU member state, separate requirements apply as to the particulars which must be included in the invoice, unless HMRC allow otherwise (*SI 1995/2518, reg 14(2);* VAT Information Sheet 10/07).

(3) *Margin schemes* – VATA 1994, s 50A applies to supplies of works of art, antiques or collectors' items, motor vehicles, second-hand goods, and any supply of goods through a person who acts as an agent, but in his own name, in relation to the supply. An invoice in relation to such supplies must include a relevant reference. Similar provisions apply to certain supplies made by tour operators (*VATA 1994, s 53*).

(4) *Relevant reference* – A 'relevant reference' is: (a) a reference to the appropriate provision of Council Directive 2006/112/EC; (b) a reference to the corresponding provision of the Act; or (c) any other reference that a margin scheme has been applied or that a reverse charge may apply. Examples of relevant references or indications that a margin scheme has been applied are if the invoice includes: 'This invoice is for a second-hand margin scheme supply' or 'This is a tour operators' margin scheme supply' (*SI 1995/2518, reg 14(8)*; see VAT Information Sheet 10/07).

## ADVISORY FUEL RATES

See **Chapter 2: Expenses and Benefits** for the latest advisory fuel rates. These rates apply for VAT, income tax and National Insurance contributions purposes. A business can reclaim the VAT element on the amount attributable to fuel of mileage allowances paid to employees or subcontractors.

## PRIVATE FUEL SCALE CHARGES

(*VATA 1994, ss 56(7), 57*)

### Fuel scale charge from 1 May 2013

Shown here on a VAT-inclusive basis (*Budget, 20 March 2013*)

| Description of vehicle: vehicle's $CO_2$ emissions figure (but see Note 2 below) | 12-month period £ | 3-month period £ | 1-month period £ |
|---|---|---|---|
| 120 or less | 675 | 168 | 56 |
| 125 | 1,010 | 253 | 84 |
| 130 | 1,080 | 269 | 89 |
| 135 | 1,145 | 286 | 95 |
| 140 | 1,215 | 303 | 101 |
| 145 | 1,280 | 320 | 106 |
| 150 | 1,350 | 337 | 112 |
| 155 | 1,415 | 354 | 118 |
| 160 | 1,485 | 371 | 123 |
| 165 | 1,550 | 388 | 129 |
| 170 | 1,620 | 404 | 134 |
| 175 | 1,685 | 421 | 140 |
| 180 | 1,755 | 438 | 146 |
| 185 | 1,820 | 455 | 151 |
| 190 | 1,890 | 472 | 157 |
| 195 | 1,955 | 489 | 163 |
| 200 | 2,025 | 506 | 168 |
| 205 | 2,090 | 523 | 174 |
| 210 | 2,160 | 539 | 179 |
| 215 | 2,225 | 556 | 185 |
| 220 | 2,295 | 573 | 191 |
| 225 or more | 2,360 | 590 | 196 |

### Fuel scale charge from 1 May 2012

Shown here on a VAT-inclusive basis (*SI 2012/882*)

See also www.hmrc.gov.uk/vat/forms-rates/rates/rates-thresholds.htm#8 and Notes below.

155

| Description of vehicle: vehicle's $CO_2$ emissions figure (but see Note 2 below) | 12-month period £ | 3-month period £ | 1-month period £ |
|---|---|---|---|
| 120 or less | 665 | 166 | 55 |
| 125 | 1,000 | 250 | 83 |
| 130 | 1,065 | 266 | 88 |
| 135 | 1,135 | 283 | 94 |
| 140 | 1,200 | 300 | 100 |
| 145 | 1,270 | 316 | 105 |
| 150 | 1,335 | 333 | 111 |
| 155 | 1,400 | 350 | 116 |
| 160 | 1,470 | 366 | 122 |
| 165 | 1,535 | 383 | 127 |
| 170 | 1,600 | 400 | 133 |
| 175 | 1,670 | 416 | 138 |
| 180 | 1,735 | 433 | 144 |
| 185 | 1,800 | 450 | 150 |
| 190 | 1,870 | 467 | 155 |
| 195 | 1,935 | 483 | 161 |
| 200 | 2,000 | 500 | 166 |
| 205 | 2,070 | 517 | 172 |
| 210 | 2,135 | 533 | 177 |
| 215 | 2,200 | 550 | 183 |
| 220 | 2,270 | 567 | 189 |
| 225 or more | 2,335 | 583 | 194 |

## Fuel scale charge from 1 May 2011 to 30 April 2012

| Description of vehicle: vehicle's $CO_2$ emissions figure (but see Note 2 below) | 12-month period £ | 3-month period £ | 1-month period £ |
|---|---|---|---|
| 120 or less | 630 | 157 | 52 |
| 125 | 945 | 236 | 78 |
| 130 | 1,010 | 252 | 84 |
| 135 | 1,070 | 268 | 89 |
| 140 | 1,135 | 283 | 94 |
| 145 | 1,200 | 299 | 99 |
| 150 | 1,260 | 315 | 105 |
| 155 | 1,325 | 331 | 110 |
| 160 | 1,385 | 346 | 115 |
| 165 | 1,450 | 362 | 120 |
| 170 | 1,515 | 378 | 126 |

| Description of vehicle: vehicle's $CO_2$ emissions figure (but see Note 2 below) | 12-month period £ | 3-month period £ | 1-month period £ |
|---|---|---|---|
| 175 | 1,575 | 394 | 131 |
| 180 | 1,640 | 409 | 136 |
| 185 | 1,705 | 425 | 141 |
| 190 | 1,765 | 441 | 147 |
| 195 | 1,830 | 457 | 152 |
| 200 | 1,890 | 472 | 157 |
| 205 | 1,955 | 488 | 162 |
| 210 | 2,020 | 504 | 168 |
| 215 | 2,080 | 520 | 173 |
| 220 | 2,145 | 536 | 178 |
| 225 or more | 2,205 | 551 | 183 |

## Fuel scale charge from 1 May 2010 to 30 April 2011

| Description of vehicle: vehicle's $CO_2$ emissions figure (but see Note 2 below) | 12-month period £ | 3-month period £ | 1-month period £ |
|---|---|---|---|
| 120 or less | 570 | 141 | 47 |
| 125 | 850 | 212 | 70 |
| 130 | 850 | 212 | 70 |
| 135 | 910 | 227 | 75 |
| 140 | 965 | 241 | 80 |
| 145 | 1,020 | 255 | 85 |
| 150 | 1,080 | 269 | 89 |
| 155 | 1,135 | 283 | 94 |
| 160 | 1,190 | 297 | 99 |
| 165 | 1,250 | 312 | 104 |
| 170 | 1,305 | 326 | 108 |
| 175 | 1,360 | 340 | 113 |
| 180 | 1,420 | 354 | 118 |
| 185 | 1,475 | 368 | 122 |
| 190 | 1,530 | 383 | 127 |
| 195 | 1,590 | 397 | 132 |
| 200 | 1,645 | 411 | 137 |
| 205 | 1,705 | 425 | 141 |
| 210 | 1,760 | 439 | 146 |
| 215 | 1,815 | 454 | 151 |
| 220 | 1,875 | 468 | 156 |
| 225 | 1,930 | 482 | 160 |
| 230 or more | 1,985 | 496 | 165 |

## Fuel scale charge from 1 May 2009 to 30 April 2010

| Description of vehicle: vehicle's CO$_2$ emissions figure (but see Note 2 below) | 12-month period £ | 3-month period £ | 1-month period £ |
|---|---|---|---|
| 120 or less | 505 | 126 | 42 |
| 125 | 755 | 189 | 63 |
| 130 | 755 | 189 | 63 |
| 135 | 755 | 189 | 63 |
| 140 | 805 | 201 | 67 |
| 145 | 855 | 214 | 71 |
| 150 | 905 | 226 | 75 |
| 155 | 960 | 239 | 79 |
| 160 | 1,010 | 251 | 83 |
| 165 | 1,060 | 264 | 88 |
| 170 | 1,110 | 276 | 92 |
| 175 | 1,160 | 289 | 96 |
| 180 | 1,210 | 302 | 100 |
| 185 | 1,260 | 314 | 104 |
| 190 | 1,310 | 327 | 109 |
| 195 | 1,360 | 339 | 113 |
| 200 | 1,410 | 352 | 117 |
| 205 | 1,465 | 365 | 121 |
| 210 | 1,515 | 378 | 126 |
| 215 | 1,565 | 390 | 130 |
| 220 | 1,615 | 403 | 134 |
| 225 | 1,665 | 416 | 138 |
| 230 | 1,715 | 428 | 142 |
| 235 or more | 1,765 | 441 | 147 |

**Notes**

(1)   *General* – If a business pays for any fuel used for private motoring by its owners, directors or employees, it has to pay VAT on the VAT-inclusive fuel scale charge listed above at the rate applicable at the time the charge is due. To calculate standard rate VAT from the VAT inclusive amount, multiply the VAT inclusive scale charge by the appropriate VAT fraction.

(2)   *CO$_2$ emissions figures* – Where the CO$_2$ emissions figure of a vehicle is not a multiple of five, the figure is rounded down to the next multiple of five to determine the level of the charge. For a bi-fuel vehicle which has two CO$_2$ emissions figures, the lower of the two figures should be used. For cars which are too old to have a CO$_2$ emissions figure, HMRC have prescribed a level of emissions by reference to the vehicle's engine capacity (VAT Notice 700/64, para 9.3).

(3)   *Further information* – Information on fuel scale charges and motor expenses generally is contained in VAT Notice 700/64.

(4)   *Prospective changes* – From Royal Assent of *FA 2013* the fuel scale charge rates will be calculated by HMRC according to a fomula set out in regulations. The table of rates will be published annually in a VAT Notice (*FB 2013, cl 190, Sch 36*).

# EU VAT RATES AND COUNTRY CODES

(*VAT Regulations, SI 1995/2518, reg 2*)

| EU country | Country code | Standard rate % | Reduced rates % |
|---|---|---|---|
| Austria | AT | 20 | 10 |
| Belgium | BE | 21 | 6 & 12 |
| Bulgaria | BG | 20 | 9 |
| Cyprus | CY | 18 | 5 & 8 |
| Czech Republic | CZ | 21 | 15 |
| Denmark | DK | 25 | – |
| Estonia | EE | 20 | 9 |
| Finland | FI | 24 | 10 & 14 |
| France | FR | 19.6 | 5.5 & 7 |
| Germany | DE | 19 | 7 |
| Greece | EL | 23 | 6.5 &13 |
| Hungary | HU | 27 | 5 & 18 |
| Ireland | IE | 23 | 9 & 13.5 |
| Italy | IT | 21 | 10 |
| Latvia | LV | 21 | 12 |
| Lithuania | LT | 21 | 5 & 9 |
| Luxembourg | LU | 15 | 6 & 12 |
| Malta | MT | 18 | 5 & 7 |
| Netherlands | NL | 21 | 6 |
| Poland | PL | 23 | 5 & 8 |
| Portugal | PT | 23 | 6 & 13 |
| Romania | RO | 24 | 5 & 9 |
| Slovak Republic | SK | 20 | 10 |
| Slovenia | SI | 20 | 8.5 |
| Spain | ES | 21 | 10 |
| Sweden | SE | 25 | 6 &12 |
| United Kingdom | GB | 20 | 5 |

## Notes

(1)   Cyprus – those areas under the control of the Government of the Republic of Cyprus and including the UK Sovereign Base Areas of Akrotiri and Dhekelia.

(2)   United Kingdom – The UK and the Isle of Man are part of the EU VAT area, but sales to the UK and/or the Isle of Man should not be included on the EC Sales List (ESL).

(3)  Spain – includes the Balearic Islands but excludes Ceuta, Melilla and the Canary Islands

(4)  Italy – excludes the communes of Livigno and Campione d'Italia and the Italian waters of Lake Lugano

(5)  Portual – includes the Azores and Madeira.

(6)  Germany – excludes Büsingen and the Isle of Heligoland

(7)  The following are not part of the EU VAT area:

- The Åland Islands

- Andorra

- The Channel Islands

- The overseas departments of France (Guadeloupe, Martinique, Reunion, St. Pierre and Miquelon, and French Guiana), but Monaco is treated as part of France.

- Gibraltar

- Liechtenstein

- Mount Athos (Agion Poros)

- San Marino

- Vatican City

(8)  See: www.hmrc.gov.uk/vat/managing/international/esl/country-codes.htm; for the VAT number formats for each EU country and links to foreign language enquiry letters, and VAT Notice 725.

## PLACE OF SUPPLY – SERVICES

*(VATA 1994, s 7A, Sch 4A)*

### Customers within the EU

From 1 January 2010 the general rule for the place of supply of services where the customer is within the EU is:

- *For business to business (B2B) supplies* – where the customer belongs (EC Sales List needs to be completed).

- *For business to customer (B2C) supplies* – where the supplier belongs.

### Customers outside the EU

Where the customer belongs outside the EU the place of supply is where the customer belongs for both B2B and B2C services.

*Exceptions*

Exceptions to the above general rule are as follows:

| Categoy of service | Place of supply of services for B2B supplies | Place of supply of services for B2C supplies |
|---|---|---|
| • relating to land and property | Where the land is situated | Where the land is situated |
| • involving physical performance. For example artistic, cultural, education and training, sporting, entertainment services, exhibitions, conferences, meetings); and | Subject to the general rule for B2B services – where the customer belongs | Where the event actually takes place |
| • ancillary services relating to such activities, including services of organisers of such activities | | |
| • in respect of admission to cultural, artistic, sporting, scientific, educational, entertainment or similar events (including fairs and exhibitions); and | Where the event actually takes place | Where the event actually takes place |
| • supplies of ancillary services relating to admission to such events | | |
| • work on, or valuation of moveable goods; and | Subject to the general rule for B2B services – where the customer belongs | Supplies are made where the services are physically performed |
| • ancillary transport services | | |
| • Restaurant and catering | Where the services are physically carried out | Where the services are physically carried out |
| • Passenger transport | The place of supply of passenger transport is where it takes place. To the extent that the transport takes place outside the UK, it is outside the scope of UK VAT. However, if a journey involves travel through another Member State, the supply of passenger transport will be made in that Member State to the extent that the transport takes place | The place of supply of passenger transport is where it takes place. To the extent that the transport takes place outside the UK, it is outside the scope of UK VAT. However, if a journey involves travel through another Member State, the supply of passenger transport will be made in that Member State to the extent that the transport takes place |

*continued*

| Categoy of service | Place of supply of services for B2B supplies | Place of supply of services for B2C supplies |
|---|---|---|
| | there. In effect VAT is due in each member state the transport passes through in proportion to the total length of the journey | there. In effect VAT is due in each member state the transport passes through in proportion to the total length of the journey |
| ● Freight transport | Subject to the general rule for B2B services – where the customer belongs | |
| ● B2C international freight transport (between the EC and non-EC countries, or wholly outside the EC) | | Where the transport takes place |
| ● B2C intra-EC freight transport | | The Member State in which the transportation begins |
| ● short-term hire of means of transport ('Short-term hire' means for a continuous period not exceeding 90 days if the means of transport is a vessel and not exceeding 30 days for any other means of transport) | Where the means of transport is put at the disposal of the hiree | Where the means of transport is put at the disposal of the hiree |
| ● Long-term hire of means of transport | Subject to the general rule for B2B services – where the customer belongs | Where the recipient/ customer belongs, unless the hire is long-term hire of a pleasure boat where it will be the place where the pleasure boat is put at the disposal of the customer |

**Notes**

(1)  *Place of supply: 'Use and enjoyment'* – There are additional rules for the letting on hire of goods, electronically supplied services, telecommunications services and radio and television broadcasting services in either of the following situations:

- the place of supply would be the UK (because the supplier or customer belongs in the UK) but the services are effectively used and enjoyed outside the EC, or

- the place of supply would be outside the EC (because the supplier or customer belongs outside the EC) but the services are effectively used and enjoyed in the UK.

In these circumstances, the place of supply is where their effective use and enjoyment takes place. Where this is the UK, the services are subject to UK VAT.

(2)   *Use and enjoyment: Accounting procedures* – The accounting procedures taking account of the use and enjoyment provisions are:

| If your B2B supply is | You are: |
|---|---|
| to a customer belonging in the UK | not required to account for UK VAT to the extent that the customer uses and enjoys the services outside the EC |
| to a customer belonging outside the EC | required to account for UK VAT to the extent that the customer uses and enjoys the services in the UK |
| to a customer belonging outside the EC and the customer uses and enjoys the services in another Member State | not required to account for UK VAT as those services are supplied in that Member State but you may be required to register and account for VAT in that Member State |

# CIVIL PENALTIES, SURCHARGES AND INTEREST

For discussion of all penalties relating to VAT see **Chapter 17**.

HMRC (or the tax tribunal) may reduce certain civil penalties to such amount (including nil) as they think proper (*VATA 1994, s 70*). For guidance on the penalties which can be mitigated, and the potential levels of mitigation, see VCP11713 and VCP11740 et seq.

*13*

# Other taxes and duties

## INSURANCE PREMIUM TAX (IPT)

*(FA 1994, Pt III, Schs 6A–7A; IPT Regulations 1994, SI 1994/1774)*

### Rates of IPT

*(FA 1994, ss 51, 51A)*

| Period | Standard Rate % | Higher Rate % |
|---|---|---|
| From 4 January 2011 | 6.0 | 20.0 |
| 1 July 1999 to 3 January 2011 | 5.0 | 17.5 |
| 1 April 1997 to 30 June 1999 | 4.0 | 17.5 |
| 1 October 1994 to 31 March 1997 | 2.5 | – |

**Notes**

(1)   *General* – Insurance premium tax (IPT) is charged on premiums received by insurers under taxable insurance contracts from 1 October 1994.

(2)   *Higher rate of IPT* – This applies to insurance sold in certain circumstances relating to motor cars or motorcycles, certain electrical or mechanical domestic appliances and travel insurance *(FA 1994, Sch 6A)*.

## LANDFILL TAX

*(FA 1996, Pt III, Sch 5; FA 2011, s 25; SI 1996/1527; SI 2011/1017)*

### Rates

*(FA 1996, s 42)*

| Disposals made or treated as made | Standard rate per tonne £ | Lower rate per tonne £ | Maximum credit % |
|---|---|---|---|
| 1 April 2014 | 80 | 2.50 | 6.2 |
| 1 April 2013–31 March 2014 | 72 | 2.50 | 6.2 |
| 1 April 2012–31 March 2013 | 64 | 2.50 | 6.2 |
| 1 April 2011–31 March 2012 | 56 | 2.50 | 6.2 |

| Disposals made or treated as made | Standard rate per tonne £ | Lower rate per tonne £ | Maximum credit % |
|---|---|---|---|
| 1 April 2010–31 March 2011 | 48 | 2.50 | 5.5 |
| 1 April 2009–31 March 2010 | 40 | 2.50 | 6.0 |
| 1 April 2008–31 March 2009 | 32 | 2.50 | 6.0 |
| 1 April 2007–31 March 2008 | 24 | 2.00 | 6.6 |

**Notes**

(1) *General* – Landfill Tax was introduced from 1 October 1996. It applies to waste disposals by way of landfill at a licensed site, unless specifically exempted. Landfill site operators are taxed on disposals of waste by reference to the weight and type of waste concerned.

(2) *Future changes* – The Government announced a floor under the standard rate of landfill tax so that the rate will not fall below £80 per tonne from 2014–15 to 2019–20.

(3) *Which rate* – The lower rate of landfill tax relates to listed inactive (or inert) wastes, as listed in the *Landfill Tax (Qualifying Material) Order, SI 2011/1017)*. The standard rate applies to all other taxable waste.

(4) *Tax credits* – Registered landfill site operators can claim a tax credit worth 90% of any qualifying contributions made to approved environmental bodies, subject to a maximum percentage of their landfill tax liability during the contribution year (*Landfill Tax Regulations, SI 1996/1527, reg 31*).

# AGGREGATES LEVY

*(FA 2001, Pt 2, Schs 4–10; FA 2011, s 24; Aggregates Levy Regulations 2002, SI 2002/761)*

## Rates

*(FA 2001, s 16)*

| Period | Rate per tonne £ |
|---|---|
| From 1 April 2013 | 2.00 |
| 1 April 2009–31 March 2013 | 2.00 |
| 1 April 2008–31 March 2009 | 1.95 |
| 1 April 2002–31 March 2008 | 1.60 |

**Notes**

(1) *General* – Aggregates levy was introduced on 1 April 2002. It is charged on aggregate (broadly rock, sand and gravel) subjected to commercial exploitation.

(2) *How much* – The levy is charged at a rate per tonne, and the amount of levy charged on a part of a tonne of aggregate shall be the proportionately reduced amount (*FA 2001, s 16(4)*).

# CLIMATE CHANGE LEVY

*(FA 2000 s 30, Sch 6; Climate Change Levy (General) Regulations 2001, SI 2001/838)*

## Rates

*(FA 2000, Sch 6, para 42; FA 2011, s 23)*

| Taxable commodity supplied | Rate at which levy payable if supply is not a reduced-rate supply | | | | | |
|---|---|---|---|---|---|---|
| | From 1 April 2014 | From 1 April 2013 | 1 April 2012–31 March 2013 | 1 April 2011–31 March 2012 | 1 April 2009–31 March 2011 | 1 April 2008–31 March 2009 |
| Electricity | £0.00541 per kilowatt hour (kWh) | £0.00524 per kilowatt hour (kWh) | £0.00509 per kilowatt hour (kWh) | £0.00485 per kilowatt hour (kWh) | £0.00470 per kilowatt hour (kWh) | £0.00456 per kilowatt hour (kWh) |
| Gas supplied by a gas utility or any gas supplied in a gaseous state that is of a kind supplied by a gas utility | £0.00188 per kWh | £0.00182 per kWh (£0.00064 in N. Ireland to 31/10/13) | £0.00177 per kWh (£0.00062 in N. Ireland) | £0.00169 per kWh (£0.00059 in N. Ireland) | £0.00164 pence per kWh | £0.00159 per kWh |
| Any petroleum gas, or other gaseous hydrocarbon, supplied in a liquid state | £0.01210 per kilogram | £0.01172 per kilogram | £0.01137 per kilogram | £0.01083 per kilogram | £0.01050 per kilogram | £0.01018 pence per kilogram |
| Any other taxable commodity | £0.01476 per kilogram | £0.01429 per kilogram | £0.01387 per kilogram | £0.01321 per kilogram | £0.01281 per kilogram | £0.01242 pence per kilogram |

## Notes

(1)   *General* – Climate change levy (CCL) was introduced from 1 April 2001, as part of a range of measures designed to help the UK meet its legally binding commitment to reduce greenhouse gas emissions. CCL is chargeable on the industrial and commercial supply of taxable commodities for lighting, heating and power by consumers in specified business sectors.

(2)   *Reduced-rate supplies (FA 2000, Sch 6, para 42(1))* – CCL is charged at 20% of the full rate for energy intensive industries that have entered into a negotiated energy efficiency Climate Change Agreement (35% for supplies on or after 1 April 2011 *(FA 2010, s 18)*).

# ROAD FUEL DUTY

*(Hydrocarbon Oil Duties Act 1979 (HODA 1979); FA 2011, ss 19, 20; FA 2009, ss 15, 16; FA 2010, ss 12, 13)*

| Description | 23 March 2011 to 1 September 2013 | 1 January 2011 to 22 March 2011 | 1 October 2010 to 31 December 2010 | 1 April 2010 to 30 September 2010 | 1 September 2009 to 31 March 2010 | 1 April 2009 to 31 August 2009 |
|---|---|---|---|---|---|---|
| Unleaded petrol and bioethanol (*HODA 1979, s 6(1A)(a)*) | 57.95p | 58.95p | 58.19p | 57.19p | 56.19p | 54.19p |
| Heavy oil and biodiesel (*HODA 1979, s 6(1A)(c)*) | 57.95p | 58.95p | 58.19p | 57.19p | 36.19p | 34.19p |
| Natural road fuel gas (including biogas) (*HODA 1979, s 8(3)(a)*) | 24.70p per kg | 26.15p per kg | 25.05p per kg | 23.60p per kg | 22.16p per kg | 19.26p per kg |
| Other road fuel gas (eg liquefied petroleum gas) (*HODA 1979, s 8(3)(b)*) | 31.61p per kg | 33.04p per kg | 31.95p per kg | 30.53p per kg | 27.67p per kg | 24.82p per kg |

## Notes

(1)　*Per litre* – Figures shown in pence per litre (unless otherwise stated).

(2)　*Biofuels* – The rate of duty on bioethanol is, since 1 April 2010, the same as that on unleaded petrol (*FA 2010, s 12(5)*). The rate for unleaded petrol is set out in *HODA 1979, s 6(1A)(a)*). The rate of duty on biodiesel is, since 1 April 2010, the same as that on heavy oil (*FA 2010, s 12(3)*). The rate for heavy oil is set out in *HODA 1979, s 6(1A)(c)*.

(3)　*Cancelled rate increases* – The fuel duty increases which were due to take effect from 1 January 2013 are cancelled, as are the duty increases due to take effect on 1 September 2013 (*Budget, 20 March 2013*).

## VEHICLE EXCISE DUTY

*(Vehicle Excise and Registration Act 1994 (VERA 1994), ss 2, 4, Sch 1; FA 2008, s 17; FA 2009, ss 13, 14; FA 2011, ss 21, 22)*

## Light passenger vehicles – General rates

*(VERA 1994, Sch 1, para 1B)*

| Band | CO$_2$ (g/km) | From 1 April 2013 Petrol and diesel cars Standard £ | From 1 April 2012 Petrol and diesel cars Standard £ | From 1 April 2011 Petrol and diesel cars Standard £ | From 1 April 2010 Petrol and diesel cars Standard £ |
|------|------|------|------|------|------|
| A | Up to 100 | 0 | 0 | 0 | 0 |
| B | 101 to 110 | 20 | 20 | 20 | 20 |
| C | 111 to 120 | 30 | 30 | 30 | 30 |
| D | 121 to 130 | 105 | 100 | 95 | 90 |
| E | 131 to 140 | 125 | 120 | 115 | 110 |
| F | 141 to 150 | 140 | 135 | 130 | 125 |
| G | 151 to 165 | 175 | 170 | 165 | 155 |
| H | 166 to 175 | 200 | 195 | 190 | 180 |
| I | 176 to 185 | 220 | 215 | 210 | 200 |
| J | 186 to 200 | 260 | 250 | 245 | 235 |
| K | 201 to 225 | 280 | 270 | 260 | 245 |
| L | 226 to 255 | 475 | 460 | 445 | 425 |
| M | Over 255 | 490 | 475 | 460 | 435 |

**Notes**

(1)   *Period of licence* – The above rates apply for 12 month vehicle licences for cars registered on and after 1 March 2001. The rate for a six-month licence is 55% of the annual rate *(VERA 1994, s 4(2))*.

(2)   *Band K* – This includes cars that have a CO$_2$ figure over 225g/km but were registered before 23 March 2006 *(VERA 1994, Sch 1, para 1B)*.

(3)   *Alternative fuels* – From 1 April 2010 there is a £10 discount for all cars that run on alternative fuels (tax class 59). This also applies to all first year licences.

(4)   *First year licence* – There is a different rate of licence for cars for the first year the car is registered – see below.

(5)   *Further information* – A full list of VED rates for all vehicles can be found at: http://carfueldata.direct.gov.uk/

## Light passenger vehicles – First year rates

*(VERA 1994, Sch 1, para 1B)*

| Band | CO$_2$ (g/km) | From 1 April 2013 Petrol and Diesel cars Standard £ | From 1 April 2012 Petrol and Diesel cars Standard £ | From 1 April 2011 Petrol and Diesel cars Standard £ |
|------|------|------|------|------|
| A | Up to 100 | 0 | 0 | 0 |
| B | 101 to 110 | 0 | 0 | 0 |
| C | 111 to 120 | 0 | 0 | 0 |
| D | 121 to 130 | 0 | 0 | 0 |
| E | 131 to 140 | 125 | 120 | 115 |
| F | 141 to 150 | 140 | 135 | 130 |
| G | 151 to 165 | 175 | 170 | 165 |
| H | 166 to 175 | 285 | 275 | 265 |
| I | 176 to 185 | 335 | 325 | 315 |
| J | 186 to 200 | 475 | 460 | 445 |
| K | 201 to 225 | 620 | 600 | 580 |
| L | 226 to 255 | 840 | 815 | 790 |
| M | Over 255 | 1,065 | 1,030 | 1,000 |

### Notes

(1) *First year rates –* From 1 April 2010, the above rates of vehicle tax apply for the first tax disc (ie taken out at first registration). From the second tax disc onwards, the normal standard or reduced rate of vehicle tax applies.

(2) *Six month licences –* These are not applicable to vehicles being registered for the first time in bands A to D. Six-month tax discs are only available where the vehicle tax rate is more than £50 *(VERA 1994, s 3(2))*. In addition, from 1 April 2010 six-month tax discs are not available for vehicles being registered in bands H to M, as the first year rate for these vehicles is higher than the normal standard rate *(VERA 1994, s 3(7))*. However, a six-month tax disc is available when re-taxing the vehicle.

## Other vehicles

*(VERA 1994, Sch 1, paras 1, 1J, 2)*

| Category | From 1 April 2013 £ | From 1 April 2012 £ | From 1 April 2011 £ | From 1 April 2010 £ |
|------|------|------|------|------|
| Light goods vehicles (Tax Class 39) (weighing no more than 3,500kg revenue weight) *(Sch 1, para 1J)* | 220 | 215 | 200 | 200 |

*continued*

| Category | From 1 April 2013 £ | From 1 April 2012 £ | From 1 April 2011 £ | From 1 April 2010 £ |
|---|---|---|---|---|
| Lower-emissions vans (light goods vehicles) (Tax Class 36) (weighing no more than 3,500kg revenue weight) *(Sch 1, para 1J)* | 140 | 135 | 125 | 125 |
| Private or light goods vehicles (PLG) registered before 1 March 2001 (Tax Class 11) *(Sch 1, para 1)* | | | | |
| • Not over 1549 cc | 140 | 135 | 130 | 125 |
| • Over 1549 cc | 225 | 220 | 215 | 205 |
| Motorcycles (with or without a sidecar) (Tax Class 17) *(Sch 1, para 2)* | | | | |
| • Not over 150cc | 17 | 16 | 15 | 15 |
| • 151 to 400cc | 37 | 36 | 33 | 33 |
| • 401 to 600cc | 57 | 55 | 50 | 50 |
| • Over 600cc | 78 | 76 | 70 | 70 |
| Motor-tricycles (weighing no more than 450kg) (Tax Class 50) *(Sch 1, para 2)* | | | | |
| • Not over 150cc | 17 | 16 | 15 | 15 |
| • Any other case | 78 | 76 | 70 | 70 |

**Note**

The lower rate of vehicle excise duty for lower emission vans applies to models which meet certain air quality pollutant emissions standards (see *VERA 1994, Sch 1, para 1K*) and were registered on or after 1 March 2003 and before 1 January 2007, or that meet the Euro 5 pollutant emissions standards and were registered on or after 1 January 2009 and before 1 January 2011 *(Sch 1, para 1M)*.

# AIR PASSENGER DUTY

*(FA 1994, ss 28–30, Sch 5A; FA 2010, s 14)*

| Band, and approximate distance in miles from London to the capital city of the destination country | Higher rate | Lower rate | | | | | Standard rate | | | |
|---|---|---|---|---|---|---|---|---|---|---|
| | From 1 April 2013 £ | From 1 April 2013 £ | From 1 April 2012 £ | From 1 Nov 2010 £ | From 1 Nov 2009 £ | | From 1 April 2013 £ | From 1 April 2012 £ | From 1 Nov 2010 £ | From 1 Nov 2009 £ |
| Band A (0–2,000) | 52 | 13 | 13 | 12 | 11 | | 26 | 26 | 24 | 22 |
| Band B (2,001–4,000) | 268 | 67 | 65 | 60 | 45 | | 134 | 130 | 120 | 90 |
| Band C (4,001–6,000) | 332 | 83 | 81 | 75 | 50 | | 166 | 162 | 150 | 100 |
| Band D (over 6,000) | 376 | 94 | 92 | 85 | 55 | | 188 | 184 | 170 | 110 |

## Notes

(1)   Air passenger duty (APD) is chargeable on the carriage of each chargeable passenger at the specified rate *(FA 1994, s 30(1))*. A four destination band structure was introduced from 1 November 2009, based on geographical distance from London, each having two rates of duty depending upon the class of travel. The countries in each band are specified in Appendix 1 of Notice 550: Air Passenger Duty).

(2)   Prior to 1 November 2009, four rates of duty applied:

*Standard rates*

●   £20 for specified European destinations; and

●   £80 for all other destinations

*Reduced rates*

●   £10 for specified European destinations; and

●   £40 for all other destinations

(3)   'Standard class travel' means:

(a)   in the case of an aircraft on which only one class of travel is available, that class of travel

(b)   in any other case, the lowest class of travel available on the aircraft *(FA 1994, s 30(10))*.

(4)   Where a seat pitch exceeds 1.016 metres (40 inches), whether the flight has a single class or more than one class, the standard rate (or 'non-standard class travel' rate) of APD applies *(FA 1994, s 30(11); HMRC Notice 550, para 2.6.5)*.

(5)   The Northern Irish Assembly can now set the APD rates on long haul routes departing from Northern Ireland (bands B, C & D). From 1 January 2013 the APD for these routes from Northern Ireland is nil. From 1 November 2011 to

171

31 December 2012, the APD for the same direct long-haul routes departing from airports in Northern Ireland was charged at the short-haul (Band A) rates (www. hmrc.gov.uk/air-passenger-duty/apd-update-ni.htm; *FA 2012, s 190, Sch 23*).

(6) From 1 April 2013, the scope of APD is extended to business jets and smaller aircraft by reducing the de minimis weight limit for exemption of aircraft from 10 tonnes to 5.7 tonnes, subject to certain exclusions (eg emergency flights).

(7) From 1 April 2013 a higher rate of APD applies to business jets carrying less than 19 passengers aboard aircraft with an authorised take-off weight of 20 tonnes or more (*FA 2012, s 190, Sch 23*).

## BANK LEVY

(*FA 2011, s 73, Sch 19*)

| Period | Short-term chargeable liabilities | Long-term chargeable equity and liabilities |
|---|---|---|
| From 1 January 2014 | 0.142% | 0.071% |
| 1 January 2013–31 December 2013 | 0.130% | 0.065% |
| 1 January 2012–31 December 2012 | 0.088% | 0.044% |
| 1 May 2011–31 December 2011 | 0.075% | 0.0375% |
| 1 March 2011–30 April 2011 | 0.1% | 0.05% |
| 1 January 2011–28 February 2011 | 0.05% | 0.025% |

**Notes**

(1) *General* – The bank levy is a tax based on total chargeable equity and liabilities as reported in the relevant balance sheets of UK banks and banking groups, building societies and building society groups, foreign banks and foreign banking groups operating in the UK and UK banks in non-banking groups, at the end of a chargeable period.

(2) *Threshold* – The bank levy is nil if the amount of chargeable equity and liabilities is £20 billion or less. If this limit is exceeded, the first £20 billion (on which no levy is charged) is apportioned between long term equities and liabilities and short term liabilities, in accordance with the proportion of chargeable equity and liabilities of each (*FA 2011, Sch 19, para 6*).

(3) *Payment* – Payment of the bank levy is treated as a payment of corporation tax (*Sch 19, Pt 6*). It is subject to corporation tax payment procedures, including the quarterly instalment payments system (see **Chapter 7: Taxation of companies**).

(4) *Commencement* – The bank levy applies to periods of account ending on or after 1 January 2011 (*Sch 19, paras 4(8), 5(4)*). Periods falling wholly before 1 January 2011 are ignored for these purposes.

# ANNUAL TAX ON ENVELOPED DWELLINGS (ATED)

*(FB 2013, cll 91–172, Schs 31–33)*

| Taxable value on relevant day £ | Annual chargeable amount 2013/14 £ |
| --- | --- |
| Up to 2,000,000 | Nil |
| 2,000,001–5,000,000 | 15,000 |
| 5,000,001–10,000,000 | 35,000 |
| 10,000,001–20,000,000 | 70,000 |
| Over £20,000,000 | 140,000 |

**Notes**

(1) *General* – Annual tax on enveloped dwellings (ATED) was introduced as part of a package of anti-avoidance measures aimed at 'non-natural persons' (NNPs) (ie companies, partnerships with at least one corporate member and collective investment schemes) who own 'high value' residential property. ATED broadly applies to NNPs with beneficial interests in UK dwellings valued at more than £2 million at the valuation date. ATED is subject to a range of reliefs (see note 5 below).

(2) *Commencement* – ATED has effect for properties under the ownership of an NNP on or after 1 April 2013, ie if the dwelling is owned, acquired, built or converted from a non-residential property from that date.

(3) *ATED charge* – The ATED rates will be increased according to the consumer prices index each year. ATED is an annual charge, unless the NNP owns the property interest for only part of the chargeable period, in which case the charge is proportionately reduced *(FB 2013, cll 91, 96–98)*.

(4) *Valuations* – The value of a property interest for ATED purposes is generally its market value on 1 April 2012, or when acquired, if later. For a new property, or an existing property which has been altered to be a dwelling, the valuation date is broadly the date of entry on the Council Tax Valuation Lists (or Northern Ireland Valuation List) or when it is first occupied, if earlier (www.hmrc.gov.uk/ATED/basics.htm#4). This valuation figure will be used for up to five ATED return periods. Thus all properties within ATED will need to be revalued on 1 April 2017, to cover ATED returns for the five return periods starting on 1 April 2018. HMRC intends introducing a 'pre-return banding check' service from 1 June 2013 *(FB 2013, cl 99)*.

(5) *Reliefs* – There are certain reliefs from ATED. These relate to property rental businesses where the dwelling is let to an unconnected third party on a commercial basis, dwellings held by property development companies or as trading stock, and farmhouses occupied by qualifying farm workers. The NNP must make a 'nil' return to claim relief from ATED *(FB 2013, cll 130–150)*.

(6) *Returns and payments* – ATED is self-assessed, and is payable by the NNP. ATED chargeable periods run for 12 months commencing 1 April each year. The ATED return and payment are both normally due by 30 April each year (eg the return and payment for the ATED period 1 April 2014 to 31 March 2015 are due by 30

April 2014). For dwellings first falling within ATED after 1 April in the relevant period, returns and payments are due within 30 days if purchased, or 90 days if the dwelling is newly built (*FB 2013, cll 157–159, 161*). If the NNP is not chargeable for a full year, a later repayment claim can be made.

(7)   *Special provision for 2013/14* – For the first year of ATED only (ie for the period 1 April 2013 to 31 March 2014), ATED returns must normally be made by 1 October 2013 (*FB 2013, Sch 33, Pt 2*), and payments must be made by 31 October 2013 (see HMRC TIIN, 11 December 2012).

(8)   *Enquiries* – ATED returns are subject to an enquiry regime. Incorrect and/or late returns may be subject to penalties. Late payment interest charges may also apply. The regime is subject to review and appeal processes (*FB 2013, cl 160, Schs 31–32*).

(9)   *Further guidance* – HMRC has published a guide to ATED and to the property banding check needed to establish the rate of the ATED: (www.hmrc.gov.uk/ated/index.htm).

## MACHINE GAMES DUTY

(*FA 2012, s 191, Sch 24; Machine Games Duty Regulations, SI 2012/2500*); HMRC Notice 452)

### Rates

(*FA 2012, Sch 24, para 9*)

| Description | Rate from 1 February 2013 |
|---|---|
| Standard rate | 20% |
| Lower rate | 5% |

### Notes

(1)   *General* – Machine games duty (MGD) is an excise duty introduced in *Finance Act 2012* to replace amusement machine licence duty. MGD is charged on total net takings from the playing of 'dutiable' machine games in the UK, ie broadly games which offer the player the opportunity to win a cash prize, the value of which exceeds the cost of playing the game. Machine games on which MGD is payable is exempt from VAT (*VATA 1994, Sch 9, Group 4, Item 1A*).

(2)   *Commencement* – MGD was introduced with effect from 1 February 2013.

(3)   *MGD rates* – The standard rate of 20% applies to 'Type 1' machine games which are not subject to the lower rate. The lower rate of 5% applies to 'Type 2' machines where the maximum stake is 10 pence, and the cash prize is £8 or less (*FA 2012, Sch 24, para 5*).

(4)   *Returns and payments* – MGD accounting periods are normally quarterly. A person who is responsible for premises where dutiable gaming machines are provided for play is required to register for MGD with HMRC. The registered person for MGD purposes must generally file returns and make payments by the 30th day

following the end of every accounting period (*SI 2012/2500, regs 12, 13*). Penalties and interest can be charged in certain circumstances (eg errors in returns, failure to register, and failure to make payments on time).

(5)     *Registration* – Applications to register for MGD may be made to HMRC online or by paper (see VAT Notice 452, para 6.6). HMRC has also published a guide to MGD online on its website (www.hmrc.gov.uk/machinegamesduty/mgd-online. htm).

(6)     *Further guidance* – The HMRC website includes a section on MGD (www.hmrc. gov.uk/machinegamesduty/), featuring basic guides, notices and publications.

*14*

# National Insurance Contributions (NICs)

## CLASS 1 PRIMARY (EMPLOYEE) CONTRIBUTIONS

*(SSCBA 1992, ss 5(1), 8, 19(4); SI 2001/1004, regs 10, 131; Pension Schemes Act 1993, ss 41, 42A; SI 2006/1009, art 3)*

| Class 1 NIC rates and thresholds | 2013–14 | 2012–13 | 2011–12 | 2010–11 | 2009–10 |
|---|---|---|---|---|---|
| Lower earnings limit (LEL) | £109 per week | £107 per week | £102 per week | £97 per week | £95 per week |
| | £473 per month | £464 per month | £442 per month | £421 per month | £412 per year |
| | £5,668 per year | £5,564 per year | £5,304 per year | £5,044 per year | £4,940 per year |
| Primary threshold (PT) | £149 per week | £146 per week | £139 per week | £110 per week | £110 per week |
| | £646 per month | £634 per month | £602 per month | £476 per month | £476 per month |
| | £7,755 per year | £7,605 per year | £7,225 per year | £5,715 per year | £5,715 per year |
| Upper accrual point (UAP) | £770 per week | £770 per week | £770 per week | £770 per week | £770 per week |
| | £3,337 per month | £3,337 per month | £3,337 per month | £3,337 per month | £3,337 per month |
| | £40,040 per year | £40,040 per year | £40,040 per year | £40,040 per year | £40,040 per year |
| Upper earnings limit (UEL) | £797 per week | £817 per week | £817 per week | £844 per week | £844 per week |
| | £3,454 per month | £3,540 per month | £3,540 per month | £3,656 per month | £3,656 per month |
| | £41,450 per year | £42,475 per year | £42,475 per year | £43,875 per year | £43,875 per year |
| Not contracted out | 12% on earnings between PT and UEL | 12% on earnings between PT and UEL | 12% on earnings between PT and UEL | 11% on earnings between PT and UEL | 11% on earnings between PT and UEL |
| | 2% on excess over UEL | 2% on excess over UEL | 2% on excess over UEL | 1% on excess over UEL | 1% on excess over UEL |

| Class 1 NIC rates and thresholds | 2013–14 | 2012–13 | 2011–12 | 2010–11 | 2009–10 |
|---|---|---|---|---|---|
| Contracted out (see Note 3 below) | 10.6% on earnings between PT and UAP | 10.6% on earnings between PT and UAP | 10.4% on earnings between PT and UAP | 9.4% on earnings between PT and UAP | 9.4% on earnings between PT and UAP |
| | 12% on earnings between UAP and UEL | 12% on earnings between UAP and UEL | 12% on earnings between UAP and UEL | 11% on earnings between UAP and UEL | 11% on earnings between UAP and UEL |
| | 2% on excess over UEL | 2% on excess over UEL | 2% on excess over UEL | 1% on excess over UEL | 1% on excess over UEL |
| Contracted out rebate – flat rate (see Note 3 below) | 1.4% | 1.4% | 1.6% | 1.6% | 1.6% |
| Reduced rate (see Note 4 below) | 5.85% on earnings between PT and UEL | 5.85% on earnings between PT and UEL | 5.85% on earnings between PT and UEL | 4.85% on earnings between PT and UEL | 4.85% on earnings between PT and UEL |
| | 2% on excess over UEL | 2% on excess over UEL | 2% on excess over UEL | 1% on excess over UEL | 1% on excess over UEL |

## CLASS 1 PRIMARY (EMPLOYEE) CONTRIBUTIONS (CONTINUED)

(*SSCBA 1992, ss 5(1), 8, 19(4)*; *SI 2001/1004, regs 10, 131*; *Pension Schemes Act 1993, ss 41, 42A*; *SI 2006/1009, art 3*)

| Class 1 NIC rates and thresholds | 2008–09 | 2007–08 |
|---|---|---|
| Lower earnings limit (LEL) | £90 per week | £87 per week |
| | £390 per month | £377 per month |
| | £4,680 per year | £4,524 per year |
| Primary threshold (PT) | £105 per week | £100 per week |
| | £453 per month | £435 per month |
| | £5,435 per year | £5,225 per year |
| Upper earnings limit (UEL) | £770 per week | £670 per week |
| | £3,337 per month | £2,904 per month |
| | £40,040 per year | £34,840 per year |
| Not contracted out | 11% on earnings between PT and UEL | 11% on earnings between PT and UEL |
| | 1% on excess over UEL | 1% on excess over UEL |

*continued*

| Class 1 NIC rates and thresholds | 2008–09 | 2007–08 |
|---|---|---|
| Contracted out | 9.4% on earnings between PT and UEL<br><br>1% on excess over UEL | 9.4% on earnings between PT and UEL<br><br>1% on excess over UEL |
| Contracted out rebate – flat rate | 1.6% | 1.6% |
| Reduced rate (see Note 4 below) | 4.85% on earnings between PT and UEL<br><br>1% on excess over UEL | 4.85% on earnings between PT and UEL<br><br>1% on excess over UEL |

**Notes**

(1) *Nil band* – No Class 1 contributions are payable on earnings between the lower earnings limit and primary threshold, but the employee is treated as having paid such contributions for the purposes of establishing or protecting entitlement to certain state benefits (*SSCBA 1992, s 6A*).

(2) *The 'Upper Accrual Point' (UAP)* – This was introduced from 6 April 2009 (*NICA 2008, s 3*). The UAP broadly represents the point at which entitlement to contributory related benefits ceases to accrue.

(3) *Contracting out* – With effect from 6 April 2012, it is no longer possible to contract out of the additional state pension on a defined contribution basis.

(4) *Married woman's rate* – This reduced rate applies to women married before 6 April 1977 who have elected to pay a reduced rate of Class 1 contributions.

## CLASS 1 SECONDARY (EMPLOYER) CONTRIBUTIONS

*(SSCBA 1992, ss 6(1)(b), 9; SI 2001/1004, reg 10; Pension Schemes Act 1993, ss 41, 42A; SI 2006/1009, arts 2, 3)*

| Class 1 NIC rates and thresholds | 2013–14 | 2012–13 | 2011–12 | 2010–11 |
|---|---|---|---|---|
| Secondary threshold (ST) | £148 per week<br>£641 per month<br>£7,696 per year | £144 per week<br>£624 per month<br>£7,488 per year | £136 per week<br>£589 per month<br>£7,072 per year | £110 per week<br>£476 per month<br>£5,715 per year |
| Not contracted out rate | 13.8% on earnings above ST | 13.8% on earnings above ST | 13.8% on earnings above ST | 12.8% on earnings above ST |
| Contracted out rates Salary related (COSR) | 10.4% | 10.4% | 10.1% | 9.1% |
| Money purchase (COMP) (see Note 2 below) | Abolished | Abolished | 12.4% | 11.4% |

| Class 1 NIC rates and thresholds | 2013–14 | 2012–13 | 2011–12 | 2010–11 |
|---|---|---|---|---|
| Contracted out rebate rates Salary related (COSR) | 3.4% | 3.4% | 3.7% | 3.7% |
| Money purchase (COMP) (see Note 2 below) | Abolished | Abolished | 1.4% | 1.4% |

| Class 1 NIC rates and thresholds | 2009–10 | 2008–09 | 2007–08 |
|---|---|---|---|
| Secondary threshold (ST) | £110 per week £476 per month £5,715 per year | £105 per week £453 per month £5,435 per year | £100 per week £435 per month £5,225 per year |
| Not contracted out rate | 12.8% on earnings above ST | 12.8% on earnings above ST | 12.8% on earnings above ST |
| Contracted out rates Salary related (COSR) | 9.1% | 9.1% | 9.1% |
| Money purchase (COMP) | 11.4% | 11.4% | 11.4% |
| Contracted out rebate rates Salary related (COSR) | 3.7% | 3.7% | 3.7% |
| Money purchase (COMP) | 1.4% | 1.4% | 1.4% |

**Notes**

(1) *General* – Class 1 contributions are not payable in respect of individuals under the age of 16 at the time of payment of the earnings. An employee who is at or over state pension age at the time of payment is not liable to pay primary Class 1 contributions, but employers must continue to pay secondary Class 1 contributions for employees over that age (*SSCBA 1992, s 6(3)*) (see *NIM1001*).

(2) *Contracting out* – With effect from 6 April 2012, it is no longer possible to contract out of the additional state pension on a defined contribution basis. All contracting out will cease from 6 April 2016 when the flat rate state pension comes into effect (*Budget, 20 March 2013*).

(3) *Regional employer NIC holiday* – This scheme is available to new businesses that start up during the period from 22 June 2010 to 5 September 2012 in certain areas of the UK. If the business qualifies, it can claim an exemption from the first £5,000 of employer's Class 1 contributions in the first 12 months of employment of up to 10 new employees. For further information see: www.hmrc.gov.uk/payerti/

getting-started/nics-holiday/index.htm (*National Insurance Contributions Act 2011, ss 4–11*).

(4)   *Disguised remuneration* – Class 1 employee and employer contributions can arise on certain 'disguised remuneration' from Employee Benefit Trusts (EBTs), unapproved pension schemes (EFRBS) and other third party intermediaries where such income would not otherwise be within the charge to NICs (see *ITEPA 2003, ss 554A–554Z20; Social Security (Contributions) Regulations, SI 2001/1004* as amended by *SI 2011/2700*).

(5)   *Teachers and instructors* – Under *The Social Security (Categorisation of Earners) 1978, SI 1978/1689*, lecturers, teachers, instructors and certain related workers at educational establishments were treated as employed for National Insurance purposes, whether or not they were employed or self-employed. For these particular categories of earners in the educational field, but not for others (eg entertainers, agency workers and office cleaners), these provisions have been revoked with effect from 6 April 2012 and those who are self-employed will be treated as such (*SI 2012/816*).

(6)   *Employment allowance* – The Government has announced that, from April 2014, businesses and charities will be entitled to an employment allowance of £2,000 per annum towards their employers' class 1 NIC liability (*Budget, 20 March 2013*).

## CLASS 1A CONTRIBUTIONS

(*SSCBA 1992, s 10*)

- Class 1A contributions are payable by employers (and certain third parties) on taxable benefits provided to employees. The Class 1A NIC charge is calculated as a percentage of the cash equivalent of the benefits.

- The Class 1A percentage is the same as the rate of secondary Class 1 contributions for the tax year in question (13.8% for 2013–14).

- No Class 1A NICs are due in some cases (see HMRC Booklet CWG5, Pt 2):

  ○   Benefits which are exempt from income tax (*SSCBA 1992, s 10(1)(a)*);

  ○   Benefits returned on form P9D (*SSCBA 1992, s 10(1)(b)*);

  ○   Benefits which are exempt from Class 1A NICs (*SI 2001/1004, Pt 3*) (see Booklet CWG5, pt 5);

  ○   Benefits covered by a dispensation (*ITEPA 2003, ss 65, 96*);

  ○   Benefits covered by an Extra-Statutory Concession (as listed in *SI 2001/1004, reg 40(7)*);

  ○   Benefits included in a PAYE Settlement Agreement (see Class 1B contributions below) (*SSCBA 1992, s 10(6)*);

  ○   Benefits provided for employment duties, where any use for private purposes is not significant (see *ITEPA 2003, s 316*);

  ○   Benefits which are already liable to Class 1 NICs (*SSCBA 1992, s 10(1)(c)*); and

  ○   Benefits which are exempt from Class 1 NICs (*SI 2001/1004, reg 40*)

## CLASS 1B CONTRIBUTIONS

*(SSCBA 1992, s 10A)*

- Class 1B contributions are payable by employers who enter into a PAYE Settlement Agreement (PSA) with HMRC. A PSA is a formal agreement between HMRC and an employer, which allows the employer to account for tax on certain expense payments and benefits in a lump sum after the end of the tax year.

- The Class 1B NIC charge applies to items contained within a PSA that would normally attract a liability for Class 1 or Class 1A NICs, and to the total tax payable under the PSA. The Class 1B charge is calculated as a percentage of the total amount chargeable.

- The Class 1B percentage is the same as the rate of secondary Class 1 contributions for the tax year in question (13.8% for 2012–13).

- Payment of Class 1B NIC is due by 19 October in the tax year following the tax year to which the PSA applies (22 October for electronic payments) *(SI 2003/2682, reg 109(2))*.

## CLASS 2 CONTRIBUTIONS

*(SSCBA 1992, ss 11, 12)*

### Rates (weekly)

*(SSCBA 1992, ss 11(1), 117(1); SI 2001/1004, regs 125(c), 152(b))*

| Tax year | Flat rate £ | Share fishermen £ | Volunteer development workers £ |
|---|---|---|---|
| 2013–14 | 2.70 | 3.35 | 5.45 |
| 2012–13 | 2.65 | 3.30 | 5.35 |
| 2011–12 | 2.50 | 3.15 | 5.10 |
| 2010–11 | 2.40 | 3.05 | 4.85 |
| 2009–10 | 2.40 | 3.05 | 4.75 |
| 2008–09 | 2.30 | 2.95 | 4.50 |
| 2007–08 | 2.20 | 2.85 | 4.35 |

**Notes**

(1) *General* – Class 2 contributions are generally payable by self-employed persons over the age of 16, but are not payable in respect of any period after the earner has reached state pension age, are excepted in certain prescribed circumstances *(SI 2001/1004, reg 43)*, and are subject to a residence test *(SI 2001/1004, reg 145(1)(c), (d))* and a small earnings exception (see below).

(2) *Due six monthly* – From April 2011, payments of Class 2 contributions are due on 31 July and 31 January, but payments can still be made by direct debit for each

181

month in arrears. Before 2011–12 Class 2 NICs were generally paid quarterly by direct debit.

(3)   *Deferment* – A person who is both employed and self-employed is liable for both Class 1 and Class 2 (and Class 4) contributions, subject to an annual maximum. If the individual expects to pay more than the annual maximum, an application can be made to defer payment of Class 2 (and Class 4) contributions (*SI 2001/1004, regs 21, 90*) (see *NIM20725*).

## Small earnings exception

*(SSCBA 1992, s 11(4); SI 2001/1004, reg 46(a))*

| Tax year | Limit £ |
|---|---|
| 2013–14 | 5,725 |
| 2012–13 | 5,595 |
| 2011–12 | 5,315 |
| 2010–11 | 5,075 |
| 2009–10 | 5,075 |
| 2008–09 | 4,825 |
| 2007–08 | 4,635 |

**Notes**

(1)   *Application for exception* – A person whose net profits from self-employment are less than the small earnings exception limit for the relevant tax year may claim exception from liability to pay Class 2 NICs. An application for exception from liability for Class 2 contributions (form CF10) is available via HMRC's website: www.hmrc.gov.uk/forms/cf10.pdf.

(2)   *Voluntary contributions* – Class 2 contributions can be paid voluntarily for weeks of self-employment covered by the small earnings exception (*SI 2001/1004, reg 46(b)*). Alternatively, an individual may pay Class 3 contributions (see below) if entitled to do so (*NIM21044*).

## CLASS 3 CONTRIBUTIONS

*(SSCBA 1992, s 13)*

| Tax Year | Weekly Rate £ |
|---|---|
| 2013–14 | 13.55 |
| 2012–13 | 13.25 |
| 2011–12 | 12.60 |
| 2010–11 | 12.05 |
| 2009–10 | 12.05 |
| 2008–09 | 8.10 |
| 2007–08 | 7.80 |

**Notes**

(1)   *Eligibility* – Individuals wishing to pay Class 3 contributions in order to meet the conditions for entitlement to certain benefits must be over the age of 16 and satisfy conditions as to residence in Great Britain or Northern Ireland in the relevant tax year (*SSCBA 1992, s 1(6)(b)*; *SI 2001/1004, regs 48(1), 145(1)(e)*).

(2)   *Earnings factor* – An individual is entitled to pay Class 3 contributions if his or her earnings factor (EF) derived from Class 1, 2 and/or 3 NICs is less than the qualifying earnings factor for the relevant tax year, subject to certain restrictions on the right to pay. A qualifying earnings factor is an amount equal to 52 times that year's lower earnings limit for Class 1 contributions (*SSCBA 1992, s 14*; *SI 1979/676, Sch 1, Pt 2*) (see *NIM25001*).

# CLASS 4 CONTRIBUTIONS

(*SSCBA 1992, s 15*)

## Class 4 NIC rates

(*SSCBA 1992, s 15(3ZA)*)

| Tax Year | Main Class 4 percentage % | Additional Class 4 percentage % |
|---|---|---|
| 2013–14 | 9 | 2 |
| 2012–13 | 9 | 2 |
| 2011–12 | 9 | 2 |
| 2010–11 | 8 | 1 |
| 2009–10 | 8 | 1 |
| 2008–09 | 8 | 1 |
| 2007–08 | 8 | 1 |

**Notes**

(1)   *General* – Class 4 contributions are payable on profits from trades, professions or vocations, which are chargeable to income tax under *ITTOIA 2005, Pt 2, Ch 2*, and are not profits from a trade, profession or vocation carried on wholly outside the UK.

(2)   *Exceptions* – The liability to pay Class 4 contributions is subject to certain exceptions in *SI 2001/1004, Pt 8*. These include individuals who are over state pension age at the beginning of the relevant tax year. Individuals who are under the age of 16 at the beginning of the tax year are also exempt if they obtain a certificate of exception from HMRC (*SI 2001/1004, regs 91, 93*).

## CLASS 4 NIC PROFIT LIMITS

*(SSCBA 1992, s 15(3))*

| Tax Year | Lower profits limit £ | Upper profits limit £ |
|---|---|---|
| 2013–14 | 7,755 | 41,450 |
| 2012–13 | 7,605 | 42,475 |
| 2011–12 | 7,225 | 42,475 |
| 2010–11 | 5,715 | 43,875 |
| 2009–10 | 5,715 | 43,875 |
| 2008–09 | 5,435 | 40,040 |
| 2007–08 | 5,225 | 34,840 |

**Notes**

(1)    *General* – Class 4 contributions are payable at the main rate on profits between the lower and upper profits limits, and at the additional rate on profits above the upper profits limit.

(2)    *Deferment* – An individual can apply to defer payment of Class 4 NIC if appropriate, in order to avoid an overpayment of contributions (eg if there are earnings from both employment and self-employment in the same tax year). However, contributions remain payable at the additional rate. An application to HMRC for deferment of payment of Class 4 (and/or Class 2) NICs is made on form CA72B, which is available via HMRC's website (www.hmrc.gov.uk/forms/ca72b.pdf).

(3)    *Annual maximum* – Class 4 contributions are subject to an annual maximum, calculated in accordance with *SI 2001/1004, reg 100*. The liability for contributions at the main rate is broadly limited to a maximum of 53 times the appropriate weekly amount of Class 2 NICs, plus the maximum amount of Class 4 contributions payable at the main rate, less any Class 2 NICs and any Class 1 NICs paid at the main rate. However, Class 4 NICs remain payable at the additional rate. An application to HMRC for a refund of Class 4 NICs (if appropriate) can be made on form CA5610, which is available via HMRC's website (www.hmrc.gov.uk/forms/ca5610.pdf).

*15*

# Tax Credits

## CHILD TAX CREDIT (CTC)

*(Child Tax Credit Regulations 2002, SI 2002/2007, reg 7, as amended)*

### Maximum amounts per year:

| Rates | 2013–14 | 2012–13 | 2011–12 |
|---|---|---|---|
| Family element (Basic) | £545 | £545 | £545 |
| Child element (for each child or qualifying young person) | £2,720 | £2,690 | £2,555 |
| Disabled child element (additional payment for each disabled child or qualifying young person) | £3,015 | £2,950 | £2,800 |
| Severely disabled child element (further additional payment for each severely disabled child or qualifying young person) | £1,220 | £1,190 | £1,130 |

**Notes**

(1) *Eligibility* – CTC is paid to the main carer for children up to 16 years old, or 18 in full-time education. CTC is separate from and additional to Child Benefit (see **Chapter 18**).

(2) *Claims* – Tax Credit claims are made provisionally for the coming year based on the previous year's income (2012–13 income forms the basis of 2013–14 claims). A Tax Credits claim must be renewed by 31 July, but estimated figures can be included, which must be finalised by the following 31 January.

(3) *Qualifying young person* – For the meaning of 'qualifying young person', see *SI 2002/2007, regs 4, 5*.

(4) *Disabled or severely disabled* – As to what constitutes disability or severe disability for these purposes, see *SI 2002/2007, reg 8*.

(5) *Further information* – Guidance for advisers including access to all the Tax Credits legislation can be found on: www.revenuebenefits.org.uk/tax-credits/

## WORKING TAX CREDIT (WTC)

(*Working Tax Credit (Entitlement and Maximum Rate) Regulations 2002, SI 2002/2005*)

### Maximum amounts per year

(*SI 2002/2005, reg 20(1), Sch 2, para 1*):

| Rates and Thresholds | 2013–14 | 2012–13 | 2011–12 |
|---|---|---|---|
| Basic element (*reg 4*) | £1,920 | £1,920 | £1,920 |
| Second adult and lone parent element (*regs 11, 12*) | £1,970 | £1,950 | £1,950 |
| 30 hour element (*reg 10*) | £790 | £790 | £790 |
| Disability element (*reg 9*) | £2,855 | £2,790 | £2,650 |
| Severe disability element (*reg 17*) | £1,220 | £1,190 | £1,130 |
| 50+ Return to work payment (16–29 hours) (*reg 18*) | – | – | £1,365 |
| 50+ Return to work payment (30+ hours) (*reg 18*) | – | – | £2,030 |

**Notes**

(1)   *Eligibility* – WTC are paid to employed and self-employed claimants on low incomes.

(2)   *50+ Tax Credits* – These elements were removed from the Tax Credits system with effect from 6 April 2012 (www.hmrc.gov.uk/budget2010/individuals.htm).

(3)   *Online tools* – An online questionnaire to assist in determining entitlement to Tax Credits is available on HMRC's website (www.hmrc.gov.uk/taxcredits/start/who-qualifies/quick-questionnaire.htm). An online Tax Credits calculator is also available via the Tax Credits section of the HMRC website (www.hmrc.gov.uk/taxcredits/payments-entitlement/entitlement/question-how-much.htm).

## CHILDCARE ELEMENT OF THE WORKING TAX CREDIT

(*Working Tax Credit (Entitlement and Maximum Rate) Regulations 2002, SI 2002/2005*)

### Maximum rates per year

(*SI 2002/2005, reg 20(2), (3)*):

| Rates and Thresholds | 2013–14 | 2012–13 | 2011–12 |
|---|---|---|---|
| Maximum eligible cost for one child (per week) | £175 | £175 | £175 |
| Maximum eligible cost for two or more children (per week) | £300 | £300 | £300 |
| Percentage of eligible costs covered | 70% | 70% | 70% |

**Notes**

(1)  *Entitlement* – The childcare element applies where the claimant pays for registered or approved childcare (*SI 2001/2005, regs 13, 14*).

(2)  *Childcare help from employers* – Employers may provide tax free child care vouchers to their employees (see **Chapter 2**). An online calculator helps Tax Credit claimants decide whether it would be beneficial to accept the employer provided childcare vouchers and how this would affect their Tax Credit entitlement (www.hmrc.gov.uk/calcs/ccin.htm).

(3)  *New childcare vouchers* – From Autumn 2015 parents will be able to buy childcare vouchers through an online scheme, with the cost subsidised by the Government at the rate of £20 for every £80 paid by the parent, up to a limit of £1,200 per child. The employer provided system of childcare vouchers will be phased out (Treasury press release: www.hm-treasury.gov.uk/press_29_13.htm).

## INCOME THRESHOLDS AND WITHDRAWAL RATES

*(Tax Credits Act 2002, ss 7, 13(2); Tax Credits (Income Thresholds and Determination of Rates) Regulations 2002, SI 2002/2008, regs 3, 7, 8)*

| **Annual Rates and Thresholds** | **2013–14** | **2012–13** | **2011–12** |
| --- | --- | --- | --- |
| First income threshold | £6,420 | £6,420 | £6,420 |
| First withdrawal (or taper) rate | 41% | 41% | 41% |
| Second income threshold | – | – | £40,000 |
| Second withdrawal rate | – | – | 41% |
| First threshold for those entitled to CTC only | £15,910 | £15,860 | £15,860 |
| Income rise disregard | £5,000 | £10,000 | £10,000 |
| Income fall disregard | £2,500 | £2,500 | – |

**Notes**

(1)  *First withdrawal rate* – Entitlement of a claimant of both WTC and CTC (or WTC only) is reduced at the first withdrawal rate on each £1 by which their income exceeds the first income threshold. Detailed guidance on calculating Tax Credits can be found on the Revenue Benefits website (www.revenuebenefits.org.uk/tax-credits/guidance/how-do-tax-credits-work/calculating-tax-credits/).

(2)  *Second withdrawal rate* – With effect from 2012–13 there is no second income threshold, and the family element starts to be reduced (still at the first withdrawal rate on each further £1 of income) as soon as all of the other credits have been withdrawn.

(3)  *Income disregards* – Claimants' awards are initially based on their previous year's income. Once they report their current year's income, the award can be finalised. For 2013–14, the first £5,000 of any excess of their current year's income over that of the previous year, or the first £2,500 of any shortfall, is disregarded when calculating their final award (see www.revenuebenefits.org.uk/tax-credits/guidance/how-do-tax-credits-work/understanding-the-disregard/).

187

## UNIVERSAL CREDIT AND TAX CREDITS REFORM

Tax Credits and a range of other state benefits are to be replaced by a new benefit called Universal Credit from October 2013, although a pilot programme will start in April 2013. The full transition from Tax Credits to Universal Credit will not be completed until the end of 2017.

**Notes**

(1)   *Payment* – Universal Credit claims will be paid monthly rather than weekly or fortnightly.

(2)   *Claims* – Couples living in the same household will make a joint claim, as is currently the case for Tax Credits.

(3)   *Cash basis reporting* – Self-employed claimants will have to report their net income for the month online every month using a cash basis of accounting.

(4)   *Use of RTI* – Employers are required to report pay and deductions for employees under real time information (RTI) generally on or before the employee is paid (see **Chapter 2**). This data will be passed to Department of Work and Pensions who will adjust the amounts paid to Universal Credit claimants on a monthly basis.

(5)   *Further information* – Guidance for advisers on Universal Credit can be found here: www.revenuebenefits.org.uk/tax-credits/transition-to-universal-credit/

# Statutory payments

## NATIONAL MINIMUM WAGE (NMW) RATES

*(NMWA 1998, s 2; SI 1999/584, Pt 2)*

| Hourly rate from | Adult rate (Aged 21 and over) | Development rate (Aged 18 to 20) | Under 18 rate | Apprentice rate |
|---|---|---|---|---|
| | £ | £ | £ | £ |
| 1 October 2012 | 6.19 | 4.98 | 3.68 | 2.65 |
| 1 October 2011 | 6.08 | 4.98 | 3.68 | 2.60 |
| 1 October 2010 | 5.93 | 4.92 | 3.64 | 2.50 |
| 1 October 2009 | 5.80 | 4.83 | 3.57 | – |
| 1 October 2008 | 5.73 | 4.77 | 3.53 | – |
| 1 October 2007 | 5.52 | 4.60 | 3.40 | – |
| 1 October 2006 | 5.35 | 4.45 | 3.30 | – |

**Notes**

(1) *Adult rate (SI 1999/584, reg 11)* – The adult NMW rate was extended to workers aged 21 or over from 1 October 2010 *(reg 13(1))*. Previously, this rate applied to workers aged 22 or over.

(2) *Development rate (SI 1999/584, reg 13(1))* – From 1 October 2010, this rate applies to workers who have reached the age of 18, but not 21. Previously, this rate applied to workers who had not reached the age of 22.

(3) *Apprentice rate (SI 1999/584, reg 13(3))* – This applies to apprentices who are either under 19, or in the first year of their apprenticeship.

(4) *Further information* – Guidance on NMW for employers see: www.hmrc.gov.uk/ payerti/payroll/pay-and-deductions/nmw.htm.

## NMW: ACCOMMODATION OFFSET RATE

*(SI 1999/584, regs 30(d), 36)*

| Period | Daily offset | Period | Daily offset |
|---|---|---|---|
| | £ | | £ |
| 1 October 2012 | 4.82 | 1 October 2008 | 4.46 |
| 1 October 2011 | 4.73 | 1 October 2007 | 4.30 |
| 1 October 2010 | 4.61 | 1 October 2006 | 4.15 |
| 1 October 2009 | 4.51 | 1 October 2005 | 3.90 |

**Notes**

(1)   *Daily rates* – The above rates represent the maximum permitted daily rate of accommodation offset by the employer in relation to the NMW.

(2)   *Further information* – An interactive calculator for the NMW rates when accommodation is provided by the employer is available on the Gov.uk website: www.gov.uk/national-minimum-wage-accommodation.

## STATUTORY SICK PAY (SSP)

(*SI 1995/512, SI 1995/513*)

| Tax year | Weekly earnings threshold | Weekly rate |
|---|---|---|
| | £ | £ |
| 2013–14 | 109 | 86.70 |
| 2012–13 | 107 | 85.85 |
| 2011–12 | 102 | 81.60 |
| 2010–11 | 97 | 79.15 |
| 2009–10 | 95 | 79.15 |
| 2008–09 | 90 | 75.40 |
| 2007–08 | 87 | 72.55 |

**Notes**

(1)   *No SSP* – If the weekly earnings do not exceed the earnings threshold no SSP is payable.

(2)   *Recovery of SSP* – Employers can recover SSP from HMRC when the total SSP paid exceeds 13% of the employers' and employees' class 1 NICs payable for the month for which SSP is paid.

(3)   *Further information* – For guidance on SSP see: www.hmrc.gov.uk/payerti/ employee/statutory-pay/ssp-overview.htm.

## STATUTORY MATERNITY PAY (SMP)

(*SI 1994/1882*)

| Tax year | Weekly earnings threshold | Weekly flat rate |
|---|---|---|
| | £ | £ |
| 2013–14 | 109 | 136.78 |
| 2012–13 | 107 | 135.45 |
| 2011–12 | 102 | 128.73 |
| 2010–11 | 97 | 124.88 |
| 2009–10 | 95 | 123.06 |

| Tax year | Weekly earnings threshold | Weekly flat rate |
|---|---|---|
| | £ | £ |
| 2008–09 | 90 | 117.18 |
| 2007–08 | 87 | 112.75 |

**Notes**

(1)  *Rates* – SMP is paid at 90% of average weekly earnings for the first six weeks and at the lower of the flat rate above and 90% of average weekly earnings for the next 33 weeks.

(2)  *No SMP* – If weekly earnings do not exceed the weekly earnings threshold no SMP is payable.

(3)  *Recovery of SMP* – Employers can recover SMP from HMRC at 92% of the amount paid if their total lass 1 NIC liability for previous tax year was more than £45,000, or the recovery amount is set a 103% if total Class 1 NIC liability for the employer was up to £45,000 in the previous tax year.

(4)  *Further information* – For guidance for employers on SMP see: www.hmrc.gov.uk/payerti/employee/statutory-pay/smp-overview.htm

## STATUTORY ADOPTION PAY (SAP)

*(SI 2002/2818)*

| Tax year | Weekly Earnings threshold | Weekly flat rate |
|---|---|---|
| | £ | £ |
| 2013–14 | 109 | 136.78 |
| 2012–13 | 107 | 135.45 |
| 2011–12 | 102 | 128.73 |
| 2010–11 | 97 | 124.88 |
| 2009–10 | 95 | 123.06 |
| 2008–09 | 90 | 117.18 |
| 2007–08 | 87 | 112.75 |

**Notes**

(1)  *Rates* – SAP is paid at the lower of the flat rate above and 90% of average weekly earnings for the 39 weeks.

(2)  *No SAP* – If weekly earnings do not exceed the weekly earnings threshold no SAP is payable.

(3)  *Recovery of SAP* – Employers can recover SAP from HMRC at the rate of 92% of SAP paid out if the employer's total Class 1 NIC liability for previous tax year was more than £45,000, or at the rate of 103% of the SAP paid, if the employer's total Class 1 NIC liability was up to £45,000 in the previous tax year.

(4)   *Further information* – For guidance for employers on SAP see: www.hmrc.gov.uk/
payerti/employee/statutory-pay/sap-overview.htm

## STATUTORY PATERNITY PAY

*(SSCBA 1992, Pt 12ZA; SI 2011/678; SI 2010/1060)*

| Tax year | Weekly earnings threshold | Weekly flat rate |
|---|---|---|
| | £ | £ |
| 2013–14 | 109 | 136.78 |
| 2012–13 | 107 | 135.45 |
| 2011–12 | 102 | 128.73 |
| 2010–11 | 97 | 124.88 |
| 2009–10 | 95 | 123.06 |
| 2008–09 | 90 | 117.18 |
| 2007–08 | 87 | 112.75 |

**Notes**

(1)   *OSPP Rates* – Ordinary Statutory Paternity Pay (OSPP) is paid at the lower of the
flat rate above and 90% of average weekly earnings for up to weeks.

(2)   *ASPP rates* – Additional statutory paternity pay (ASPP) is payable at the same
rates as OSPP. It is paid when either the mother/adopter dies, or when the child is
at least 20 weeks old and the mother has returned to work before the end of their
maternity or adoption leave pay period.

(3)   *No SPP* – If the employee's weekly earnings do not exceed the weekly earnings
threshold no OSPP or ASPP is payable.

(4)   *Recovery of SPP* – Employers can recover OSPP and ASPP from HMRC at the
rate of 92% in total Class 1 NIC liability for previous tax year was more than
£45,000, or at the rate of 103% if the employer's total Class 1 NIC liability was up
to £45,000.

(5)   *Further information* – For guidance on both types of paternity pay see: www.hmrc.
gov.uk/payerti/employee/statutory-pay/spp-overview.htm.

# HMRC Powers and Penalties

## NEW PENALTY REGIME

HMRC may impose penalties on taxpayers in the following circumstances:

- Late payment of tax or duty
- Late filing of returns
- Failure to notify chargeability to tax
- Errors on returns and documents
- Failure to keep or retain records
- VAT and excise wrong-doing
- Failure to submit returns online

**Notes**

(1) *General* – The structure of these penalties is now generally the same across all the taxes administered by HMRC, but the new penalty regime came into force at various times for different taxes as outlined below.

(2) *Record keeping*:

- *Main taxes* – The rules apply from 1 April 2009 in respect of income tax, CGT, corporation tax, direct tax claims not included in a return and VAT.

- *Other taxes (from 1 April 2010)* – IPT, SDLT, aggregates levy, climate change levy and landfill tax. In addition, record keeping requirements apply to bank payroll tax from 8 April 2010, and excise duties from 1 April 2011 (CH10100).

(3) *Time limits (for assessments, claims etc)* – The time limits entered into force from 1 April 2009 (VAT), 1 April 2010 (direct taxes, and IPT, aggregates levy, climate change levy and landfill tax) and 1 April 2011 (SDLT, SDRT, PRT, excise duty and IHT), subject to transitional provisions (in *SI 2009/403, art 10*) whereby in some cases the change in time limits does not apply until 1 April 2012.

(4) *Payment and enforcement: Taking control of goods etc – FA 2008, s 127, Sch 43* to be brought into force (England and Wales) by Statutory Instrument alongside the commencement of *TCEA 2007, Part 3*.

(5) *Penalties for errors*:

- *Main taxes* – Income tax (including PAYE and CIS), CGT, corporation tax, VAT, NICs.

- *Other taxes* – Including IPT, IHT, SDLT, SDRT, PRT and environmental taxes (aggregates levy, climate change levy, landfill tax); see CH81013 and CH81020.

(6)   *Penalties for failure to pay tax – Finance Act 2009, Sch 56 (Appointed Day and Consequential Provisions) Order, SI 2010/466* appoints 6 April 2010 as the day on which the penalty provisions apply in respect of PAYE and CIS payments, and tax charges payable by scheme administrators under *FA 2004, Pt 4*.

(7)   *Late payment Interest – Taxes and Duties (Interest Rate) (Amendment) Regulations, SI 2009/2032*, which align rates for those taxes where HMRC charged and paid interest, came into force on 12 August 2009.

(8)   *Other Taxes Interest –* The interest regime in *FA 2009, s 103* came into force on 31 August 2010 for bank payroll tax *(SI 2010/1878)*, 31 October 2011 for income tax self assessment *(SI 2011/701)* and CIS *(SI 2011/2391)*, and on 6 October 2011 for other taxes generally *(SI 2011/2401)*.

## MATTERS APPLYING TO ALL PENALTIES

### Classification of territories

- The categories are classified in accordance with the penalty regime for errors (in *FA 2007, Sch 24, para 21A*).

- *Category 1 information –* This is information involving:

  (a)   A domestic matter; or

  (b)   An offshore matter, where the territory is in Category 1 or it is information which would enable or assist HMRC to assess a tax other than income tax or CGT. Category 1 and Category 3 territories are designated by Treasury order *(SI 2011/976)*. A list of Category 1 and Category 3 territories is available on HMRC's website: www.hmrc.gov.uk/news/territories-category.htm.

- *Category 2 information –* This is information involving an offshore matter, in a *Category 2* territory, which would enable or assist HMRC to assess an income tax or CGT liability. *A Category 2 territory* is one that is neither a Category 1 nor a Category 3 territory.

- *Category 3 information –* This is information involving an offshore matter, in a *Category 3* territory, which would enable or assist HMRC to assess an income tax or CGT liability.

## SELF ASSESSMENT PENALTY PROVISIONS

*(TMA 1970, ss 59A(6), 93, 93A; FA 2007, s 97, Sch 24; FA 2008, s 113, Sch 36; s 115, Sch 37; s 123, Sch 41; FA 2009, s 106, Sch 55; FA 2009, s 107, Sch 56; FA 2011, s 86, Sch 23)*

### Late payments: 2010–11 and later tax years

*(FA 2009, s 107, Sch 56)*

| Length of delay | Penalty |
| --- | --- |
| 30 days | 5% of the unpaid tax |
| 6 months | 5% of the unpaid tax (additional) |
| 12 months | 5% of the unpaid tax (additional) |

**Notes**

(1)  *General* – The penalty regime for failure to make payments on time was introduced in *FA 2009, s 107, Sch 56*. The above penalties apply to late balancing payments of income tax and late payments of capital gains tax under self-assessment (ie based on tax returns for individuals or trustees etc, and in certain other circumstances) with effect from 6 April 2011, in relation to 2010–11 and later tax years, following its entry into force by Treasury order (*SI 2011/702, art 3*).

The above penalties replace the surcharge provisions on unpaid income tax and capital gains tax (TMA 1970, s 59C), which apply to balancing payments for tax years up to 2009–10 (see **Surcharges** below).

(2)  *Assessments and appeals* – HMRC must assess the late payment penalty, and notify the person liable. The penalty notice must state the period to which the penalty relates. The penalty is payable within 30 days from the day on which the penalty notice is issued. There is a right of appeal against both the imposition of a penalty, and the amount involved (*FA 2009, Sch 56, paras 11, 13*).

(3)  *Penalty reduction and suspension* – HMRC may reduce a late payment penalty in 'special circumstances', which does not include inability to pay (*FA 2009, Sch 56, para 9*). In addition, a defence of 'reasonable excuse' may be available (*Sch 56, para 16*).

## Surcharges (up to 2009–10)

*(TMA 1970 s 59C)*

| Tax Overdue | Surcharge amount |
| --- | --- |
| 28 days following the due date | 5% of the unpaid tax |
| 6 months following the due date | 5% of the unpaid tax (additional) |

**Notes**

(1)  *General* – Surcharges apply to any balancing payment of income tax (and class 4 NIC) or capital gains tax payable for a tax year, in respect of personal tax returns up to 2009–10 inclusive. Surcharges attract interest if paid late.

(2)  *Appeals* – An appeal against a surcharge can be made within 30 days of the date on which the surcharge was imposed.

(3)  *Exceptions* – A surcharge is not imposed if a penalty has been incurred based on the same tax, or if agreement has been reached with HMRC in advance to pay the tax by instalments, where those instalments are duly paid in accordance with the agreement.

(4)  *New regime* – As to penalties for the late payment of income tax and capital gains tax for 2010–11 and later years, see Late payments: 2010–11 and later tax years above.

## PAYMENTS ON ACCOUNT

*(TMA 1970, s 59A(6))*

The maximum penalty for fraudulent or negligent claims by taxpayers to reduce payments on account is the difference between the correct amount payable on account and the amount of any payment on account made by him.

## RECOVERY OF HMRC DEBTS THROUGH PAYE

*(ITEPA 2003, s 684(2), (3A); SI 2011/1585)*

- PAYE regulations may provide (among other things) for deductions to be made in respect of 'relevant debts' (see below) of a payee. Deductions up to £3,000 may be made from a payee's income for a tax year, without the payee's consent.

- The £3,000 limit was increased with effect from 20 July 2011. The previous limit was £2,000.

- 'Relevant debts' are defined as including any debt payable to the Commissioners for HMRC, excluding tax credits *(ITEPA 2003, s 684(7AA))*.

- HMRC may determine an employee's PAYE code, to recover all or part of a relevant debt up to the above limit *(SI 2003/2682, reg 14A(1))*, with effect from 6 April 2012 *(SI 2011/1584, reg 2(2))*.

## Late returns: 2010–11 and later years

*(FA 2009, s 106, Sch 55)*

| Period | Penalty | Notes |
|---|---|---|
| Up to 3 months late | £100 | Fixed penalty |
| More than 3 months late | £10 per day | • Daily penalties apply for up to 90 days (maximum £900). <br> • Payable only if HMRC give notice of the penalty, and the notice specifies the date from which the penalty is payable. |
| More than 6 months late | Greater of: <br> • 5% of tax liability; and <br> • £300 | 'Tax liability' refers to any tax which would have been shown in the return in question. |
| More than 12 months late: <br> Any case except below | Greater of: <br> • 5% of tax liability; and <br> • £300 | |
| Information withheld | Greater of: <br> • Relevant % of tax liability; and <br> • £300 | See percentages below |
| Deliberate but not concealed | | |
| Deliberate and concealed | Greater of: <br> • Relevant % of tax liability; and <br> • £300 | See percentages below |

| Period | Penalty | | Notes | |
|---|---|---|---|---|
| Information withheld deliberately | **Unprompted disclosure** | | **Prompted disclosure** | |
| | **Max. Penalty** | **Min. Penalty** | **Max. Penalty** | **Min. Penalty** |
| Category 1 information | | | | |
| Deliberate but not concealed | 70% | 20% | 70% | 35% |
| Deliberate and concealed | 100% | 30% | 100% | 50% |
| Category 2 information | | | | |
| Deliberate but not concealed | 105% | 30% | 105% | 52.5% |
| Deliberate and concealed | 150% | 45% | 150% | 75% |
| Category 3 information | | | | |
| Deliberate but not concealed | 140% | 40% | 140% | 70% |
| Deliberate and concealed | 200% | 60% | 200% | 100% |

**Notes**

(1)  *General –* The above penalty regime for the late filing of income tax self-assessment returns (and certain others returns etc) introduced in *FA 2009, s 106, Sch 55* was brought into force by Treasury order (*SI 2011/702*; see also CH61120).

The *FA 2009, s 106, Sch 55* provisions were introduced with effect from 6 April 2011, in respect of returns for 2010–11 and later years, and were subsequently amended in respect of the offshore income penalty regime (see below).

As to the penalty provisions for earlier returns, see: **Late returns: 2009–10 and earlier years** below.

For 2010–11 returns, the penalty percentages where information is withheld are those which applied when the regime in *FA 2009, Sch 55* was originally introduced (ie prior to the introduction of the offshore income penalty regime from 6 April 2011 – see below). The penalty percentages are the same as shown in Category 1 above.

(2)  *Offshore income etc –* The penalty regime for late returns was amended (by *FA 2010, s 35, Sch 10*) in relation to offshore income etc. The amendments were introduced by Treasury order (SI 2011/975) with effect from 6 April 2011. The provisions apply to returns etc for 2011–12 onwards.

(3)  *Penalty aggregation –* A taxpayer may become liable to more than one category of penalty in respect of the same return etc (*FA 2009, Sch 55, para 1(3)*). However, where more than one tax-geared penalty arises, the aggregate must not exceed the following (*FA 2009, Sch 55, para 17(3)*):

- Deliberate withholding of Category 3 information – 200%
- Deliberate withholding of Category 2 information – 150%
- All other cases – 100%

(4)  *Penalty reductions –* HMRC may reduce a penalty in 'special circumstances' which does not include inability to pay (*FA 2009, Sch 55, para 16*). In addition, a defence of 'reasonable excuse' may be available (*Sch 55, para 23*).

(5)   *Penalty aggregation* – A taxpayer may become liable to more than one category of penalty in respect of the same return etc (*FA 2009, Sch 55, para 1(3)*). However, where more than one tax-geared penalty arises, the aggregate must not exceed the following (*FA 2009, Sch 55, para 17(3)*):

- Deliberate withholding of Category 3 information – 200%

- Deliberate withholding of Category 2 information – 150%

- All other cases – 100%

(6)   *Penalty reductions* – HMRC may reduce a penalty in 'special circumstances' which does not include inability to pay (*FA 2009, Sch 55, para 16*). In addition, a defence of 'reasonable excuse' may be available (*Sch 55, para 23*).

## Late returns: 2009–10 and earlier years

(*TMA 1970, s 93*)

(1)   *General* – The following penalties apply to the failure to make a tax return (for individuals and trustees) for 2009–10 and earlier years:

- £100 if the return is not delivered by the filing date (see **Chapter 1: Personal Taxation**);

- A further penalty of up to £60 per day if the failure continues and HMRC obtain a direction from the tribunal to charge daily penalties;

- A further £100 (where a daily penalty is not imposed) if the failure continues more than six months from the filing date.

- A tax-related penalty if the failure continues more than one year from the filing date, of up to the amount of any tax liability which would have been shown on the return.

(2)   *Penalty 'cap'* – The above fixed penalties of £100 cannot exceed the tax liability which would be shown in the return (*TMA 1970, s 93(7)*), or the amount of tax outstanding at the due date if the return had been delivered on the filing date (*s 93(9)*), ie any payments on account (under *TMA 1970, s 59A*) or payments otherwise made before the filing date are taken into account, as is any PAYE or other tax deducted at source in respect of that year (EM4562).

(3)   *Reasonable excuse* – The above fixed penalties of £100 can be set aside by the tribunal if the taxpayer had a reasonable excuse for not delivering the return throughout the period of default (*TMA 1970, s 93(8)*). Information on what HMRC consider to be a 'reasonable excuse' is available on the HMRC website (see www.hmrc.gov.uk/sa/deadlines-penalties.htm#3).

(4)   *Penalty exception* – Following the decision in *Steeden v Carver* [1999] STC (SCD) 283, HMRC will not charge a penalty where a return is delivered on the day after the filing date (see SALF208 and SAM120650).

(5)   *Partnerships (TMA 1970, s 93A)* – The following penalties apply to the failure to make a partnership tax return:

- £100 per 'relevant partner' (ie each person who was a partner at any time during the period covered by the return) if the return is not delivered by the filing date;

- A further penalty of up to £60 per day per relevant partner if the failure continues and HMRC obtain a direction from the tribunal to charge daily penalties;

- A further £100 per relevant partner (where a daily penalty is not imposed) if the failure continues more than six months from the filing date.

The fixed £100 penalties are not subject to the potential reduction described in note 2 above. However, there is no tax-related penalty for the late filing of partnership returns, as the partnership itself is not liable to tax.

## Failure to notify liability, etc

*(FA 2008, s 123, Sch 41)*

*Category 1 Territory*

| Behaviour | Unprompted disclosure | | | Prompted disclosure | | |
|---|---|---|---|---|---|---|
| | Maximum penalty | Minimum penalty | | Maximum penalty | Minimum penalty | |
| | | Case A | Case B | | Case A | Case B |
| Any other case* | 30% | 0% | 10% | 30% | 10% | 20% |
| Deliberate but not concealed | 70% | 20% | – | 70% | 35% | – |
| Deliberate and concealed | 100% | 30% | – | 100% | 50% | – |

*Category 2 Territory*

| Behaviour | Unprompted disclosure | | | Prompted disclosure | | |
|---|---|---|---|---|---|---|
| | Maximum penalty | Minimum penalty | | Maximum penalty | Minimum penalty | |
| | | Case A | Case B | | Case A | Case B |
| Any other case* | 45% | 0% | 15% | 45% | 15% | 30% |
| Deliberate but not concealed | 105% | 30% | – | 105% | 52.5% | – |
| Deliberate and concealed | 150% | 45% | – | 150% | 75% | – |

*Category 3 Territory*

| Behaviour | Unprompted disclosure | | | Prompted disclosure | | |
|---|---|---|---|---|---|---|
| | Maximum penalty | Minimum penalty | | Maximum penalty | Minimum penalty | |
| | | Case A | Case B | | Case A | Case B |
| Any other case* | 60% | 0% | 20% | 60% | 20% | 40% |
| Deliberate but not concealed | 140% | 40% | – | 140% | 70% | – |
| Deliberate and concealed | 200% | 60% | – | 200% | 100% | – |

* *Case A and Case B* – These apply to 'any other case'. Case A applies if HMRC become aware of the failure less than 12 months after the tax first becomes unpaid due to the failure. Otherwise, Case B applies *(FA 2008, Sch 41, para 13(3))*.

**Notes**

(1) *General* – The penalties regime for failure to notify (and certain VAT and excise wrongdoing – see note (3) below) generally applies (except in relation to offshore income – see note (2) below) where the obligation to notify arises on or after 1 April 2010. For direct tax purposes, the first tax periods for which the penalties will therefore apply are 2009–10 (income tax and capital gains tax) and accounting periods ending from 31 March 2010 (corporation tax). For indirect tax purposes, the new penalty regime applies where the obligation to notify arises on or after 1 April 2010 (*SI 2009/511; see also CH71120*).

The maximum penalty levels when the regime in *FA 2008, Sch 41* was originally introduced (ie prior to the introduction of the penalty regime for offshore income from 6 April 2011) are the same as in *Category 1* above, ie:

- Deliberate and concealed act or failure – 100%;

- Deliberate but not concealed – 70%; and

- Any other case – 30%.

The 30% penalty is subject to the following possible reductions for disclosure:

- Unprompted – A minimum of 0% if HMRC become aware of the failure less than 12 months after the tax first becomes unpaid due to the failure; or a minimum of 10% in any other case;

- Prompted – A minimum of 10% if HMRC become aware of the failure less than 12 months after the tax first becomes unpaid due to the failure; or a minimum of 20% in any other case;

(2) *Offshore income etc* – The penalty regime for failure to notify etc was amended (by *FA 2010, s 35, Sch 10*) in relation to offshore income etc. The amendments were introduced by Treasury order (*SI 2011/975*) with effect from 6 April 2011.

(3) *Other penalties* – Separate penalty provisions apply in respect of the unauthorised issue of an invoice showing VAT (*FA 2008, Sch 41, para 2*), and certain excise wrongdoings (*FA 2008, Sch 41, paras 2, 3, 4, 6B–6C*). These are treated as Case B.

(4) *Reductions and exceptions* – HMRC may reduce a penalty in 'special circumstances', which does not include inability to pay, and a defence of 'reasonable excuse' may also be available in some cases (*FA 2008, Sch 41, paras 14, 20*).

# Errors in returns and documents

## Errors in VAT returns, etc

(*FA 2007, s 97, Sch 24*)

| Behaviour | Unprompted disclosure | | Prompted disclosure | |
|---|---|---|---|---|
| | Maximum penalty | Minimum penalty | Maximum penalty | Minimum penalty |
| Careless | 30% | 0% | 30% | 15% |
| Deliberate but not concealed | 70% | 20% | 70% | 35% |
| Deliberate and concealed | 100% | 30% | 100% | 50% |

**Notes**

(1) *General* – For penalties to apply, the inaccuracy must be careless or deliberate and result in an underpayment of tax. Where a document contains more than one inaccuracy, a penalty is payable for each inaccuracy (*FA 2007, Sch 24, paras 1, 4(1)*).

(2) *Scope* – For VAT purposes, penalties can apply in relation to the following:

● VAT returns under regulations made under *VATA 1994, Sch 11, para 2*;

● Returns, statements or declaration in connection with a claim; and

● Any document which is likely to be relied upon by HMRC to determine, without further inquiry, a question about: (a) a person, P's liability to tax; (b) payments by P by way of or in connection with tax; (c) any other payment by P (including penalties); or (d) repayments, or any other kind of payment or credit, to P.

(3) *Commencement* – The above penalties generally apply to returns for tax periods commencing from 1 April 2008, and for which the filing date is on or after 1 April 2009 (*SI 2008/568*). Exceptions to this general rule include those below; the filing date for these documents must be on or after 1 April 2009 (see CH81012):

● Claims under the Thirteenth Council Directive (arrangements for the refund of VAT to persons not established in Community territory) must be for years commencing on or after 1 July 2008.

● Claims under the Eighth Council Directive (arrangements for the refund of VAT to taxable persons not established in the territory of the country) must be for years commencing on or after 1 January 2009.

(3) *Type and quality of disclosure* – The maximum penalties above are subject to potential reduction, depending on whether the disclosure of the inaccuracy is 'prompted' or 'unprompted', and reflecting the quality of the disclosure.

(4) *Error by another person* – A penalty can also apply to an error in a taxpayer's document which is attributable to another person (*FA 2007, Sch 24, para 1A*). Penalties range from 30% to 100% for unprompted disclosure, and 50% to 100% for prompted disclosure.

(5) *Special reductions and suspensions* – HMRC may reduce a penalty in 'special circumstances', and penalties may be suspended at HMRC's discretion in appropriate cases (*FA 2007, Sch 24, paras 11, 14*).

## Under-assessment by HMRC

(*FA 2007, Sch 24, paras 2, 4C*)

● *General* – A penalty can be charged on a person if an HMRC assessment understates the tax payable, and the person fails to take reasonable steps to notify HMRC of the under-assessment within 30 days from the date of the assessment.

● *Level of penalty* – The maximum penalty payable is 30% of the potential lost revenue. The penalty may be reduced in the same way as for errors in returns where the person would otherwise be liable to a penalty at the 30% rate.

● *Commencement* – The penalty provisions generally apply to assessments for tax periods commencing from 1 April 2008 (*SI 2008/568, art 2(b)*).

- *Special reductions* – HMRC may reduce a penalty because of 'special circumstances' (*FA 2007, Sch 24, para 11*).

*Category 1 Territory*

| Behaviour | Unprompted disclosure | | Prompted disclosure | |
|---|---|---|---|---|
| | Maximum penalty | Minimum penalty | Maximum penalty | Minimum penalty |
| Careless | 30% | 0% | 30% | 15% |
| Deliberate but not concealed | 70% | 20% | 70% | 35% |
| Deliberate and concealed | 100% | 30% | 100% | 50% |

*Category 2 Territory*

| Behaviour | Unprompted disclosure | | Prompted disclosure | |
|---|---|---|---|---|
| | Maximum penalty | Minimum penalty | Maximum penalty | Minimum penalty |
| Careless | 45% | 0% | 45% | 22.5% |
| Deliberate but not concealed | 105% | 30% | 105% | 52.5% |
| Deliberate and concealed | 150% | 45% | 150% | 75% |

*Category 3 Territory*

| Behaviour | Unprompted disclosure | | Prompted disclosure | |
|---|---|---|---|---|
| | Maximum penalty | Minimum penalty | Maximum penalty | Minimum penalty |
| Careless | 60% | 0% | 60% | 30% |
| Deliberate but not concealed | 140% | 40% | 140% | 70% |
| Deliberate and concealed | 200% | 60% | 200% | 100% |

**Notes**

(1)   *General* – The penalties regime for errors generally applies (except in relation to offshore income – see note (4) below) to returns for tax periods commencing from 1 April 2008, and for which the filing date is on or after 1 April 2009 (*SI 2008/568*; see also CH81012).

The levels of penalty applicable when the regime was originally introduced (ie for periods prior to the introduction of the penalty regime in respect of offshore income from 6 April 2011) are the same as in *Category 1* above.

(2)   *Disclosure* – The maximum penalties above are subject to potential reduction, depending on whether the disclosure of the inaccuracy is 'prompted' or 'unprompted', and reflecting the quality of the disclosure.

(3)   *Other penalties* – A penalty can also apply to an error in a taxpayer's document which is attributable to another person (*FA 2007, Sch 24, para 1A*). Penalties range from 30% to 100% for unprompted disclosure, and 50% to 100% for prompted disclosure.

In addition, a penalty can apply if the taxpayer fails to notify HMRC of the under assessment of a relevant tax liability within 30 days from the date of the assessment

(*FA 2007, Sch 24, para 2*). Penalties range from 0% to 30% for unprompted disclosure, and 15% to 30% for prompted disclosure.

(4)    *Offshore income etc* – The penalty regime for errors was amended (by *FA 2010, s 35, Sch 10*) in relation to offshore income etc. The amendments were introduced by Treasury order (*SI 2011/975*) with effect from 6 April 2011.

(5)    *Special reductions and suspensions* – HMRC may reduce a penalty in 'special circumstances', which does not include inability to pay, and penalties may be suspended at HMRC's discretion in appropriate cases (*FA 2007, Sch 24, paras 11, 14*).

# FAILURE TO KEEP OR RETAIN TAX RECORDS

(*TMA 1970, s 12B, FA 2008, s 115, Sch 37*)

(1)    The maximum penalty for failing to keep and preserve records (in accordance with *TMA 1970, s 12B*) is £3,000 per tax year (or accounting period) (*s 12B(5)*).

(2)    The record keeping requirements introduced in *Finance Act 2008* apply for direct tax and VAT purposes from 1 April 2009 (*SI 2009/402*) and for other taxes and duties generally from 1 April 2010 (*SI 2010/815*).

# PENALTIES FOR 2009–10 AND EARLIER YEARS

## Late returns

(*TMA 1970, s 93*)

(1)    *General* – The following penalties apply to the failure to make a tax return (for individuals and trustees) for 2009–10 and earlier years:

- £100 if the return is not delivered by the filing date (see **Chapter 1: Personal Taxation**);

- A further penalty of up to £60 per day if the failure continues and HMRC obtain a direction from the tribunal to charge daily penalties;

- A further £100 (where a daily penalty is not imposed) if the failure continues more than six months from the filing date.

- A tax-related penalty if the failure continues more than one year from the filing date, of up to the amount of any tax liability which would have been shown on the return.

(2)    *Penalty 'cap'* – The above fixed penalties of £100 cannot exceed the tax liability which would be shown in the return (*TMA 1970, s 93(7)*), or the amount of tax outstanding at the due date if the return had been delivered on the filing date (*s 93(9)*), ie any payments on account (under *TMA 1970, s 59A*) or payments otherwise made before the filing date are taken into account, as is any PAYE or other tax deducted at source in respect of that year (EM4562).

(3)    *Reasonable excuse* – The above fixed penalties of £100 can be set aside by the tribunal if the taxpayer had a reasonable excuse for not delivering the return throughout the period of default (*TMA 1970, s 93(8)*). Information on what HMRC

consider to be a 'reasonable excuse' is available here: www.hmrc.gov.uk/sa/deadlines-penalties.htm#3.

(4)   *Penalty exception* – Following the decision in *Steeden v Carver* [1999] STC (SCD) 283, HMRC will not charge a penalty where a return is delivered on the day after the filing date (see SALF208 and SAM120650).

(5)   *Partnerships (TMA 1970, s 93A)* – The following penalties apply to the failure to make a partnership tax return:

- £100 per 'relevant partner' (ie each person who was a partner at any time during the period covered by the return) if the return is not delivered by the filing date;

- A further penalty of up to £60 per day per relevant partner if the failure continues and HMRC obtain a direction from the tribunal to charge daily penalties;

- A further £100 per relevant partner (where a daily penalty is not imposed) if the failure continues more than six months from the filing date.

The fixed £100 penalties are not subject to the potential reduction described in note 2 above. However, there is no tax-related penalty for the late filing of partnership returns, as the partnership itself is not liable to tax.

## Interest on underpaid VAT (default interest)

(*VATA 1994, s 74*; HMRC Departmental interest rates; VAT Notice 700/43)

| Period from | Interest rate applicable |
|---|---|
|  | % |
| 29/9/09 | 3.00 |
| 24/3/09 | 2.50 |
| 27/1/09 | 3.50 |
| 6/1/09 | 4.50 |
| 6/12/08 | 5.50 |
| 6/11/08 | 6.50 |
| 6/1/08 | 7.50 |
| 6/8/07 | 8.50 |
| 6/9/06 | 7.50 |
| 6/9/05 | 6.50 |
| 6/9/04 | 7.50 |
| 6/12/03 | 6.50 |

**Notes**

(1)   *General* – Default interest is charged where appropriate on any amount of VAT which has been underdeclared or overclaimed, from the time the amount should have been paid to the time it is assessed. It is intended to provide 'commercial restitution' for the loss of understated or overclaimed VAT and should not be considered a penalty (see VAT Notice 700/43, para 1.2).

(2)   *Payment of interest* – If all the VAT liable to interest is not paid within 30 days of a notification from HMRC, further interest is chargeable. Interest continues to be charged on a monthly basis until all the VAT liable to interest is paid. HMRC will issue notification of these additional interest charges on a Notice of Assessment of Further Interest Form (VAT Notice 700/43, para 2.8).

## Interest on overpaid VAT in certain cases of official error

(*VATA 1994, s 78*; HMRC Departmental interest rates – 'Statutory interest')

| Period from | Interest rate |
|---|---|
| | % |
| 29/9/09 | 0.5 |
| 27/1/09 | 0.0 |
| 6/1/09 | 1.0 |
| 6/12/08 | 2.0 |
| 6/11/08 | 3.0 |
| 6/1/08 | 4.0 |
| 6/8/07 | 5.0 |
| 6/9/06 | 4.0 |
| 6/9/05 | 3.0 |
| 6/9/04 | 4.0 |
| 6/12/03 | 3.0 |

**Notes**

(1)   In addition to interest relating to errors, HMRC also pay interest if the mistake meant that the recipient had to wait an unreasonable time before receiving payment of an amount related to VAT. A separate claim must be made for any interest from HMRC, as it is not paid automatically (see www.hmrc.gov.uk/vat/managing/problems/corrections/receiving-interest.htm).

(2)   An interest claim (under *VATA 1994, s 78*) must be made not more than 4 years after the end of the applicable period to which it relates (*s 78(11)*).

## VAT Default surcharge

(*VATA 1994, ss 59–59B, 71*; VAT Notice 700/50)

| Defaults | Surcharge | Surcharge period |
|---|---|---|
| First default | No surcharge<br><br>Surcharge Liability Notice issued. | 12 months |
| Second default in a surcharge period | 2% (unless it is less than £400)* | 12 months from the date of the most recent default |
| Third default in a surcharge period | 5% (unless it is less than £400)* | 12 months from the date of the most recent default |

*continued*

| Defaults | Surcharge | Surcharge period |
|---|---|---|
| Fourth default in a surcharge period | 10% | 12 months from the date of the most recent default |
| Fifth and subsequent defaults in a surcharge period | 15% | 12 months from the date of the most recent default |

\* HMRC do not issue a surcharge at the 2% and 5% rates if it is calculated to be less than £400 (VAT Notice 700/50, para 4.5)

**Notes**

(1)   *General* – A default surcharge can apply to the failure to submit a return or amount of VAT payable on time, or the amount due under the payment on account scheme on time. The surcharge is calculated as a percentage of the unpaid VAT in default.

(2)   *Small businesses* – HMRC apply special arrangements to 'small businesses' (ie those with a taxable turnover of £150,000 or less) to help when the business first has difficulties paying VAT on time. HMRC will send a letter offering help and support rather than a Surcharge Liability Notice following the first default (VAT Notice 700/50, para 4.2).

(3)   *Minimum surcharge* – There is a minimum surcharge of £30 for surcharges calculated at the 10% or 15% rates (*VATA 1994, s 59(4); see* VAT Notice 700/50, para 4.5).

(4)   *Reasonable excuse* – A surcharge liability does not arise if HMRC or the tribunal are satisfied that there is a reasonable excuse for the return or VAT payment being late (*VATA 1994, s 59(7)*). As to circumstances which cannot constitute a 'reasonable excuse' for these purposes, see *VATA 1994, s 71(1)*.

(5)   *Payments on account* – Surcharges can apply to late payments on account; see *VATA 1994, s 59A* and VAT Notice 700/50, para 4.4).

(6)   *Further information* – For further information on default surcharges, and on VAT penalties generally, see www.hmrc.gov.uk/vat/managing/problems/penalties.htm.

## Unauthorised issue of VAT invoice

*(FA 2008, Sch 41, paras 2, 6)*

- *General* – A penalty is payable by a person who makes an unauthorised issue of a VAT invoice, ie where an 'unauthorised person' (eg a person not registered under *VATA 1994*) issues an invoice showing an amount of VAT or a VAT inclusive amount).

- *Commencement* – The provisions apply to any unauthorised issue of an invoice taking place from 1 April 2010 (*SI 2009/511, art 3*).

- *Level of penalty* – The same penalties apply as for failure to notify (see **Failure to notify** above), except that the lower penalties for non-deliberate behaviour (ie 0% (unprompted) and 10% (prompted)) do not apply.

- *Special reductions and reasonable excuse* – HMRC may reduce a penalty in 'special circumstances' and penalties do not arise if HMRC or the tribunal are satisfied that there is a 'reasonable excuse' for the act or failure (*FA 2008, Sch 41, paras 14, 20*).

## Incorrect certificates as to zero-rating etc

(*VATA 1994, s 62*)

- *General* – The penalty is charged in respect of incorrect certificates within *VATA 1994, s 62(1)*, or in respect of acquisitions of goods from other member states within the fiscal warehousing regime; see *s 62(1A)*.

- *Person liable* – The person giving or preparing the certificate is liable to the penalty.

- *Level of penalty* – The penalty is equal to the difference between the VAT chargeable if the certificate had been correct and any VAT actually charged, or (in respect of acquisitions from other member states within the fiscal warehousing regime) the amount of VAT actually chargeable on the acquisition.

## Inaccuracies in EC sales statements, etc

(*VATA 1994, s 65*)

- *General* – A penalty may be charged for material inaccuracies in EC sales statements, or in statements relating to *VATA 1994, s 55A* ('Customers to account for tax on supplies of goods or services of a kind used in missing trader intra-community fraud').

- *Amount of penalty* – A penalty of £100 is charged for a material inaccuracy on a statement submitted within two years after a penalty notice has been issued by HMRC. The penalty applies if the trader submits a third EC sales statement containing a material inaccuracy within the two-year period, and only relates to the third list containing an inaccuracy (see VCP11044).

## Failure to submit EC sales statements, etc

(*VATA 1994, s 66*)

- *General* – A penalty may be charged for the late submission of EC sales statements, or of statements relating to *VATA 1994, s 55A* ('Customers to account for tax on supplies of goods or services of a kind used in missing trader intra-community fraud').

- *Level of penalties* – Penalties may be charged if HMRC has served a default notice and the statement to which the notice relates is not submitted within 14 days after the notice is served. The penalty is the greater of £50 or the following daily penalties (each up to a maximum of 100 days):

  ○ First default (or the default to which the notice relates) – £5 per day;

  ○ Second default – £10 per day; and

  ○ Any other case – £15 per day.

## Breach of walking possession agreements

(*VATA 1994, s 68*)

- *General* – A penalty can be imposed for the breach of an undertaking contained in a walking possession agreement (NB a penalty under *VATA 1994, s 68* does not extend to Scotland).

- *Amount of penalty* – The person in default is liable to a penalty equal to 50% of VAT due or any amount recoverable as if it were VAT due.

## Breaches of regulatory provisions

*(VATA 1994, s 69; VCP11100 et seq)*

- *General* – Subject to certain exceptions in *VATA 1994, s 69(4)* (eg if the trader is liable to a default surcharge for the same failure), the penalty for a failure to comply with any regulatory requirement is determined according to the number of occasions in the previous 2 years on which the person has failed to comply with that requirement. The regulatory requirements in question are listed in *VATA 1994, s 69* (eg failure to notify HMRC of cessation of trading by a registered person, or failure to comply with any requirement set out in the VAT Regulations and any other regulations made under *VATA 1994*).

- *Amount of penalty* – The penalty is generally the greater of £50 and an amount equal to the prescribed rate multiplied by the number of days on which the failure continues, up to a maximum of 100. The 'prescribed rate' depends upon the number of failures to comply, as follows:

  o    No previous failure to comply in the above period – £5

  o    One previous failure in that period – £10

  o    Any other case – £15

- *Late payments or late submission of VAT returns* – Where the breach is a late payment failure or the late furnishing of a return, the prescribed penalty rate is the greater of the penalty above, and the amounts as follows (*VATA 1994, s 69(5)*):

  o    No previous failure in the above period – One-sixth of 1% of the VAT due or assessed in respect of that period

  o    One previous failure in that period – One-third of 1% of the VAT due

  o    Any other case – One-half of 1% of the VAT due

  A late payment or filing penalty cannot be assessed if a default surcharge is to be assessed for the same failure (VCP11134).

## Failure to preserve records

*(VATA 1994, s 69(2))*

- *General* – HMRC may require records to be preserved for a period specified in writing, but not exceeding 6 years (*VATA 1994, Sch 11, para 6(3)*). A penalty may be charged for a failure to comply.

- *Amount of penalty* – The penalty for failing to comply with a requirement imposed under *VAT 1994, Sch 11, para 6(3)* is £500, unless HMRC or the tribunal is satisfied that there is a reasonable excuse for the failure.

## Failure to keep records or provide information: specified gold transactions

*(VATA 1994, s 69A)*

- *General* – The provisions apply to a person who fails to comply with certain record and information requirements in respect of specified gold transactions (ie in respect of regulations made under *FA 1999, s 13(5)(a)* or *(b)*).

- *Penalty* – The maximum penalty is 17.5% of the value of the transactions to which the failure relates, unless HMRC or the tribunal is satisfied that there is a reasonable excuse for the failure.

## Breach of HMRC direction to keep records

*(VATA 1994, s 69B, Sch 11, para 6A(1), (6))*

- *General* – Penalties can arise in respect of the following compliance failures:

  (a)   To comply with a HMRC direction to keep specified records;

  (b)   To comply with a requirement by HMRC to preserve records for a period of up to 6 years.

- *Penalties* – The penalties for failing to comply with the above requirements (unless HMRC or the tribunal is satisfied that there is a reasonable excuse for the failure) are as follows:

  (a)   In respect of (a) above – The penalty is £200 for each day the failure continues (up to a maximum of 30 days);

  (b)   In respect of (b) above – The penalty is £500.

## Evasion of import VAT (and other relevant duties)

*(FA 2003, ss 24(2)(d), 25)*

- *General* – A penalty can be imposed where a person engages in conduct to evade import VAT, or by which he contravenes a legislative duty, obligation, requirement or condition in relation to import VAT.

- *Penalty* – The penalty for evasion involving dishonesty is an amount equal to the import VAT evaded or sought to be evaded.

- Other relevant duties – The same penalty provisions that apply to import VAT apply to other relevant duties.

## Contravention of relevant rules

*(FA 2003, ss 26, 27, 29; Customs (Contravention of a Relevant Rule) Regulations 2003, SI 2003/3113)*

- *General* – A penalty can arise for contravening a 'relevant rule' (see *FA 2003, s 26(8), SI 2003/3113, reg 3, Sch*).

- *Penalty* – A penalty of up to £2,500 (or other amount prescribed by Treasury Order) can be imposed (unless HMRC or the tribunal are satisfied that there is a reasonable excuse for the failure, or unless the penalty is reduced or cancelled by HMRC or the tribunal).

## Online filing – Failure of a specified person to file VAT returns electronically (prescribed accounting periods ending from 31 March 2011)

*(Value Added Tax Regulations 1995, SI 1995/2518, reg 25A)*

| Annual VAT exclusive turnover | Penalty | Annual VAT exclusive turnover | Penalty |
|---|---|---|---|
| £22,800,001 and above | £400 | £100,001 to £5,600,000 | £200 |
| £5,600,001 to £22,800,000 | £300 | £100,000 and under | £100 |

**Notes**

(1)   *Specified person* – A 'specified person' is one who became VAT registered on or after 1 April 2010, or is registered before that date and at 31 December 2009 or any later date has an annual turnover of £100,000 or more (exclusive of VAT), whether or not that person's turnover subsequently falls below that level, and who in either case is notified by HMRC as being a specified person. A 'specified person' is charged a penalty if they submit a paper return for any accounting period ending on or after 31 March 2011.

(2)   *Commencement* – Specified persons can be liable to penalties in relation to returns made for prescribed accounting periods ending on or after 31 March 2011 *(SI 1995/2518, reg 25A(15))*.

(3)   *Digital by default* – All VAT registered persons are required to submit online VAT returns from 1 April 2012. Those first required to do so from that date will be charged a penalty if they submit a paper return for any accounting period ending on or after 31 March 2013.

(4)   *Exceptions* – A person who has a reasonable excuse for failing to comply is not liable to a penalty. There is also an exemption for businesses run by individuals who have a religious conscience objection to the use of computers and the internet.

## PENALTIES FOR CORPORATION TAX

*(FA 1998, Sch 18; FA 2007, s 97, Sch 24; FA 2008, s 113, Sch 36, s 123, Sch 41)*

| Offence | Maximum penalty |
|---|---|
| **Failure to notify chargeability** | |
| *(FA 2008, s 123; Sch 41, paras 1, 6, 6A; SI 2009/511)* | |
| ● Deliberate and concealed act or failure | 100% of potential lost revenue |
| ● Deliberate but not concealed act or failure | 70% of potential lost revenue |
| ● Any other case | 30% of potential lost revenue |
| **Failure to deliver a return** | *Flat rate penalty* |
| *(FA 1998, Sch 18, paras 17, 18)* | |
| ● Up to 3 months after filing date | £100 |
| | Persistent failure, ie a third successive failure £500 |

| Offence | Maximum penalty |
|---|---|
| ● More than 3 months after filing date | A further £100 |
| | Persistent failure (see above) |
| | A further £500 |
| | *Tax related penalty* |
| ● At least 18 months but less than 24 months after end of return period | 10% of tax unpaid at 18 months after end of return period |
| ● 24 months or more after end of return period | A further 10% of tax unpaid at 18 months after end of return period |
| **Errors in returns etc** | |
| *(FA 2007, s 97; Sch 24, para 4; SI 2008/568)* | |
| ● Reasonable care taken | No penalty liability |
| ● Careless inaccuracy | 30% of potential lost revenue |
| ● Deliberate but not concealed inaccuracy | 70% of potential lost revenue |
| ● Deliberate and concealed inaccuracy | 100% of potential lost revenue |
| **Failure to keep and preserve records** | Up to £3,000 |
| *(FA 1998, Sch 18, para 23)* | |
| **Failure to comply with information notice, or obstruction during an inspection** | |
| *(FA 2008, s 113, Sch 36, paras 39, 40, 50)* | |
| ● Initial failure | £300 |
| ● Continued failure | Up to £60 per day |
| ● Continued failure where significant tax is at risk | Penalty may be decided by the Upper Tribunal (See Note 4) |
| **Inaccurate information and documents** | Up to £3,000 for each inaccuracy |
| *(FA 2008, Sch 36, para 40A)* | |
| **Failure to notify coming within the charge to corporation tax within 3 months of first accounting period** – repealed from 1 April 2010 *(FA 2008, Sch 41, para 25(a)(ii))* | Up to £300 <br> Up to £60 per day for continued failure |
| *(FA 2004, s 55; TMA 1970, s 98)* | |
| **Quarterly Instalment Payments** <br> **('Large' companies)** <br><br> ● Deliberate or reckless failure to pay the correct amount on an instalment date; <br><br> ● Fraudulent or negligent claim for repayment (under reg 6(2) of the instalment regulations) | Up to twice the amount of interest charged on any unpaid amount in respect of the company's total liability for the accounting period |
| *(TMA 1970, s 59E(4); SI 1998/3175, reg 13)* | |

**Notes**

(1)    *Failure to notify* – The failure to notify chargeability provisions took effect from 1 April 2010 (NB penalties were previously charged under *FA 1998, Sch 18, para 2(3)*, up to a maximum of 100% of tax payable for the accounting period and remaining unpaid 12 months after the end of the period).

(2)   *Failure to make returns etc* – A new fixed and tax related penalty regime will apply for the late filing of corporation tax returns from a date to be specified by Treasury Order *(FA 2009, s 106, Sch 55)*.

(3)   *Failure to deliver a return* – The above flat rate penalties do not apply if the return period is one for which the company must deliver accounts under the *Companies Act 2006*, and the return is filed by the date allowed by Companies House *(FA 1998, Sch 18, para 19)*. This has no effect on the tax geared penalties which may arise.

(4)   *Information notices and inspections* – In relation to a failure to comply with an information notice, or a deliberate obstruction during an inspection:

(a)   A penalty for obstruction is only due in relation to an inspection which has been approved by the tribunal.

(b)   If the failure or obstruction continues after an initial penalty is charged (under *FA 2008, Sch 36, para 39*), an additional tax-related penalty can be imposed if an HMRC officer has reason to believe that the failure or obstruction may result in a significant loss of tax. However, HMRC must first apply to the Upper Tribunal for the imposition of the additional penalty (see *FA 2008, Sch 36, para 50*).

## SDLT penalties

*(FA 2003, Schs 10, 11; FA 2008, Sch 36, paras 39, 40, 40A, 50)*

| Offence | Penalty |
| --- | --- |
| Failure to deliver a return by the filing date *(FA 2003, Sch 10, paras 3, 4)* | Up to 3 months late – £100 |
| | Over 3 months late – £200 |
| | Over 12 months – tax related penalty not exceeding the tax chargeable |
| Failure to comply with a notice to deliver a return *(FA 2003, Sch 10, para 5)* | Up to £60 for each day on which the failure continues |
| Failure to keep and preserve records *(FA 2003, Sch 10, para 11; Sch 11, para 6)* | Up to £3,000 (unless other satisfactory documentary evidence provided) |
| Failure to comply with an information notice, or<br><br>Deliberate obstruction of HMRC officer in the course of a tribunal approved inspection *(FA 2008, Sch 36, paras 39, 40, 50)* | • Initial penalty £300<br>• Up to £60 for each day on which the failure or obstruction continues<br>• Tax related penalty if HMRC officer has reason to believe that a significant loss of tax will result from continued failure or obstruction. |
| Inaccurate information and documents *(FA 2008, Sch 36, para 40A)* | Up to £3,000 for each inaccuracy |

### Notes

(1)   The penalty for failure to comply with an information notice or the deliberate obstruction of an HMRC officer during a tribunal approved inspection applies with effect from 1 April 2010 *(FA 2009, s 96, Sch 48; SI 2009/3054, art 2)*. For

information notices issued before 1 April 2010, penalties may be charged as follows (*FA 2003, Sch 10, para 16; SI 2009/3054, art 7*):

- Initial penalty £50; and

- Up to £30 (if determined by HMRC) or £150 (if determined by courts) for each day on which the failure continues.

(2) The tax related penalty for failure to comply with an information notice, or the deliberate obstruction of an HMRC officer in the course of a tribunal approved inspection, requires HMRC to make an application to the Upper Tribunal within certain time limits (*FA 2008, Sch 36, para 50(1)*).

## SDLT AND SDRT PENALTIES – ERRORS

(*FA 2007, Sch 24*)

| Unprompted disclosure | Penalty |
|---|---|
| Careless error | 0% to 30% of potential lost revenue |
| Deliberate but not concealed error | 20% to 70% of potential revenue lost |
| Deliberate and concealed error | 30% to 100% of potential revenue lost |
| **Prompted disclosure** | |
| Careless error | 15% to 30% of potential lost revenue |
| Deliberate but not concealed error | 35% to 70% of potential lost revenue |
| Deliberate and concealed error | 50% to 100% of potential lost revenue |

**Notes**

(1) The above penalties apply with effect for inaccuracies in returns or other documents to be filed on or after 1 April 2010 (*SI 2009/571, art 5*).

(2) A penalty may also be charged if an error in a return is attributable to another person (*FA 2007, Sch 24, para 1A*). Penalties in such circumstances range from 30% to 100% for unprompted disclosure, and 50% to 100% for prompted disclosure. They apply where the inaccuracy is contained in a return or other document which is due to be filed from 1 April 2010, and which relates to a tax period beginning from 1 April 2009.

## STAMP DUTY PENALTIES – LATE STAMPING

(*SA 1891, s 15B*)

| Offence | Penalty |
|---|---|
| Document not presented within 30 days after: | The lower of: |
| • Execution in the UK; or | • £300; or |
| • It is first received in the UK (if executed outside the UK) | • the amount of duty |
| Document presented more than 1 year after the above 30 day period | The greater of: |
| | • £300; or |
| | • the amount of duty |

**Notes**

(1)   The above penalties apply with effect for instruments executed from 1 October 1999.

(2)   Penalties are rounded down to the nearest multiple of £5 (STM 3.27).


# INFORMATION NOTICES AND DATA-GATHERING
*(FA 2011, s 86, Schs 23, 24)*

## Penalties
*(FA 2011, Sch 23, Pt 4)*

| Offence | Penalty |
| --- | --- |
| **Failure to comply with a data-holder notice** | |
| *(FA 2011, Sch 23, paras 30, 31)* | |
| • Initial penalty | £300 |
| • Continued failure | Up to £60 per day on which the failure continues |
| • Provision of inaccurate data | Up to £3,000 per inaccuracy |
| (ie where condition A, B or C is met in *FA 2011, Sch 23, para 32*) | |

**Notes**

(1)   *General* – An HMRC officer may require a 'relevant data-holder' to provide 'relevant data' (both as defined). Penalties apply to a failure by the data-holder to comply with a data-holder notice. The above penalty regime generally applies with effect from 1 April 2012, to relevant data with a bearing on any period (ie before, on or after that date) *(FA 2011, Sch 23, para 65)*. There is a right of appeal against the liability to, or amount of, the penalties listed in the table above *(para 36)*.

(2)   *Daily penalties* – If daily penalties have been assessed as above and the failure continues for more than 30 days, an HMRC officer may apply to the tribunal for penalties of up to £1,000 per day to be applied instead *(FA 2011, Sch 23, para 38)*.

(3)   *Reasonable excuse* – The £300 fixed penalty, and the penalties of up to £60 per day, do not apply if there is a 'reasonable excuse' for the failure *(FA 2011, Sch 23, para 34)*.

# INFORMATION AND INSPECTION POWERS

*(FA 2008, s 113, Sch 36)*

| Offence | Penalty |
|---|---|
| **Failure to comply with an information notice or obstruction** | |
| *(FA 2008, Sch 36, paras 39, 40, 50)* | |
| • Initial penalty | £300 |
| • Continued failure | Up to £60 per day on which failure or obstruction continues |
| • Continued failure where significant tax is at risk | Penalty may be decided by the Upper Tribunal (See Note 3) |
| Inaccurate information and documents | Up to £3,000 for each inaccuracy |
| *(FA 2008, Sch 36, para 40A)* | |

**Notes**

(1)  The above penalty regime applies with effect for information notices issued or inspections carried out from 1 April 2009 for direct tax (and VAT) purposes (*SI 2009/404, art 2*), and for other taxes and duties generally from 1 April 2010 (*FA 2009, s 96, Sch 48; SI 2009/3054*).

(2)  Penalties for the above offences do not arise if there is a 'reasonable excuse' for the failure or obstruction (*FA 2008, Sch 36, para 45*).

(3)  Information notices and inspections – In relation to a failure to comply with an information notice, or a deliberate obstruction during an inspection:

(a)  A penalty for obstruction is only due in relation to an inspection which has been approved by the tribunal.

(b)  If the failure or obstruction continues after an initial penalty is charged (under *FA 2008, Sch 36, para 39*), an additional tax-related penalty can be imposed if an HMRC officer has reason to believe that the failure or obstruction may result in a significant loss of tax. However, HMRC must first apply to the Upper Tribunal for the imposition of the additional penalty (see *FA 2008, Sch 36, para 50*).

# DISCLOSURE OF TAX AVOIDANCE SCHEMES (DOTAS)

*(FA 2004, Pt 7 (as amended); SSAA 1992, s 132A; VATA 1994, Sch 11A and secondary legislation (see below))*

**DOTAS forms** (for income tax, capital gains tax, corporation tax, national insurance contributions, stamp duty land tax and inheritance tax schemes)

| Form | Description |
|---|---|
| AAG1 | Disclosure of avoidance scheme (Notification by scheme promoter) |
| AAG2 | Disclosure of avoidance scheme (Notification by scheme user where offshore promoter does not notify) |

*continued*

| Form | Description |
|------|-------------|
| AAG3 | Disclosure of avoidance scheme (Notification by scheme user where no promoter, or promoted by lawyer unable to make full notification) |
| AAG4* | Disclosure of avoidance scheme (Notification of scheme reference number by scheme user) |
| AAG4(SDLT)* | Disclosure of SDLT avoidance scheme – notification of scheme reference number |
| AAG4(IHT)* | Disclosure of avoidance scheme (Notification of scheme reference number by scheme user) |
| AAG5 | Continuation sheet |
| AAG6 | Disclosure of avoidance scheme (Notification of scheme reference number) |
| AAG6 (SDLT) | Disclosure of SDLT avoidance scheme – Notification of scheme reference number |
| AAG6(IHT) | Disclosure of avoidance scheme – Notification of scheme reference number |

\* *Online submissions* – Online notifications can generally be made via the HMRC website (www.hmrc.gov.uk/aiu/form-aag4.htm). However, a different online notification is required for SDLT purposes (www.hmrc.gov.uk/aiu/form-aag4sdlt.htm), and also for IHT purposes (https://online.hmrc.gov.uk/shortforms/form/AAG4IHT?dept-name=&sub-dept-name=&location=35&origin=http://www.hmrc.gov.uk).

**Notes**

(1)   *General* – The DOTAS regime was originally introduced from 1 August 2004, although its scope has been progressively widened. A tax arrangement is broadly notifiable if it falls within a description ('hallmark') prescribed by regulations, it enables (or might be expected to enable) any person to obtain a 'tax advantage' as defined (and/or an NIC advantage), and it is such that the main benefit (or one of them) that might be expected to arise from the arrangement is the obtaining of that advantage (*FA 2004, s 306(1)*). The scheme 'promoter' (or in certain circumstances the scheme user, or someone who designs and implements their own 'in-house' scheme) must generally disclose the relevant scheme within a prescribed period, normally five days beginning with one of certain trigger events (*SI 2004/1864, reg 4*). HMRC will issue a scheme reference number, which users of the scheme must include on their returns or form AAG4. A promoter must also provide HMRC with periodic lists of persons to whom they become liable to issue a scheme reference number.

The DOTAS obligations are underpinned by a penalty regime, subject to a right of appeal. DOTAS penalties broadly fall into three categories. Firstly, disclosure penalties apply for failure to disclose a scheme. Secondly, information penalties apply to all other compliance failures except user penalties. Thirdly, user penalties apply to failure by a scheme user to report a scheme reference number to HMRC. No penalty generally arises if there is a 'reasonable excuse' for the compliance failure. See '**Further information**' below.

(2)   *Forms and notifications* – Disclosures must be made in a form and manner specified by HMRC. The DOTAS forms for income tax, capital gains tax, corporation tax, national insurance contributions, stamp duty land tax and inheritance tax schemes,

including an online filing facility, can be accessed via HMRC's website (www. hmrc.gov.uk/aiu/forms-tax-schemes.htm). Paper forms should be submitted to:

Anti Avoidance Group (Intelligence)
HM Revenue & Custom
CTIAA Intelligence S0528
PO Box 194
Bootle
L69 9AA

(3)    *Legislation* – A list of primary and secondary legislation concerning DOTAS is included on HMRC's website (www.hmrc.gov.uk/aiu/legislation.htm).

(4)    *Further information* – Detailed HMRC guidance on DOTAS, including how to make a disclosure, the time limits for doing so and details of penalties for non-disclosure, can be downloaded from the HMRC website (www.hmrc.gov.uk/aiu/dotas.pdf).

HMRC's Anti-Avoidance Group can be contacted by email: aag@hmrc.gov. uk. An online facility for general enquiries about the disclosure rules is also available on HMRC's website: https://online.hmrc.gov.uk/shortforms/form/ AAGGeneral_N?dept-name=&sub-dept-name=&location=35&origin=http:// www.hmrc.gov.uk.

## Disclosure of tax avoidance schemes (VAT)

(*VATA 1994, Sch 11A, paras 10, 11*; *The VAT (Disclosure of Avoidance Schemes) Regulations 2004, SI 2004/1929*; *Value Added Tax (Disclosure of Avoidance Schemes) (Designations) Order 2004, SI 2004/1933*; VAT Notice 700/8).

(1)    *General* – A penalty can apply to the failure to disclose the following (within the statutory time limit in *SI 2004/1929, reg 2;* see VAT Notice 700/8, section 5):

*    The use of a designated avoidance scheme, unless the taxable person has already notified HMRC; or

*    A notifiable scheme that is not a designated scheme.

(2)    *Amount of penalty* – The penalties for failing to comply with the notification requirements (unless there is a reasonable excuse for the failure) are as follows:

*    Notifiable scheme that is not a designated scheme – £5,000; or

*    Designated scheme – 15% of the VAT saving.

(3)    *Making a notification* – Guidance on how to make notifications for VAT purposes is contained in VAT Notice 700/8 ('Disclosure of VAT avoidance schemes'). Notifications should be posted or emailed to the addresses given in the VAT Notice 700/8. Notifications should be posted to:

VAT Avoidance Disclosures Unit, Anti Avoidance Group (Intelligence)
HM Revenue & Custom
CTIAA Intelligence S0528
PO Box 194
Bootle
L69 9AA

or emailed to: vat.avoidance.disclosures.bst@hmrc.gsi.gov.uk.

(4)   *Further information* – Detailed guidance on the disclosure of VAT avoidance schemes is contained in VAT Notice 700/8.

## TAX AGENTS: DISHONEST CONDUCT

(*FA 2012, s 223, Sch 38*)

| HMRC powers | Right of appeal? |
|---|---|
| Obtain working papers from tax agent voluntarily or under a file access notice. Penalties apply if the notice is not complied with. | No appeal against file access notice, but can appeal against the penalties. |
| Issue a Conduct Notice which includes evidence of the dishonest conduct. | Yes, within 30 days. |
| Charge civil penalties of between £5,000 and £50,000, plus interest on late paid penalties (*SI 2013/280*). | Yes, against the amount of the penalty but not against the imposition of the penalty. |
| Disclose details of the agent's dishonest conduct to the agent's professional body. | No appeal. |
| 'Name and shame' by publishing details of the tax agent on the HMRC website, where the agent has been charged a penalty of more than £5,000. | No appeal. |

**Notes**

(1)   *Who these powers apply to* – A tax agent is an individual who, in the course of business, assists other persons (ie clients) with their tax affairs, and these terms are defined widely (*FA 2012, Sch 38, para 2*).

(2)   *What is dishonest conduct* – An individual engages in dishonest conduct if, in the course of acting as a tax agent, the individual does something dishonest with a view to bringing about a loss of tax revenue (*FA 2012, Sch 38, para 3*).

(3)   *Commencement* – The powers listed above came into force on 1 April 2013 (*SI 2013/279*).

(4)   *Further information* – For a summary of the dishonest conduct powers see www. hmrc.gov.uk/agents/strategy/dishonestconduct.htm. Technical guidance is found in the HMRC Compliance Handbook at paras CH180000–186220. A factsheet is available: www.hmrc.gov.uk/agents/strategy/tafs.pdf.

*18*

# State Benefits

SOCIAL SECURITY BENEFIT RATES

*(ITEPA 2003, Pts 9, 10)*

| Benefit (weekly rates) | April 2013 £ | April 2012 £ | April 2011 £ |
|---|---|---|---|
| **Attendance allowance (N)** | | | |
| ● Higher rate | 79.15 | 77.45 | 73.60 |
| ● Lower rate | 53.00 | 51.85 | 49.30 |
| **Bereavement Benefit (N)** | | | |
| ● Bereavement Payment (lump sum) | 2000.00 | 2,000.00 | 2,000.00 |
| ● Widowed Parent's Allowance | 108.30 | 105.95 | 100.70 |
| ● Bereavement Allowance (Standard rate) | 108.30 | 105.95 | 100.70 |
| **Carer's Allowance (T)** | 59.75 | 58.45 | 55.55 |
| **Disability Living Allowance (N)** | | | |
| Care component | | | |
| ● Highest | 79.15 | 77.45 | 73.60 |
| ● Middle | 53.00 | 51.85 | 49.30 |
| ● Lowest | 21.00 | 20.55 | 19.55 |
| Mobility component | | | |
| ● Higher | 55.25 | 54.05 | 51.40 |
| ● Lower | 21.00 | 20.55 | 19.55 |
| **Employment and Support Allowance (ESA) (T)** | | | |
| Personal Allowances | | | |
| Single | | | |
| ● under 25 | 56.80 | 56.25 | 53.45 |
| ● 25 or over | 71.70 | 71.00 | 67.50 |
| Lone parent | | | |
| ● under 18 | 56.80 | 56.25 | 53.45 |
| ● 18 and over | 71.70 | 71.00 | 67.50 |

*continued*

| Benefit (weekly rates) | April 2013 £ | April 2012 £ | April 2011 £ |
|---|---|---|---|
| Couple | | | |
| ● Both under 18 | 56.80 | 56.25 | 53.45 |
| ● Both under 18 – with child | 85.80 | 84.95 | 80.75 |
| ● Both under 18 (main phase), | 71.70 | 71.00 | 67.50 |
| ● One under 18, or both over 18 | 112.55 | 111.45 | 105.95 |
| ● claimant under 25 partner under 18 | 56.80 | 56.25 | 53.45 |
| ● claimant 25+ partner under 18 | 71.70 | 71.00 | 67.50 |
| claimant (main phase) partner under 18 | 71.70 | 71.00 | 67.50 |
| **Income support (see note 9)** | | | |
| **Personal Allowances** | | | |
| Single | | | |
| ● Under 25 | 56.80 | 56.25 | 53.45 |
| ● 25 or over | 71.70 | 71.00 | 67.50 |
| Lone parent | | | |
| ● Under 18 | 56.80 | 56.25 | 53.45 |
| ● 18 or over | 71.70 | 71.00 | 67.50 |
| Couple | | | |
| ● Both under 18 | 56.80 | 56.25 | 53.45 |
| ● Both under 18 – higher rate | 85.80 | 84.95 | 80.75 |
| ● One under 18, one under 25 | 56.80 | 56.25 | 53.45 |
| ● One under 18, one 25 and over | 71.70 | 71.00 | 67.50 |
| ● Both 18 or over | 112.55 | 111.45 | 105.95 |
| ● Dependent children | 65.62 | 64.99 | 62.33 |
| **Premiums** | | | |
| Family/lone parent | 17.40 | 17.40 | 17.40 |
| Pensioner (applies to couples only) | 109.50 | 106.45 | 103.75 |
| Disability | | | |
| ● Single | 31.00 | 30.35 | 28.85 |
| ● Couple | 44.20 | 43.25 | 41.10 |
| Enhanced disability (also for ESA) | | | |
| ● Single | 15.15 | 14.80 | 14.05 |
| ● Disabled child | 23.45 | 22.89 | 21.63 |
| ● Couple | 21.75 | 21.30 | 20.25 |
| Severe disability (also for ESA) | | | |
| ● Single | 59.50 | 58.20 | 55.30 |
| ● Couple (lower rate) | 59.50 | 58.20 | 55.30 |
| ● Couple (higher rate) | 119.00 | 116.40 | 110.60 |
| Disabled child | 57.89 | 56.63 | 53.62 |
| Carer (also for ESA claims) | 33.30 | 32.60 | 31.00 |
| Relevant sum for strikers | 39.00 | 38.00 | 36.00 |

| Benefit (weekly rates) | April 2013 £ | April 2012 £ | April 2011 £ |
|---|---|---|---|
| **Industrial Death Benefit (T)** | | | |
| Widow's pension (T) | | | |
| ● Higher rate | 110.15 | 107.45 | 102.15 |
| ● Lower rate | 33.05 | 32.24 | 30.65 |
| Widower's pension (T) | 110.15 | 107.45 | 102.15 |
| **Jobseeker's Allowance (JSA)(T)** | | | |
| Contribution-based JSA – Personal rates | | | |
| ● Under 25 | 56.80 | 56.25 | 53.45 |
| ● 25 or over | 71.70 | 71.00 | 67.50 |
| Income-based JSA – personal allowances | | | |
| ● Under 25 | 56.80 | 56.25 | 53.45 |
| ● 25 or over | 71.70 | 71.00 | 67.50 |
| Lone parent | | | |
| ● Under 18 | 56.80 | 56.25 | 53.45 |
| ● 18 or over | 71.70 | 71.00 | 67.50 |
| Couple | | | |
| ● Both under 18 | 56.80 | 56.25 | 53.45 |
| ● Both under 18 – higher rate | 85.80 | 84.95 | 80.75 |
| ● One under 18, one under 25 | 56.80 | 56.25 | 53.45 |
| ● One under 18, one 25 and over | 71.70 | 71.00 | 67.50 |
| ● Both 18 or over | 112.55 | 111.45 | 105.95 |
| Dependent children | 65.62 | 64.99 | 62.33 |
| Premiums (see Income Support rates) | | | |
| **Maternity Allowance(N)** | | | |
| ● Standard rate | 136.78 | 135.45 | 128.73 |
| ● Maternity Allowance threshold | 30.00 | 30.00 | 30.00 |
| **Pension Credit (N)** | | | |
| Standard minimum guarantee | | | |
| ● Single | 145.40 | 142.70 | 137.35 |
| ● Couple | 222.05 | 217.90 | 209.70 |
| Additional amount for severe disability | | | |
| ● Single | 59.50 | 58.20 | 55.30 |
| ● Couple (one qualifies) | 59.50 | 58.20 | 55.30 |
| ● Couple (both qualify) | 119.00 | 116.40 | 110.60 |
| Additional amount for carers | 33.30 | 32.60 | 31.00 |

*continued*

221

| Benefit (weekly rates) | April 2013 £ | April 2012 £ | April 2011 £ |
|---|---|---|---|
| Savings credit | | | |
| ● Threshold – single | 115.30 | 111.80 | 103.15 |
| ● Threshold – couple | 183.90 | 178.35 | 164.55 |
| ● Maximum – single | 18.06 | 18.54 | 20.52 |
| ● Maximum – couple | 22.89 | 23.73 | 27.09 |
| Amount for claimant and first spouse in polygamous marriage | 222.05 | 217.90 | 209.70 |
| Additional amount for additional spouse | 76.65 | 75.20 | 72.35 |
| **Severe Disablement Allowance (N)** | | | |
| Basic rate | 71.80 | 69.00 | 62.95 |
| Age-related addition | | | |
| ● Higher rate | 10.70 | 11.70 | 13.80 |
| ● Middle rate | 6.00 | 5.90 | 7.10 |
| ● Lower rate | 6.00 | 5.90 | 5.60 |
| **Widow's Benefit (T)** | | | |
| Widowed Mother's Allowance | 108.30 | 105.95 | 100.70 |
| Widow's Pension (Standard rate) | 108.30 | 105.95 | 100.70 |

**Notes**

(1)  *General* – The above represents a selection of state benefit rates. A more comprehensive list of rates can be accessed on the Gov.uk website.

(2)  *Commencement* – The benefit rates from April 2013 above are as announced by DWP press release on 6 December 2012.

The benefit rates for 2013 were uprated by The Social Security Benefits Up-rating Regulations, SI 2013/599819 (www.legislation.gov.uk/uksi/2013/599/contents/made).

(3)  *Uprating of benefits* – The annual uprating of benefits take place for State Pensions and most other benefits in the first full week of the tax year.

(4)  *Taxable or not* – in the table above (**T**) indicates a taxable benefit, (**N**) indicates a non-taxable benefit. Only those UK social security benefits that are specified in Table A at *ITEPA 2003, s 660(1)* are taxable as social security income under *ITEPA 2003, Pt 10*. Some other social security benefits, specified at *ITEPA 2003, s 577*, are taxable as pension income under *ITEPA 2003, Pt 9*.

(5)  *Foreign benefits* – Certain foreign social security payments are exempt from UK tax (see *ITEPA 2003, Pt 10, Ch 7*).

(6)  *Statutory payments* – Details of statutory sick pay, maternity pay, paternity pay and adoption pay are given in **Chapter 16**.

(7)  *Industrial Death Benefit scheme pensions* – Industrial death benefit is not payable in respect of deaths occurring on or after 11 April 1988 (see EIM76200).

(8)  *Incapacity benefit* – ESA has replaced Incapacity Benefit and Income Support paid on incapacity grounds for anyone starting a claim from 27 October 2008. Existing

recipients of Incapacity Benefit or Income Support continue to receive that benefit until they are moved to ESA (EIM76180).

(9) *Income support* – For further information on taxable and non-taxable parts of income support, see EIM76190.

(10) *Widowed Parent's Allowance* – Replaced Widowed Mother's Allowance (WMA) from 9 April 2001, although WMA is still paid to widows whose entitlement arose before 9 April 2001 (see EIM76172, EIM76177).

(11) *Widow's Pension* – Replaced by Bereavement Allowance (see EIM76173) for new claimants on or after 9 April 2001. However, widows in receipt of widow's pension before that date continue to receive widow's pension (see EIM76178).

# NON-TAXABLE SOCIAL SECURITY BENEFITS

*(ITEPA 2003, Pt 10)*

## Summary

- Attendance Allowance
- Back to Work Bonus
- Bereavement Payment
- Child Benefit (but see Note 10 below)
- Child's Special Allowance
- Child Tax Credit
- Cold Weather Payments (see also Winter Fuel payment)
- Council Tax Benefit
- Constant Attendance Allowance (see Industrial Injuries Benefits)
- Disability Living Allowance
- Income-related Employment and Support Allowance
- Employment and Support Allowance (income related)
- Exceptionally Severe Disablement Allowance (see Industrial Injuries Benefits)
- Guardian's Allowance
- Health in pregnancy grant
- Housing Benefit
- Incapacity Benefit (for first 28 weeks of entitlement, taxable thereafter)
- Income Support (certain payments)
- Income-related employment and support allowance
- Industrial Injuries Benefits (ie industrial injuries pension, reduced earnings allowance, retirement allowance, constant attendance allowance and exceptionally severe disablement allowance)

- Invalidity Benefit
- In-work credit
- In-work emergency discretion fund payment
- In-work emergency fund payment
- Maternity Allowance
- Payments to reduce under-occupation by housing benefit claimants
- Pensioner's Christmas Bonus
- Reduced Earnings Allowance (see Industrial Injuries Benefits)
- Retirement Allowance (see Industrial Injuries Benefits)
- Return to work credit
- Severe Disablement Allowance
- Social Fund Payments
- State Pension credit
- War Widow's pension
- Winter Fuel payment
- Working Tax Credit

*(Sources – ITEPA 2003, s 677 (Table B); EIM76100; Gov.uk (www.gov.uk))*

**Notes**

(1) *Bereavement Payment* – replaced Widow's Payment from 9 April 2001.

(2) *Industrial injuries benefits* – The above excludes industrial death benefit, which is taxable (*ITEPA 2003, ss 577(1), 677(2)*).

(3) *Payments out of the Social Fund* – Payments are made to people on low incomes to help with maternity expenses, funeral costs, financial crises and as community care grants. The fund also makes interest-free loans.

(4) *Return to work credit* – Includes the self-employment credit.

(5) *War Widow's pension* – Where a pension or allowance is not paid or only a reduced amount is paid because the claimant gets a different benefit (eg widowed mother's allowance or widow's pension), the amount of that other benefit that equals the amount of pension withheld, is exempt from income tax (*ITEPA 2003, s 640*; see EIM76103).

With regard to wounds and disability pensions for service with the forces, see EIM74302. For allowances payable to civilians in respect of war injuries, see EIM74700.

(6) *Foreign benefits* – Certain foreign social security payments are exempt from UK tax (see *ITEPA 2003, Pt 10, Ch 7*).

# CHILD BENEFIT AND GUARDIAN'S ALLOWANCE

*(Child Benefit (Rates) Regulations: SI 2006/965)*

| Weekly rates | First child rate | Additional children rate | Guardian's allowance |
|---|---|---|---|
| | £ | £ | £ |
| 2013–14 | 20.30 | 13.40 | 15.90 |
| 2012–13 | 20.30 | 13.40 | 15.55 |
| 2011–12 | 20.30 | 13.40 | 14.75 |
| 2010–11 | 20.30 | 13.40 | 14.30 |
| 2009–10 | 20.00 | 13.20 | 14.10 |

(1)  *General* – Child benefit is not income related and is automatically paid to the claimant (usually the mother) after a single claim, until the child is no longer eligible.

(2)  *Not taxable* – Child benefit is not taxable, and it does not form part of the recipient's taxable income. However, child benefit paid after 7 January 2013 can be clawed-back from high earners, see **Chapter 1: High Income Child Benefit Charge.**

(3)  *Election not to receive* – The child benefit claimant may elect not to receive child benefit, but will retain an entitlement to the benefit (see **Chapter 1**).

(4)  *NI credits* – A person who claims child benefit for a child under 12 years and who does not earn above the LEL will automatically receive national insurance credits which can help make up qualifying years for the State pension.

(5)  *Guardian's allowance* – This is a tax free payment for people who are bringing up children whose parents have died.

(6)  *Further information* – For child benefit and guardian's allowance see www.hmrc. gov.uk/childbenefit/index.htm.

# STATE PENSION

*(Pensions Act 2011)*

| Weekly rates | Basic single person: category A | Spouse's pension: category B | Non-contributory: category C or D | Addition at age 80 |
|---|---|---|---|---|
| | £ | £ | £ | £ |
| 2013–14 | 110.15 | 66.00 | 66.00 | 0.25 |
| 2012–13 | 107.45 | 64.40 | 64.40 | 0.25 |
| 2011–12 | 102.15 | 61.20 | 61.20 | 0.25 |
| 2010–11 | 97.65 | 58.50 | 58.50 | 0.25 |
| 2009–10 | 95.25 | 57.05 | 58.50 | 0.25 |

(1)  *General* – the State retirement pension is payable when a person reaches state pension age (SPA). The SPA varies for men and women and for younger people the SPA is gradually increasing to 68. Use the calculator on gov.uk website to work out the SPA: www.gov.uk/calculate-state-pension.

(2)   *Deferment* – An individual who qualifies for the State pension may choose to defer claiming the State pension. If the person defers for a period of 12 months or more, that person may opt to receive either the pension foregone as a lump sum or a higher pension.

(3)   *Taxable* – The state pension is taxable as is any state pension lump sum received due to deferment *(F(No 2)A 2005, ss 7–10*; see EIM74650).

(4)   *NI contributions* – An individual qualifies for the full basic state pension if they have paid sufficient NI contributions, or received NI credits, in a tax year (a qualifying year), and have accumulated a minimum number qualifying years when he or she reaches SPA. The minimum number of qualifying years required depends on the date SPA is achieved, and for people reaching SPA today is 30 years.

(5)   *Pension forecast* – An individual can request a forecast of their state pension either online or by completing DWP form BR19: www.gov.uk/state-pension-statement.

(6)   *Proposed reforms* – The Government is planning to reform the State Pension from April 2016, when it will introduce a flat rate pension for all new pensioners which will replace pension credit and the second state pension (*Budget, 20 March 2013*).

## 19

# Indexes, exchanges, DTAs etc

## RETAIL PRICES INDEX (RPI)

(1)   RPI is the most familiar general purpose domestic measure of inflation in the UK. Historically, the Government has used it for the uprating of pensions, benefits and index-linked gilts, and for certain tax purposes (see below). However, with effect from 2012–13 the Consumer Prices Index (CPI) is to be used instead as the measure of inflation for pensions and most tax and NIC purposes (see **Consumer Prices Index (CPI)** below).

(2)   The RPI series used for tax purposes is the all items RPI table rebased at Jan 1987 = 100 (code CHAW). This can be viewed here: http://www.ons.gov.uk/ons/datasets-and-tables/data-selector.html?cdid=CHAW&dataset=mm23&table-id=2.1

(3)   RPI factors are used in the calculation of indexation allowance for companies within the charge to corporation tax (*TCGA 1992, s 52A*). Indexation allowance tables are published here: www.hmrc.gov.uk/rates/cg-indexation-allowance/index.htm

(4)   For individuals, trustees and personal representatives, indexation allowance was abolished for disposals from 6 April 2008. The allowance was frozen for disposals between 6 April 1998 and 5 April 2008.

(5)   For indexation allowance tables, and as to the calculation of the allowance (*TCGA 1992, s 54(1)*), see **Chapter 8: Indexation allowance.**

## CONSUMER PRICES INDEX (CPI)

From 2012–13 the underlying indexation of thresholds and limits for direct taxes and national insurance contributions will gradually be changed from the RPI to the CPI, as follows:

- National insurance contributions (NIC) – NIC rates, limits and thresholds (from 2012–13);

- Individual savings accounts (ISAs) – Increases in the annual ISA subscription limit (from 2012–13);

- Capital gains tax (CGT) – The CGT annual exempt amount (from 2013–14);

- Inheritance tax (IHT) – The IHT threshold (or 'nil rate band') (from 2015–16).

Where the legislation provides for the automatic indexation of the CPI (or RPI), this may be subject to override if Parliament determines that a different amount should apply, such as for CGT (*TCGA 1992, s 3(3)*) or IHT (*IHTA 1984, s 8(1)*) purposes.

The CPI annual inflation figure for a particular month can be accessed from the Office for National Statistics (ONS) website (www.ons.gov.uk). A table of CPI (and RPI) indices for the last three years can also be downloaded (in Excel format) from the ONS website.

## BANK BASE RATES

| Date changed | Rate % |
|---|---|
| Thu, 05 Mar 2009 | 0.50 |
| Thu, 05 Feb 2009 | 1.00 |
| Thu, 08 Jan 2009 | 1.50 |
| Thu, 04 Dec 2008 | 2.00 |
| Thu, 06 Nov 2008 | 3.00 |
| Wed, 08 Oct 2008 | 4.50 |
| Thu, 10 Apr 2008 | 5.00 |
| Thu, 07 Feb 2008 | 5.25 |
| Thu, 06 Dec 2007 | 5.50 |

**Note**

Source: Bank of England Statistical Interactive Database – official Bank Rate history (www.bankofengland.co.uk/mfsd/iadb/Repo.asp).

## CERTIFICATES OF TAX DEPOSIT

**Notes** to the table on page 229

(1)   *Who can use it* – The certificate of tax deposit scheme is open to individuals, partnerships (to pay liabilities of the partnership), individual partners (to pay liabilities that apply solely to them), companies, personal representatives (to pay liabilities of a deceased individual's estate) and trustees (to pay liabilities of the trust). Tax deposits can be used to pay liabilities relating to income tax, Class 4 NICs, capital gains tax, petroleum revenue tax, petroleum royalty and inheritance tax, but cannot be used to pay corporation tax liabilities.

(2)   *Value of deposits* – The first tax deposit must be for a minimum of £500. The minimum for subsequent deposits is the lower of £250 and the amount needed to bring total deposits with HMRC back to £500 if it has dropped below that level. There is no maximum amount for a tax deposit.

(3)   *Further information* – Details of the scheme and the rates of interest back to 1988 can be found at: www.hmrc.gov.uk/payinghmrc/cert-tax-deposit.htm.

| Deposits From | Deposits of £100,000 or more | | | | | | | | | | Deposits under £100,000 | |
|---|---|---|---|---|---|---|---|---|---|---|---|---|
| | Deposits held for under 1 month | | Deposits held for 1 to under 3 months | | Deposits held for 3 to under 6 months | | Deposits held for 6 to under 9 months | | Deposits held for 9 to 12 months | | | |
| | Applied in payment of tax % | Cash value % | Applied in payment of tax % | Cash value % | Applied in payment of tax % | Cash value % | Applied in payment of tax % | Cash value % | Applied in payment of tax % | Cash value % | Applied in payment of tax % | Cash value % |
| 6 Mar. 2009 | 0.00 | 0.00 | 0.75 | 0.25 | 0.75 | 0.25 | 0.75 | 0.25 | 0.75 | 0.25 | 0.00 | 0.00 |
| 6 Feb. 2009 | 0.00 | 0.00 | 1.00 | 0.50 | 1.00 | 0.50 | 1.00 | 0.50 | 0.75 | 0.25 | 0.00 | 0.00 |
| 9 Jan. 2009 | 0.00 | 0.00 | 1.50 | 0.75 | 1.25 | 0.50 | 1.25 | 0.50 | 1.25 | 0.50 | 0.00 | 0.00 |
| 5 Dec. 2008 | 0.00 | 0.00 | 2.50 | 1.25 | 2.50 | 1.25 | 2.50 | 1.25 | 2.25 | 1.00 | 0.00 | 0.00 |
| 7 Nov. 2008 | 1.75 | 0.75 | 4.50 | 2.25 | 4.25 | 2.00 | 4.25 | 2.00 | 4.00 | 2.00 | 1.75 | 0.75 |
| 9 Oct. 2008 | 2.50 | 1.25 | 5.25 | 2.50 | 5.00 | 2.50 | 5.00 | 2.50 | 4.75 | 2.25 | 2.50 | 1.25 |
| 11 Apr. 2008 | 2.00 | 1.00 | 4.75 | 2.25 | 4.50 | 2.25 | 4.25 | 2.00 | 4.25 | 2.00 | 2.00 | 1.00 |
| 8 Feb. 2008 | 2.00 | 1.00 | 4.50 | 2.25 | 4.25 | 2.25 | 4.00 | 2.00 | 3.75 | 1.50 | 2.00 | 1.00 |
| 7 Dec. 2007 | 3.00 | 1.50 | 5.50 | 2.75 | 5.00 | 2.50 | 4.75 | 2.25 | 4.50 | 2.25 | 3.00 | 1.50 |
| 6 Jul. 2007 | 2.25 | 1.10 | 5.00 | 2.50 | 4.75 | 2.25 | 4.75 | 2.25 | 4.75 | 2.25 | 2.25 | 1.10 |
| 11 May 2007 | 2.00 | 1.00 | 4.75 | 2.25 | 4.50 | 2.25 | 4.50 | 2.25 | 4.50 | 2.25 | 2.00 | 1.00 |
| 12 Jan. 2007 | 1.50 | 0.75 | 4.25 | 2.00 | 4.00 | 2.00 | 4.00 | 2.00 | 4.00 | 2.00 | 1.50 | 0.75 |
| 10 Nov. 2006 | 1.50 | 0.75 | 4.00 | 2.00 | 4.00 | 2.00 | 3.75 | 1.75 | 3.75 | 1.75 | 1.50 | 0.75 |
| 4 Aug. 2006 | 1.75 | 0.75 | 4.25 | 2.00 | 4.25 | 2.00 | 4.00 | 2.00 | 4.00 | 2.00 | 1.75 | 0.75 |
| 5 Aug. 2005 | 1.00 | 0.50 | 3.50 | 1.75 | 3.25 | 1.50 | 3.00 | 1.50 | 3.00 | 1.50 | 1.00 | 0.50 |
| 6 Aug. 2004 | 1.25 | 0.50 | 3.75 | 1.75 | 3.75 | 1.75 | 3.75 | 1.75 | 3.75 | 1.75 | 1.25 | 0.50 |
| 11 Jun. 2004 | 1.00 | 0.50 | 3.75 | 1.75 | 3.50 | 1.75 | 3.75 | 1.75 | 3.75 | 1.75 | 1.00 | 0.50 |
| 7 May 2004 | 0.75 | 0.25 | 3.25 | 1.50 | 3.25 | 1.50 | 3.25 | 1.50 | 3.25 | 1.50 | 0.75 | 0.25 |
| 6 Feb. 2004 | 0.50 | 0.25 | 3.00 | 1.50 | 3.00 | 1.50 | 3.00 | 1.50 | 3.00 | 1.50 | 0.50 | 0.25 |

229

FOREIGN EXCHANGE RATES

| Average for the year to 31 December 2012 | | Country/Currency | | Average for the year to 31 March 2013 | |
|---|---|---|---|---|---|
| Sterling value of Currency Unit £ | Currency Units per £1 | Country | Unit of Currency | Sterling value of Currency Unit £ | Currency Units per £1 |
| 0.8107 | 1.233473 | European Community | Euro | 0.804 | 1.243802 |
| 0.1464 | 6.831167 | Abu Dhabi | Dirham | 0.1412 | 7.081095 |
| 0.013 | 76.767648 | Afghanistan | Afghani | 0.0128 | 78.380992 |
| 0.0058 | 171.529816 | Albania | Lek | 0.0058 | 172.781275 |
| 0.0081 | 123.093387 | Algeria | Dinar | 0.008 | 124.78715 |
| 0.0066 | 150.805061 | Angola | Readj Kwanza | 0.0066 | 151.5323 |
| 0.2341 | 4.271626 | Antigua | E Caribbean Dollar | 0.2333 | 4.2866025 |
| 0.1392 | 7.181784 | Argentina | Peso | 0.1362 | 7.343248 |
| 0.0016 | 635.239489 | Armenia | Dram | 0.0016 | 643.669 |
| 0.3531 | 2.831951 | Aruba | Florin | 0.3519 | 2.84188 |
| 0.6534 | 1.530380 | Australia | Dollar | 0.6475 | 1.544287 |
| 0.8107 | 1.233473 | Austria | Euro | 0.804 | 1.243802 |
| 0.8054 | 1.241604 | Azerbaijan | New Manat | 0.8028 | 1.2456 |
| 0.6318 | 1.582875 | Bahamas | Dollar | 0.629 | 1.589812 |
| 1.6765 | 0.596475 | Bahrain | Dinar | 1.6707 | 0.59856 |
| 0.0077 | 129.561714 | Bangladesh | Taka | 0.0077 | 129.431575 |
| 0.316 | 3.164138 | Barbados | Dollar | 0.3149 | 3.175235 |
| 0.0001 | 13228.889795 | Belarus | Rouble | 0.0001 | 13327.6875 |
| 0.8107 | 1.233473 | Belgium | Euro | 0.804 | 1.243802 |
| 0.3278 | 3.050991 | Belize | Dollar | 0.3267 | 3.061117 |
| 0.0012 | 809.512836 | Benin | CFA Franc | 0.0012 | 815.514775 |
| 0.6318 | 1.582875 | Bermuda | Dollar (US) | 0.629 | 1.589812 |

| Average for the year to 31 December 2012 | | Country/Currency | | Average for the year to 31 March 2013 | |
|---|---|---|---|---|---|
| Sterling value of Currency Unit £ | Currency Units per £1 | Country | Unit of Currency | Sterling value of Currency Unit £ | Currency Units per £1 |
| 0.0118 | 84.532805 | Bhutan | Ngultrum | 0.0116 | 86.500239 |
| 0.0915 | 10.931695 | Bolivia | Boliviano | 0.0912 | 10.969937 |
| 0.4143 | 2.413702 | Bosnia-Herzegovinia | Marka | 0.4113 | 2.431597 |
| 0.0813 | 12.296653 | Botswana | Pula | 0.0797 | 12.544555 |
| 0.3235 | 3.091557 | Brazil | Real | 0.3123 | 3.2019 |
| 0.5055 | 1.978051 | Brunei | Dollar | 0.5058 | 1.977255 |
| 0.4143 | 2.413708 | Bulgaria | Lev | 0.4113 | 2.43159 |
| 0.0012 | 809.512836 | Burkina Faso | CFA Franc | 0.0012 | 815.514775 |
| 0.0004 | 2278.453877 | Burundi | Franc | 0.0004 | 2315.584 |
| 0.0002 | 6389.105714 | Cambodia | Riel | 0.0002 | 6412.63325 |
| 0.0012 | 809.512836 | Cameroon Republic | CFA Franc | 0.0012 | 815.514775 |
| 0.6315 | 1.583601 | Canada | Dollar | 0.6296 | 1.588204 |
| 0.0074 | 135.763795 | Cape Verde Islands | Escudo | 0.0073 | 136.691475 |
| 0.7708 | 1.297328 | Cayman Islands | Dollar | 0.7681 | 1.301877 |
| 0.0012 | 809.512836 | Central African | CFA Franc | 0.0012 | 815.514775 |
| 0.0012 | 809.512836 | Chad | CFA Franc | 0.0012 | 815.514775 |
| 0.0013 | 770.0784489 | Chile | Peso | 0.0013 | 771.85795 |
| 0.1001 | 9.988053 | China | Yuan | 0.0998 | 10.017312 |
| 0 | 60320.529387 | Colombia | Peso | 0 | 73260.12825 |
| 0.0016 | 607.134714 | Comoros | Franc | 0.0016 | 611.6362 |
| 0.0012 | 809.512836 | Congo (Brazaville) | CFA Franc | 0.0012 | 815.514775 |
| 0.0007 | 1454.9075510204 | Congo (DemRep) | Congo Fr | 0.0007 | 1459.6485 |

*continued*

231

| Average for the year to 31 December 2012 | | Country/Currency | | Average for the year to 31 March 2013 | |
|---|---|---|---|---|---|
| Sterling value of Currency Unit £ | Currency Units per £1 | Country | Unit of Currency | Sterling value of Currency Unit £ | Currency Units per £1 |
| 0.0013 | 795.48502040816 | Costa Rica | Colon | 0.0013 | 795.054275 |
| 0.0012 | 809.51283673469 | Cote d'Ivoire | CFA Franc | 0.0012 | 815.514775 |
| 0.1078 | 9.276048 | Croatia | Kuna | 0.1072 | 9.3297425 |
| 0.6321 | 1.582097 | Cuba | Peso | 0.6299 | 1.58765 |
| 0.8107 | 1.233473 | Cyprus | Euro | 0.804 | 1.243802 |
| 0.0322 | 31.050883 | Czech Republic | Koruna | 0.032 | 31.29844 |
| 0.1089 | 9.181059 | Denmark | Krone | 0.108 | 9.262117 |
| 0.0036 | 277.746816 | Djibouti | Franc | 0.0036 | 279.107975 |
| 0.2341 | 4.271626 | Dominica | E Caribbean Dollar | 0.2333 | 4.286602 |
| 0.0161 | 61.943573 | Dominican Republic | Peso | 0.016 | 62.354487 |
| 0.1464 | 6.831167 | Dubai | Dirham | 0.1412 | 7.081095 |
| 0.6318 | 1.582875 | Ecuador | Dollar | 0.629 | 1.589812 |
| 0.1042 | 9.598010 | Egypt | Pound | 0.1036 | 9.654277 |
| 0.0723 | 13.839181 | El Salvador | Colon | 0.072 | 13.887712 |
| 0.0012 | 809.512836 | Equatorial Guinea | CFA Franc | 0.0012 | 815.514775 |
| 0.0421 | 23.730136 | Eritrea | Nakfa | 0.042 | 23.813152 |
| 0.8107 | 1.233473 | Estonia | Euro | 0.804 | 1.243802 |
| 0.0355 | 28.144177 | Ethiopia | Birr | 0.0352 | 28.445622 |
| 0.3528 | 2.834738 | Fiji Islands | Dollar | 0.3505 | 2.853422 |
| 0.8107 | 1.233473 | Finland | Euro | 0.804 | 1.243802 |
| 0.0068 | 147.266612 | Fr. Polynesia | CFP Franc | 0.0067 | 148.35845 |
| 0.8107 | 1.233473 | France | Euro | 0.804 | 1.243802 |

| Average for the year to 31 December 2012 | | Country/Currency | | Average for the year to 31 March 2013 | |
|---|---|---|---|---|---|
| Sterling value of Currency Unit £ | Currency Units per £1 | Country | Unit of Currency | Sterling value of Currency Unit £ | Currency Units per £1 |
| 0.0012 | 809.512836 | Gabon | CFA Franc | 0.0012 | 815.514775 |
| 0.0203 | 49.346304 | Gambia | Dalasi | 0.02 | 50.012227 |
| 0.0203 | 49.320938 | Georgia | Lari | 0.0201 | 49.854902 |
| 0.8107 | 1.233473 | Germany | Euro | 0.804 | 1.243802 |
| 0.3407 | 2.9353 | Ghana | Cedi | 0.3318 | 3.013477 |
| 0.8107 | 1.233473 | Greece | Euro | 0.804 | 1.243802 |
| 0.2341 | 4.271626 | Grenada | E Caribbean Dollar | 0.2333 | 4.286602 |
| 0.0806 | 12.402746 | Guatemala | Quetzal | 0.0801 | 12.477575 |
| 0.0012 | 809.512836 | Guinea Bissau | CFA Franc | 0.0012 | 815.514775 |
| 0.0001 | 11031.342216 | Guinea Republic | Franc | 0.0001 | 10987.181715 |
| 0.0031 | 318.159979 | Guyana | Dollar | 0.0031 | 319.1083 |
| 0.0152 | 65.880948 | Haiti | Gourde | 0.015 | 66.633315 |
| 0.0327 | 30.551165 | Honduras | Lempira | 0.0325 | 30.81541 |
| 0.0814 | 12.279098 | Hong Kong | Dollar | 0.0811 | 12.330680 |
| 0.0028 | 356.920591 | Hungary | Forint | 0.0028 | 357.2737 |
| 0.0055 | 181.907653 | Iceland | Krona | 0.0056 | 179.505475 |
| 0.0118 | 84.532805 | India | Rupee | 0.0116 | 86.500239 |
| 0.0001 | 14803.457142 | Indonesia | Rupiah | 0.0001 | 15015.7875 |
| 0.0001 | 19282.640816 | Iran | Rial | 0.0001 | 19509.6825 |
| 0.0005 | 1838.802040 | Iraq | Dinar | 0.0005 | 1844.89425 |
| 0.8107 | 1.233473 | Ireland | Euro | 0.804 | 1.243802 |
| 0.1637 | 6.108028 | Israel | Shekel | 0.1623 | 6.162295 |

*continued*

233

| Average for the year to 31 December 2012 | | Country/Currency | | Average for the year to 31 March 2013 | |
|---|---|---|---|---|---|
| Sterling value of Currency Unit £ | Currency Units per £1 | Country | Unit of Currency | Sterling value of Currency Unit £ | Currency Units per £1 |
| 0.8107 | 1.233473 | Italy | Euro | 0.804 | 1.243802 |
| 0.0072 | 139.787857 | Jamaica | Dollar | 0.0071 | 141.45215 |
| 0.0079 | 126.15025 | Japan | Yen | 0.0078 | 127.557341 |
| 0.8923 | 1.120644 | Jordan | Dinar | 0.8893 | 1.124432 |
| 0.0042 | 235.948204 | Kazakhstan | Tenge | 0.0042 | 237.301475 |
| 0.0075 | 133.743897 | Kenya | Schilling | 0.0074 | 134.4561 |
| 0.4862 | 2.056610 | Korea (North) | Won | 0.4845 | 2.063802 |
| 1.5948 | 0.627044 | Kuwait | Dinar | 1.4907 | 0.67081 |
| 0.0203 | 49.320938 | Kyrgyz Republic | Som | 0.0201 | 49.854902 |
| 0.0001 | 12601.877551 | Lao People's Dem Rep | Kip | 0.0001 | 12647.16 |
| 1.1621 | 0.860487 | Latvia | Lat | 1.1542 | 0.866422 |
| 0.0004 | 2380.240816 | Lebanon | Pound | 0.0004 | 2388.616 |
| 0.0769 | 13.0064102 | Lesotho | Loti | 0.0753 | 13.279955 |
| 0.6318 | 1.582875 | Liberia | Dollar (US) | 0.629 | 1.589812 |
| 0.5056 | 1.977814 | Libya | Dinar | 0.5021 | 1.991437 |
| 0.2347 | 4.261118 | Lithuania | Litas | 0.233 | 4.29271 |
| 0.8107 | 1.233473 | Luxembourg | Euro | 0.804 | 1.243802 |
| 0.0791 | 12.640185 | Macao | Pataca | 0.0788 | 12.683102 |
| 0.0132 | 76.0009671 | Macedonia | Denar | 0.0131 | 76.625557 |
| 0.0003 | 3479.529183 | Madagascar | Malagasy Ariary | 0.0003 | 3499.89 |
| 0.0025 | 395.980142 | Malawi | Kwacha | 0.0023 | 440.306325 |
| 0.2045 | 4.889942 | Malaysia | Ringgit | 0.2033 | 4.919212 |

| Average for the year to 31 December 2012 | | Country/Currency | | Average for the year to 31 March 2013 | |
|---|---|---|---|---|---|
| Sterling value of Currency Unit £ | Currency Units per £1 | Country | Unit of Currency | Sterling value of Currency Unit £ | Currency Units per £1 |
| 0.0411 | 24.315871 | Maldive Islands | Rufiyaa | 0.041 | 24.396255 |
| 0.0012 | 809.512836 | Mali Republic | CFA Franc | 0.0012 | 815.514775 |
| 0.8107 | 1.233473 | Malta | Euro | 0.804 | 1.243802 |
| 0.0021 | 469.061795 | Mauritania | Ouguiya | 0.0021 | 472.82065 |
| 0.021 | 47.713481 | Mauritius | Rupee | 0.0207 | 48.321222 |
| 0.0479 | 20.875711 | Mexico | Mexican Peso | 0.0476 | 20.991612 |
| 0.0522 | 19.169014 | Moldova | Leu | 0.0517 | 19.35355 |
| 0.0005 | 2149.365918 | Mongolia | Tugrik | 0.0005 | 2159.64525 |
| 0.2341 | 4.271626 | Montserrat | E Caribbean Dollar | 0.2333 | 4.286602 |
| 0.0731 | 13.681197 | Morocco | Dirham | 0.0726 | 13.772027 |
| 0.0224 | 44.731187 | Mozambique | Metical | 0.022 | 45.448342 |
| 0.001 | 998.850914 | Myanmar | Kyat | 0.0008 | 1290.06751 |
| 0.0074 | 135.203061 | Nepal | Rupee | 0.0072 | 138.2563 |
| 0.8107 | 1.233473 | Netherland | Euro | 0.804 | 1.243802 |
| 0.0068 | 147.266612 | New Caledonia | CFP Franc | 0.0067 | 148.35845 |
| 0.5102 | 1.959825 | New Zealand | Dollar | 0.5074 | 1.970724 |
| 0.0269 | 37.239314 | Nicaragua | Gold Cordoba | 0.0266 | 37.603287 |
| 0.0012 | 809.512836 | Niger Republic | CFA Franc | 0.0012 | 815.514775 |
| 0.004 | 251.436428 | Nigeria | Naira | 0.004 | 251.94395 |
| 0.1083 | 9.233155 | Norway | Norwegian Krone | 0.108 | 9.256758 |
| 1.6416 | 0.609144 | Oman | Rial | 1.6359 | 0.611292 |
| 0.0068 | 147.702285 | Pakistan | Rupee | 0.0067 | 149.7295 |

*continued*

235

| Average for the year to 31 December 2012 | | Country/Currency | | Average for the year to 31 March 2013 | |
|---|---|---|---|---|---|
| Sterling value of Currency Unit £ | Currency Units per £1 | Country | Unit of Currency | Sterling value of Currency Unit £ | Currency Units per £1 |
| 0.6321 | 1.582097 | Panama | Balboa | 0.6299 | 1.58765 |
| 0.3067 | 3.260636 | Papua New Guinea | Kina | 0.3063 | 3.26458 |
| 0.0001 | 7021.556938 | Paraguay | Guarani | 0.0001 | 7014.83425 |
| 0.2394 | 4.177540 | Peru | New Sol | 0.24 | 4.16687 |
| 0.0149 | 66.912084 | Philippines | Peso | 0.015 | 66.694146 |
| 0.1934 | 5.169414 | Poland | Zloty | 0.1928 | 5.18775 |
| 0.8107 | 1.233473 | Portugal | Euro | 0.804 | 1.243802 |
| 0.1736 | 5.760416 | Qatar | Riyal | 0.173 | 5.780567 |
| 0.1814 | 5.512736 | Romania | New Leu | 0.1789 | 5.590047 |
| 0.0203 | 49.320938 | Russia | Rouble | 0.0201 | 49.854902 |
| 0.001 | 971.315836 | Rwanda | Franc | 0.001 | 979.919575 |
| 0 | 29877.959183 | Saotome & Principe | Dobra | 0 | 29991.6275 |
| 0.1685 | 5.936051 | Saudi Arabia | Riyal | 0.1677 | 5.962043 |
| 0.0012 | 809.512836 | Senegal | CFA Franc | 0.0012 | 815.514775 |
| 0.0072 | 139.699734 | Serbia | Dinar | 0.007 | 142.497325 |
| 0.0461 | 21.708744 | Seychelles | Rupee | 0.0462 | 21.640117 |
| 0.0001 | 6872.885714 | Sierra Leone | Leone | 0.0001 | 6887.74925 |
| 0.5048 | 1.980832 | Singapore | Dollar | 0.5054 | 1.978721 |
| 0.8107 | 1.233473 | Slovakia | Euro | 0.804 | 1.243802 |
| 0.8107 | 1.233473 | Slovenia | Euro | 0.804 | 1.243802 |
| 0.0891 | 11.224248 | Soloman Islands | Dollar | 0.0888 | 11.25496 |
| 0.0004 | 2491.090204 | Somali Republic | Schilling | 0.0004 | 2497.6395 |

| | Average for the year to 31 December 2012 | | Country/Currency | | Average for the year to 31 March 2013 | |
|---|---|---|---|---|---|---|
| | Sterling value of Currency Unit £ | Currency Units per £1 | Country | Unit of Currency | Sterling value of Currency Unit £ | Currency Units per £1 |
| | 0.0769 | 13.006967 | South Africa | Rand | 0.0753 | 13.288097 |
| | 0.0006 | 1785.194230 | South Korea | Won | 0.0006 | 1786.164390 |
| | 0.8107 | 1.233473 | Spain | Euro | 0.804 | 1.243802 |
| | 0.0049 | 202.164448 | Sri Lanka | Rupee | 0.0048 | 207.29165 |
| | 0.2341 | 4.271626 | St Christopher & | E Caribbean Dollar | 0.2333 | 4.286602 |
| | 0.2341 | 4.271626 | St Lucia | E Caribbean Dollar | 0.2333 | 4.286602 |
| | 0.2341 | 4.271626 | St Vincent | E Caribbean Dollar | 0.2333 | 4.286602 |
| | 0.1787 | 5.594983 | Sudan Republic | Pound | 0.1651 | 6.056327 |
| | 0.1915 | 5.220865 | Surinam | Dollar | 0.1909 | 5.239172 |
| | 0.0769 | 13.006410 | Swaziland | Lilangeni | 0.0753 | 13.279955 |
| | 0.0931 | 10.741259 | Sweden | Krona | 0.0929 | 10.7687 |
| | 0.6725 | 1.486984 | Switzerland | Franc | 0.6675 | 1.498065 |
| | 0.01 | 100.277797 | Syria | Pound | 0.0096 | 103.983882 |
| | 0.0213 | 46.858536 | Taiwan | Dollar | 0.0213 | 46.947095 |
| | 0.0203 | 49.320938 | Tajikistan | Somoni | 0.0201 | 49.854902 |
| | 0.0004 | 2509.602040 | Tanzania | Schilling | 0.0004 | 2514.73725 |
| | 0.0203 | 49.223330 | Thailand | Baht | 0.0202 | 49.412148 |
| | 0.0012 | 809.512836 | Togo Republic | CFA Franc | 0.0012 | 815.514775 |
| | 0.6534 | 1.530380 | Tonga Islands | Pa'anga (AUS) | 0.6475 | 1.544287 |
| | 0.0986 | 10.137330 | Trinidad/Tobago | Dollar | 0.0983 | 10.17442 |
| | 0.4037 | 2.476826 | Tunisia | Dinar | 0.3987 | 2.50812 |
| | 0.3509 | 2.850042 | Turkey | Turkish Lira | 0.3494 | 2.862235 |

*continued*

| | Average for the year to 31 December 2012 | | Country/Currency | | Average for the year to 31 March 2013 |
|---|---|---|---|---|---|
| **Country** | **Sterling value of Currency Unit £** | **Currency Units per £1** | **Unit of Currency** | **Sterling value of Currency Unit £** | **Currency Units per £1** |
| Turkmenistan | 0.2222 | 4.500820 | New Manat | 0.2213 | 4.518597 |
| UAE | 0.1464 | 6.831167 | Dirham | 0.1412 | 7.081095 |
| Uganda | 0.0003 | 3956.551836 | Schilling | 0.0002 | 4032.06325 |
| Ukraine | 0.0782 | 12.792736 | Hryvnia | 0.0778 | 12.860747 |
| Uruguay | 0.0311 | 32.104220 | Peso | 0.0308 | 32.491295 |
| USA | 0.6318 | 1.582875 | Dollar | 0.629 | 1.589812 |
| Uzbekistan | 0.0003 | 2986.947755 | Sum | 0.0003 | 3036.15975 |
| Vanuatu | 0.0067 | 149.246306 | Vatu | 0.0067 | 150.209575 |
| Venezuela | 0.1472 | 6.794202 | Bolivar Fuerte | 0.1467 | 6.81797 |
| Vietnam | 0 | 33021.285714 | Dong | 0 | 33125.295 |
| Wallis & Futuna Islands | 0.0068 | 147.266612 | CFP Franc | 0.0067 | 148.35845 |
| Western Samoa | 0.2754 | 3.631644 | Tala | 0.2738 | 3.65195 |
| Yemen (Rep of) | 0.0029 | 341.023040 | Rial | 0.0029 | 341.167225 |
| Zambia | 0.0001 | 8132.805510 | Kwacha | 0.0001 | 8138.50675 |
| Zimbabwe | 0.0017 | 598.385187 | Dollar | 0.0017 | 600.613974 |

**Note**

This table is reproduced from information provided by HMRC (www.hmrc.gov.uk/exrate/exchangerates-1213.pdf) and is Crown copyright.

| Table of spot rates on 31 December 2012 and 31 March 2013 | | | | | |
|---|---|---|---|---|---|
| **31 December 2012** | | **Country/Currency** | | **31 March 2013** | |
| **Sterling value of Currency Unit £** | **Currency Units per £1** | **Country** | **Unit of currency** | **Sterling value of Currency Unit £** | **Currency Units per £1** |
| 0.6387 | 1.5657 | Australia | AUD Dollar | 0 | 0 |
| 0.6179 | 1.6185 | Canada | CAD Dollar | 0 | 0 |
| 0.1087 | 9.1989 | Denmark | DKK Krone | 0 | 0 |
| 0.811 | 1.233 | European Community | EUR Euro | 0 | 0 |
| 0.0794 | 12.5991 | Hong Kong | HKD Dollar | 0 | 0 |
| 0.0071 | 140.549 | Japan | JPY Yen | 0 | 0 |
| 0.1105 | 9.0463 | Norway | NOK Norwegian Krone | 0 | 0 |
| 0.0725 | 13.7914 | South Africa | ZAR Rand | 0 | 0 |
| 0.0946 | 10.5746 | Sweden | SEK Krona | 0 | 0 |
| 0.6721 | 1.4879 | Switzerland | CHF Franc | 0 | 0 |
| 0.6152 | 1.6255 | USA | USD Dollar | 0 | 0 |

**Notes**

(1)   This table is reproduced from information provided by HMRC (http://www.hmrc. gov.uk/exrate/exchangerates-1213.pdf) and is Crown copyright.

(2)   At the time of writing (31 March 2013) HMRC had not yet published their table of spot rates for 31 March 2013.


## RECOGNISED STOCK EXCHANGES

(*ITA 2007, s 1005*; *CTA 2010, s 1137*)

A 'recognised stock exchange' is one which is either:

● A recognised investment exchange designated as a recognised stock exchange by an order of the Commissioners for HMRC; or

● any designated market outside the UK.

A recognised stock exchange within *ITA 2007, s 1005* is also treated as such for corporation tax purposes (*CTA 2010, s 1137(1)*).


## Stock exchanges designated as recognised stock exchanges

| Stock exchange | Date of recognition |
|---|---|
| The Athens Stock Exchange | 14 June 1993 |
| The Australian Stock Exchange (and any of its stock exchange subsidiaries) | 22 September 1988 |
| Bahamas International Securities Exchange (BISX) | 19 April 2010 |
| The Bermuda Stock Exchange | 4 December 2007 |

*continued*

| Stock exchange | Date of recognition |
|---|---|
| The Bond Exchange of South Africa | 16 April 2008 |
| The Cayman Islands Stock Exchange | 4 March 2004 |
| The Colombo Stock Exchange | 21 February 1972 |
| The Copenhagen Stock Exchange | 22 October 1970 |
| The Cyprus Stock Exchange | 22 June 2009 |
| European Wholesale Securities market | 18 January 2013 |
| The Helsinki Stock Exchange | 22 October 1970 |
| The Iceland Stock Exchange | 31 March 2006 |
| The Johannesburg Stock Exchange | 22 October 1970 |
| The Korea Stock Exchange | 10 October 1994 |
| The Kuala Lumpur Stock Exchange | 10 October 1994 |
| The London International Financial Futures and Options Exchange Administration and Management (LIFFE A&M) | 26 September 2011 |
| The London Stock Exchange | 19 July 2007 |
| The Malta Stock Exchange | 29 December 2005 |
| The Mexico Stock Exchange | 10 October 1994 |
| The MICEX Stock Exchange | 5 January 2011 |
| NASDAQ OMX Tallinn (except its First North market) | 5 May 2010 |
| NASDAQ OMX Vilnius (except securities quoted solely on its First North market) | 12 March 2012 |
| The New Zealand Stock Exchange | 22 September 1988 |
| The Plus-listed Market | 19 July 2007 |
| The Rio De Janeiro Stock Exchange | 17 August 1995 |
| The Sao Paulo Stock Exchange | 11 December 1995 |
| The Singapore Stock Exchange | 30 June 1977 |
| The Stockholm Stock Exchange | 16 July 1985 |
| The Stock Exchange of Mauritius | 31 January 2011 |
| The Stock Exchange of Thailand | 10 October 1994 |
| The Swiss Stock Exchange | 12 May 1997 |
| The Warsaw Stock Exchange | 25 February 2010 |

## Recognised stock exchange countries

The following are countries where any stock exchange in that country that is a stock exchange within the law of that country is a recognised stock exchange.

| Stock exchange | Date of recognition |
|---|---|
| Austria | 22 October 1970 |
| Belgium | 22 October 1970 |
| Canada | 22 October 1970 |
| France | 22 October 1970 |
| Germany | 5 August 1971 |
| Guernsey | 10 December 2002 |
| Hong Kong | 26 February 1971 |

| Stock exchange | Date of recognition |
|---|---|
| Ireland (Republic of) | 22 October 1970 |
| Italy | 3 May 1972 |
| Japan | 22 October 1970 |
| Luxembourg | 21 February 1972 |
| Netherlands | 22 October 1970 |
| Norway | 22 October 1970 |
| Portugal | 21 February 1972 |
| Spain | 5 August 1971 |
| USA | See note |

**Note**

*USA* – A stock exchange in the USA is a recognised stock exchange for UK tax purposes if it meets the following:

'Any exchange registered with the Securities and Exchange Commission of the United States (SEC) as a national securities exchange under Section 6 of the Securities Exchange Act of 1934 is a recognised stock exchange for UK tax purposes.'

The American Stock Exchange was a recognised stock exchange between 22 October 1970 and 1 October 2008, but following its split into new markets, it is no longer a recognised stock exchange in its own right.

## Alternative finance investment bonds

*(ITA 2007 s 564G)*

The following is a list of recognised stock exchanges designated solely for the purposes of *ITA 2007, s 564G* (alternative finance arrangements: investment bonds). The date of recognition in all cases is 1 April 2007:

- Abu Dhabi Securities Market
- Bahrain Stock Exchange
- Dubai Financial Market
- NASDAQ Dubai (formerly Dubai International Financial Exchange)
- Labuan International Financial Exchange
- Saudi Stock Exchange (Tadawul)
- Surabaya Stock Exchange

## Recognised futures exchanges

*(TCGA 1992, s 288(6))*

| Tax year of recognition | Exchange |
|---|---|
| 1985–86 | [The Baltic International Freight Futures Exchange] |
| | The International Petroleum Exchange London |

*continued*

| Tax year of recognition | Exchange |
|---|---|
| 1985–86 – *contd* | [The London Cocoa Terminal Market] |
| | [The London Coffee Terminal Market] |
| | [The London Grain Futures Market] |
| | [The London Meat Futures Market] |
| | The London Metal Exchange |
| | [The London Potato Futures Market] |
| | The London Rubber Market |
| | [The London Soya Bean Meal Futures Market] |
| | [The London Sugar Terminal Market] |
| | The London Gold Market |
| | The London Silver Market |
| 1986–87 | The Chicago Mercantile Exchange |
| | The Philadelphia Board of Trade |
| | The New York Mercantile Exchange |
| 1987–88 | The Chicago Board of Trade |
| | The Montreal Exchange |
| | The Mid America Commodity Exchange |
| | The Hong Kong Futures Exchange |
| | The Coffee, Sugar and Cocoa Exchange Inc, New York |
| 1988–89 | The Commodity Exchange, Inc (COMEX) |
| | The Citrus Associates of the New York Cotton Exchange, Inc |
| | The New York Cotton Exchange |
| | The Sydney Futures Exchange Ltd |
| 1991–92 | The London International Financial Futures and Options Exchange |
| | London FOX |
| | OM London |
| | OM Stockholm AB |

**Notes**

(1)   Recognised futures exchange means the London International Financial Futures Exchange and any other futures exchange which is designated (for the purposes of *TCGA 1992* by order of the Board.

(2)   The exchanges shown in brackets above have been part of the London FOX since January 1991. This in turn merged into the London International Financial Futures and Options Exchange in 1996.

(3)   The above exchanges are accepted as recognised futures exchanges for the tax year of recognition onwards (CG56120).

## Recognised investment exchanges

*(ITEPA 2003, s 702)*

| Date of recognition | Exchange |
|---|---|
| 22 November 2001 | ICE Futures Europe |
| 19 July 2007 | ICAP Securities & Derivatives Exchange Limited |
| 22 November 2001 | LIFFE Administration and Management |
| 22 November 2001 | London Stock Exchange plc |
| 22 November 2001 | The London Metal Exchange Limited |

## Recognised overseas investment exchanges

*(ITEPA 2003, s 702)*

| Date of recognition | Exchange |
|---|---|
| 30 January 2002 | Australian Securities Exchange Limited |
| 23 November 2001 | Chicago Board of Trade (CBOT) |
| 23 November 2001 | EUREX [Zurich] |
| 17 May 2007 | ICE Futures US Inc |
| 23 November 2001 | National Association of Securities Dealers Automated Quotations (NASDAQ) |
| 23 November 2001 | New York Mercantile Exchange Inc. [NYMEX Inc.] |
| 29 September 2009 | NYSE Liffe US |
| 23 November 2001 | SIX Swiss Exchange AG |
| 23 November 2001 | The Chicago Mercantile Exchange [CME] |

### Notes for recognised investment and overseas investment exchanges

(1)   Source: The Financial Services Authority (FSA) Register: (www.fsa.gov.uk/ register/exchanges.do)

(2)   The definition of 'readily convertible asset' *(ITEPA 2003, s 702)* includes an asset capable of being sold or otherwise realised on a recognised investment exchange, within the meaning of the *Financial Services and Markets Act 2000*. The FSA has recognised and supervises a number of Recognised Overseas Investment Exchanges.

## DOUBLE TAXATION AGREEMENTS

*(TIOPA 2010, Pt 2, Ch 1; HMRC Double Taxation Relief Manual DT2140 et seq)*

## Countries with a Double Taxation Agreement with the UK

| Country | Authority | Coverage |
|---|---|---|
| Algeria | SI 1984/362 | ATP |
| Antigua & Barbuda | SRO 1947/2865 Amended by SI 1968/1096 | C |

*continued*

243

| Country | Authority | Coverage |
|---|---|---|
| Argentina | SI 1997/1777 | C |
| | Amended by Protocol of 3 January 1996 | |
| Armenia | SI 2011/2722 | C |
| Australia | SI 2003/3199 | C |
| Austria | SI 1970/1947 | C |
| | Amended by Protocols SI 1979/117, SI 1994/768 and SI 2010/2688 | |
| Azerbaijan | SI 1995/762 | C |
| Bahrain | SI 2012/3075 | C |
| Bangladesh | SI 1980/708 | C |
| Barbados | SI 2012/3076 | C |
| Belarus | SI 1974/1269 (not superseded) | ATP |
| | SI 1986/224 [SI 1995/2706 not yet in force] | C |
| Belgium | SI 1987/2053 | C |
| | Amended by protocol SI 2010/2979 | |
| Belize | SRO 1947/2866 | C |
| | Amended by Protocols SI 1968/573 and SI 1973/2097 | |
| Bolivia | SI 1995/2707 | C |
| Bosnia Herzegovina | SI 1981/1815 | C |
| Botswana | SI 2006/1925 | C |
| Brazil | SI 1968/572 | S, ATP |
| British Virgin Islands | SI 2009/3013 | IT |
| Brunei | SI 1950/1977 | C |
| | Amended by Protocols SI 1968/306 and SI 1973/2098 | |
| Bulgaria | SI 1987/2054 | C |
| Burma (Myanmar) | SI 1952/751 including Protocol | C |
| Cameroon | SI 1982/1841 | ATP |
| Canada | SI 1980/709 | C |
| | Amended by Protocols SI 1980/1528, SI 1985/1996 and SI 2003/2619 | |
| Cayman Islands | SI 2010/2973 | IT |
| Chile | SI 2003/3200 | C |
| China | SI 1981/1119 (not superseded) | ATP |
| | SI 1984/1826 | C |
| | Amended by Protocol SI 1996/3164 | |
| Croatia | SI 1981/1815 | C |
| Cyprus | SI 1975/425 | C |
| | Amended by Protocol SI 1980/1529 | |
| Czech Republic | SI 1991/2876 | C |

| Country | Authority | Coverage |
|---|---|---|
| Denmark | SI 1980/1960 | C |
| | Amended by Protocols SI 1991/2877 and SI 1996/3165 | |
| Egypt | SI 1980/1091 | C |
| Estonia | SI 1994/3207 | C |
| Ethiopia | SI 1977/1297 | ATP |
| Falkland Islands | SI 1997/2985 | C |
| Faroes | SI 2007/3469 | C |
| Fiji | SI 1976/1342 | C |
| Finland | SI 1970/153 | C |
| | Amended by Protocols SI 1973/1327, SI 1980/710, SI 1985/1997, 1991/2878 and 1996/3166 | |
| France | SI 2009/226 | C |
| Gambia | SI 1980/1963 | C |
| Georgia | SI 2004/3325 | C |
| Germany | SI 2010/2975 | C |
| Ghana | SI 1993/1800 | C |
| Greece | SI 1954/142 | C |
| Grenada | SI 1949/361 | C |
| | Amended by Protocol SI 1968/1867 | |
| Guernsey | SI 1952/1215 | C |
| | Amended by Protocol SI 1994/3209, Supplementary Arrangement 2009/3011 | |
| Guyana | SI 1992/3207 | C |
| Hong Kong | SI 2010/2974 including Protocol | C |
| Hungary | SI 2011/2726 | C |
| Iceland | SI 1991/2879 | C |
| India | SI 1993/1801 | C |
| Indonesia | SI 1994/769 | C |
| Iran | SI 1960/2419 | ATP |
| Ireland | SI 1976/2151 | C |
| | Amended by Protocols SI 1976/2152, SI 1995/764 and SI 1998/3151 | |
| Isle of Man | SI 1955/1205 | C |
| | Amended by Supplementary Arrangements SI 1991/2880, SI 1994/3208 and SI 2009/228 | |
| Israel | SI 1963/616 | C |
| | Amended by Protocol – SI 1971/391 | |
| Italy | SI 1990/2590 | C |
| Ivory Coast | SI 1987/169 | C |
| Jamaica | SI 1973/1329 | C |
| Japan | SI 2006/1924 | C |

*continued*

| Country | Authority | Coverage |
|---------|-----------|----------|
| Jersey | SI 1952/1216 | C |
| | Amended by Arrangements SI 1994/3210 and SI 2009/3012 | |
| Jordan | SI 2001/3924 | C |
| Kazakhstan | SI 1994/3211 | C |
| | Amended by Protocol SI 1998/2567 | |
| Kenya | SI 1977/1299 | C |
| Kiribati | SI 1950/750 | C |
| | Amended by Arrangements SI 1968/309 and SI 1974/1271 | |
| Korea (Republic of) | SI 1996/3168 | C |
| Kuwait | SI 1999/2036 | C |
| Latvia | SI 1996/3167 | C |
| Lebanon | SI 1964/278 | S, ATP |
| Lesotho | SI 1997/2986 | C |
| Libya | SI 2010/243 | C |
| Liechtenstein | SI 2012/3077 | C |
| Lithuania | SI 2001/3925 | C |
| | Amended by Protocol SI 2002/2847 | |
| Luxembourg | SI 1968/1100 | C |
| | Amended by Protocols SI 1980/567, SI 1984/364 and SI 2010/237 | |
| Macedonia | SI 2007/2127 | C |
| Malawi | SI 1956/619 | C |
| | Amended by Protocols SI 1964/1401, 1968/1101 and SI 1979/302 | |
| Malaysia | SI 1997/2987 | C |
| Malta | SI 1995/763 | C |
| Mauritius | SI 1981/1121 | C |
| | Amended by Protocols SI 1987/467, SI 2003/2620 and SI 2011/2442 | |
| Mexico | SI 1994/3212 | C |
| Moldova | SI 2008/1795 | C |
| Mongolia | SI 1996/2598 | C |
| Montenegro | SI 1981/1815 | C |
| Montserrat | SRO 1947/2869 | C |
| | Amended by Protocol SI 1968/576 | |
| | SI 2011/1083 | |
| Morocco | SI 1991/2881 | C |
| Namibia | SI 1962/2352 | C |
| | Extended by SI 1962/2788 – Amended by Protocol SI 1967/1489 as extended by SI 1967/1490 | |

| Country | Authority | Coverage |
|---|---|---|
| Netherlands | SI 2009/227 | C |
| New Zealand | SI 1984/365 | C |
| | Amended by Protocols SI 2004/1274, SI 2008/1973 | |
| Nigeria | SI 1987/2057 | C |
| Norway | SI 2000/3247 | C |
| Oman | SI 1998/2568 | C |
| | Amended by Protocol SI 2010/2687 | |
| Pakistan | SI 1987/2058 | C |
| Papua New Guinea | SI 1991/2882 | C |
| Philippines | SI 1978/184 | C |
| Poland | SI 2006/3323 | C |
| Portugal | SI 1969/599 | C |
| Qatar | SI 2010/241 | C |
| Romania | SI 1977/57 | C |
| Russia | SI 1994/3213 | C |
| St. Christopher (St. Kitts) and Nevis | SRO 1947/2872 | C |
| Saudi Arabia | SI 1994/767 (not superseded) | ATP |
| | SI 2008/1770 including Protocol | C |
| Serbia | SI 1981/1815 | C |
| Sierra Leone | SRO 1947/2873 | C |
| | Amended by Protocol SI 1968/1104 | |
| Singapore | SI 1997/2988 | C |
| | Amended by Protocols SI 2010/2685 and SI 2012/3078 | |
| Slovak Republic | SI 1991/2876 | C |
| Slovenia | SI 2008/1796 | C |
| Solomon Islands | SI 1950/748 | C |
| | Amended by Arrangements SI 1968/574 and SI 1974/1270 | |
| South Africa | SI 2002/3138 | C |
| | Amended by Protocol SI 2011/2441 | |
| Spain | SI 1976/1919 | C |
| | Amended by Exchange of Notes SI 1995/765 | |
| Sri Lanka | SI 1980/713 | C |
| Sudan | SI 1977/1719 | C |
| Swaziland | SI 1969/380 | C |
| Sweden | SI 1984/366 | C |
| Switzerland | SI 1978/1408 | C |
| | Amended by Protocols SI 1982/714, SI 1994/3215, SI 2007/3465, SI 2010/2689 and exchange of letters from 19 December 2012. | |

*continued*

| Country | Authority | Coverage |
|---------|-----------|----------|
| Taiwan | SI 2002/3137 | C |
| Tajikistan | SI 1974/1269 (not superseded) | ATP |
|  | SI 1986/224 | C |
| Thailand | SI 1981/1546 | C |
| Trinidad and Tobago | SI 1983/1903 | C |
| Tunisia | SI 1984/133 | C |
| Turkey | SI 1988/932 | C |
| Turkmenistan | SI 1974/1269 (not superseded) | ATP |
|  | SI 1986/224 | C |
| Tuvalu | SI 1950/750 | C |
|  | Amended by Arrangements SI 1968/309 and SI 1974/1271 | |
| Uganda | SI 1993/1802 | C |
| Ukraine | SI 1993/1803 | C |
| USA | SI 2002/2848 including Protocol and Exchange of Notes | C |
| Uzbekistan | SI 1994/770 | C |
| Venezuela | SI 1996/2599 | C |
| Vietnam | SI 1994/3216 | C |
| Zambia | SI 1972/1721 | C |
|  | Amended by Protocol SI 1981/1816 | |
| Zimbabwe | SI 1982/1842 | C |

**Notes**

(1)   Key to coverage of agreements

   ATP   Air Transport Profits

   C   Comprehensive

   S   Shipping Profits

   IT   Income taxes only

(2)   The text of many DTAs can be accessed via HMRC's website: www.hmrc.gov.uk/taxtreaties/in-force/index.htm.

(3)   HMRC publishes a Digest of Double Taxation Treaties (pdf format), which can be downloaded from the HMRC website: www.hmrc.gov.uk/taxtreaties/dtdigest.pdf.

(4)   *Liechtenstein* – The Liechtenstein Disclosure Facility (LDF) allows people with unpaid tax linked to investments or assets in Liechtenstein to settle their tax liability under this special arrangement. The LDF will now run from 1 September 2009 until 5 April 2016. Further information about the LDF can be found at www.hmrc.gov.uk/disclosure/liechtenstein-disclosure.htm.

(5)    *Switzerland* – A Taxation Cooperation Agreement between the UK and Switzerland, aimed at resolving long-standing issues arising from Swiss banking secrecy came into force on 1 January 2013. Under the terms of the agreement, UK taxpayers who hold existing funds in Switzerland have the choice of authorising the bank to make full disclosure to HMRC or suffer a one-off tax deduction calculated according to an agreed formula, and withholding tax from future income and gains (*FA 2012, s 218, Sch 36*; for further details see www.hmrc.gov.uk/taxtreaties/ukswiss.htm and factsheet: www.hmrc.gov.uk/taxtreaties/swiss-dis-factsheet.pdf).

(6)    *Switzerland* – Letters exchanged constitute an agreement between the UK and Switzerland, which came into force on 19 December 2012, and concerning the provisions for the exchange of information under the pre-existing Double Tax Convention (*SI 1978/1408*) as amended by subsequent protocols.

## DTAs signed/not in force

(1)    *Brunei* – An agreement amended the double tax agreement was signed on 11 December 2012. The Agreement will come into effect as soon as both countries have completed their legislative procedures and notified each other through diplomatic channels.

(2)    *Brazil* – An agreement between the UK and Brazil to avoid the double taxation of the salaries of members of the crew of aircraft operated in international traffic was signed in Brasilia on 2 September 2010. The Agreement will come into effect as soon as each government has completed the necessary procedures to give effect to it under their domestic laws.

(3)    *China* – A double taxation agreement was signed in London on 27 June 2011. The agreement has not yet entered into force. This will happen when both countries have completed their Parliamentary procedures and exchanged diplomatic notes.

(4)    *Ethiopia* – A double taxation convention was signed in London on 9 June 2011. The Convention will enter into force once both countries have completed their Parliamentary procedures and exchanged diplomatic notes.

(5)    *Germany* – A new Bank Levy Agreement between the UK and the Federal Republic of Germany was signed on 7 December 2011. The purpose of the Agreement is to eliminate double charging where a bank is chargeable to the bank levy in both countries. There is also a specific measure providing for the exchange of information in relation to the levies covered by the Agreement. The Agreement will enter into force once both countries have completed their legislative procedures.

(6)    *India* – A Protocol to the Double Taxation Agreement of 1993 was signed on 30 October 2012. This will enter into force once both countries have completed their legislative procedures.

*An updated list of DTAs signed/not in force for 2012 and earlier years is available here: www.hmrc.gov.uk/taxtreaties/signed.htm.*

## Double Taxation Conventions (DTCs): Inheritance Tax

(*IHTA 1984, s 158*; IHTM 27161 *et seq*)

| Country | Authority |
|---|---|
| France | SI 1963/1319 |
| India | SI 1956/998 |
| Ireland | SI 1978/1107 |
| Italy | SI 1968/304 |
| Netherlands | SI 1980/706 |
| | Amended by Protocol SI 1996/730 |
| Pakistan | SI 1957/1522 |
| South Africa | SI 1979/576 |
| Sweden | SI 1981/840 |
| | Amended by Protocol SI 1989/986 |
| Switzerland | SI 1994/3214 including Protocol |
| USA | SI 1979/1454 |

### Note

The UK Government may enter into a DTC with the Government of any territory outside the UK. Where the deceased was domiciled in a DTC territory or owned property situate in one of those territories, the terms of the relevant DTC should be considered in relation to IHT and any tax imposed by the laws of that territory which is of a similar character or is chargeable by reference to death or gifts made *inter vivos* (*IHTA 1984, s 158*; IHTM27161).

## Tax Information Exchange Agreements (TIEAs)

*TIEAs in force*

An updated list of TIEAs in force is available on: www.hmrc.gov.uk/taxtreaties/tiea/inforce.htm

| Country | Authority | Scope |
|---|---|---|
| Anguilla | SI 2010/2677 | B |
| | Agreement effective 28 October 2004 | NR |
| Antigua and Barbuda | SI 2011/1075 | B |
| Aruba | SI 2011/2435 | B |
| | | R |
| Bahamas | SI 2010/2684 | B |
| Bermuda | SI 2008/1789 | B |
| Belize | SI 2011/1685 | B |
| British Virgin Islands | SI 2005/1457 | R |
| | SI 2009/3013 | B |
| Cayman Islands | Agreement effective 16 April 2005 | NR |

| Country | Authority | Scope |
|---|---|---|
| Curaçao, Sint Maarten and the BES Islands (Bonaire, Saba and Sint Eustatius) (formerly the Netherlands Antilles) | SI 2011/2433 | B |
| Dominica | SI 2011/1686 | B |
| Gibraltar | SI 2006/1453 | R |
| | SI 2010/2680 | B |
| Grenada | SI 2011/1687 | B |
| Guernsey | SI 2005/1262 | R |
| | SI 2009/3011 | B |
| Isle of Man | SI 2005/1263 | R |
| | SI 2009/228 | B |
| Jersey | SI 2005/1261 | R |
| | SI 2009/3012 | B |
| Liberia | SI 2011/2434 | B |
| Liechtenstein | SI 2010/2678 | B |
| Montserrat | SI 2005/1459 | R |
| Netherlands Antilles | SI 2005/1460 | R |
| San Marino | SI 2011/1688 | B |
| St Christopher (St Kitts) and Nevis | SI 2011/1077 | B |
| St Lucia | SI 2011/1076 | B |
| St Vincent and the Grenadines | SI 2011/1078 | B |
| Turks and Caicos Islands | SI 2010/2679 | B |
| | Agreement effective 15 January 2005 | NR |

## Notes

Key to scope of TIEAs

B     Bilateral agreements for co-operation in tax matters through exchange of information

NR     Non-reciprocal Agreements relating to the EU Directive on taxation of savings income in the form of interest payments

R     Reciprocal Agreements relating to the EU Directive on taxation of savings income in the form of interest payments

*TIEAs signed/not in force*

| Country | Signed |
|---|---|
| Marshall Islands | 2012 |
| Brazil | 2012 |
| Netherlands Antilles | 2010 |

An updated list of TIEAs signed/not in force is available on: www.hmrc.gov.uk/taxtreaties/tiea/signed.htm

## CLEARANCES

### Non-Statutory Clearances

*(1)   Non-Statutory Business Clearances*

(www.hmrc.gov.uk/cap/links-dec07.htm; HMRC Non-Statutory Business Clearance Guidance Manual (NBCG))

(a)   *General* – The non-statutory business clearance service is available to businesses and their advisers about the tax consequences of transactions affecting the business in the circumstances below:

- Where there is 'material uncertainty' arising within four Finance Acts of the introduction of any new legislation; or

- On legislation older than the last four Finance Acts where there is material uncertainty around the tax outcome of a real issue of commercial significance to the business itself.

Clearance applications can be made both pre-transaction (where evidence is supplied that the transaction is genuinely contemplated) and post-transaction.

(b)   *Suitability* – Circumstances where HMRC will not accept non-statutory business clearance applications include:

- Personal tax matters (eg Inheritance Tax or residence status);

- Employment contract matters (although applications may ask for confirmation on the tax treatment of salary sacrifice arrangements put in place);

- If the application concerns tax or NICs planning arrangements;

- Minor variations of previous applications in respect of the same person and the same transaction;

- If the application is about arrangements primarily to gain a tax or NICs advantage rather than being primarily commercially motivated;

- If there is no material uncertainty (eg the point at issue is covered in published HMRC guidance);

- If HMRC have already opened an enquiry etc into the subject matter of the clearance application or the self-assessment return for the year to which it relates, or if the 'enquiry window' has closed;

- If the application deals with matters not involving interpretations of tax law or its application (eg asset valuations or transfer pricing);

- If the application asks questions about the application of customs rules;

- Applications requesting HMRC's view on whether a particular Research and Development (R&D) project qualifies for relief in relation to R&D tax incentives;

- Applications concerning the tax consequences of executing trust deeds or settlements, and whether the 'settlements' anti-avoidance provisions apply (*ITTOIA 2005, Pt 5, Ch 5*).

(c)   *Contents of application* – HMRC publish a checklist of information required in support of a non-statutory business clearance application, and they ask that it be used as a cover sheet or its order be adhered to in any covering letter. The checklist can be downloaded (in pdf format) here: www.hmrc.gov.uk/cap/annex-a-checklist. pdf

For further guidance see: www.hmrc.gov.uk/cap/links-dec07.htm#4

(d)   *Submission of applications* – Non-statutory business clearance applications can be submitted to HMRC as follows:

● Large businesses – applications should be submitted to the HMRC Client Relationship Manager (CRM) assigned to that business.

● Other businesses:

HMRC Clearances Team,
Alexander House,
21 Victoria Avenue
Southend on Sea
Essex
SS99 1BD

By Email: hmrc.southendteam@hmrc.gsi.gov.uk

*Note* – In the case of market sensitive information, contact HMRC in advance: large businesses via their Customer Relationship Manager, others by telephone to 01733 317030.

## (2)   *HMRC CAP 1 (Clearances and Approvals)*

(www.hmrc.gov.uk/cap/cap1.htm)

CAP 1 replaced HMRC Code of Practice 10 (Information and advice) (COP10) and VAT Notice 700/6 (VAT rulings for non-business customers) from 31 October 2011.

(a)   *General* – Applications for a ruling under CAP 1 can be made only by non-business persons (or persons who are contacting HMRC with non-business queries) about HMRC's interpretation of recent tax legislation, and advisors acting on their behalf,

(b)   *When HMRC will respond* – HMRC undertake to provide non-business pre- and post-transaction rulings on request in most cases where the taxpayer or their adviser is uncertain about the meaning of tax legislation enacted in the last four years, as it applies to a specific issue, transaction or intended transaction and cannot find the information they need from HMRC's online guidance or telephone helplines.. However, HMRC will give a view on earlier provisions where a query raises uncertainty about the right tax treatment and the matter is not covered in their published guidance.

(c)   *When HMRC will not respond* – Circumstances in which HMRC may not give advice under this service include:

● If the application fails to provide the necessary information. (In this case HMRC will say what further information they need.)

● If HMRC do not think that there are genuine points of uncertainty. (In this case HMRC will explain why they think this and direct the applicant to the relevant online guidance.)

● If the application relates to a future transaction and HMRC are not reasonably satisfied that the transaction, as described, will indeed take place.

- If the application concerns tax planning.

- If the application relates to transactions which, in HMRC's view, are for the purposes of avoiding tax.

- If HMRC are checking the taxpayer's return for the period in question.

- If, in the case of a self assessment return, the time limit for HMRC to notify their intention to begin an enquiry into the return to which the transaction in question relates has passed.

(c)   *Contents of application* – HMRC publish a checklist of information required in support of a CAP 1 application, and they ask that it be used as a cover sheet or its order be adhered to in any covering letter. The checklist can be downloaded here: www.hmrc.gov.uk/cap/annex-a-cap1-checklist.pdf.

(d)   *Submission of applications*:

There is no single point of contact at HMRC to which applications under CAP 1 should be sent, given the very wide range of tax regimes covered by this service and the number of applications received.

If the applicant has an existing point of contact within HMRC, for example a Customer Manager or their local tax office, or are already in contact with HMRC on the subject of the query, they should address their application to the contact address which they have been given.

In all other cases, applicants are asked to use the contact details and postal addresses for specialist departments or other parts of HMRC, see 5) below.


*(3)   CG34-post-transaction valuation checks for capital gains*

(www.hmrc.gov.uk/forms/cg34.pdf)

(a)   *General* – This service allows taxpayers (including companies) to ask HMRC to check valuations required to compute capital gains tax, or corporation tax on chargeable gains. It can be used after a disposal, or after a deemed disposal following a claim that an asset has become of negligible value, but before the related tax return is submitted. If HMRC have agreed a valuation, they will not challenge the subsequent use of it in a tax return.

(b)   *Contents of application* – Form CG34 must be completed for each valuation which HMRC are asked to check, and submitted together with the information listed on the form. Copies of Form CG34 can be downloaded from: www.hmrc.gov.uk/forms/cg34.pdf

(c)   *Submission of applications* – Applicants should allow at least two months for HMRC to check valuations. Completed forms CG34 should be submitted by post as follows:

- For individuals, partnerships and personal representatives:

    HMRC Local Compliance
    Individuals and Public Bodies
    PO Box 3900
    GLASGOW
    G70 6AA

- For taxpayers dealt with by High Net Worth Units or Public Department 1:

  To the appropriate office dealing with the taxpayer's affairs

- For taxpayers dealt with by Trust Offices:

  Trusts and Estates
  Compliance SO923
  PO Box 204
  BOOTLE
  L69 9AQ

- For companies:

  To the appropriate office dealing with the company's affairs.

## (4) IHT clearance service for business owners

(www.hmrc.gov.uk/cap/clearanceiht.htm)

(a)  *General* – This service allows business owners (or their advisers) to make clearance applications in respect of IHT business property relief (BPR), if HMRC is satisfied that there is material uncertainty over the application of the law, and that the issue is commercially significant to the business itself. Applications can be made post-transaction, or pre-transaction if evidence is supplied that the transaction is genuinely contemplated.

HMRC will also provide a view on the tax consequences of a transfer of value that involves a change of ownership of a business (succession) where this transfer (ignoring BPR) would result in an immediate IHT charge. Clearances in these succession cases will only remain valid for a limited period of six months.

(b)  *Suitability* – HMRC will not accept IHT business clearance service applications in the following circumstances:

- Applications for tax planning advice, or for HMRC's approval of tax planning arrangements;

- Applications involving minor variations of previous one for the same persons on the same transactions;

- If HMRC take the view that the arrangements are primarily to gain a tax advantage rather than being primarily commercially motivated;

- Applications where there is no actual uncertainty;

- If HMRC have already opened an enquiry into the transaction that is the subject of your clearance application, or where an enquiry into an IHT return has already been opened;

- Applications on issues not involving the interpretation of tax law or its application to particular circumstances;

- Applications concerning the tax consequences of executing trust deeds or settlements, and whether the 'settlements' anti-avoidance provisions apply (*ITTOIA 2005, Pt 5, Ch 5*);

- If the disposition of property under a will is conditional on the availability of BPR.

255

(c)   *Contents of application*

HMRC publish a checklist of information required in support of an IHT business clearance service application, and they ask that it be used as a cover sheet or its order be adhered to in any covering letter. The checklist can be downloaded from: www.hmrc.gov.uk/cap/Checklist.pdf.

For further guidance see www.hmrc.gov.uk/cap/clearanceiht.htm#4.

If the application involves a transaction for which there is also the disclosure of an avoidance scheme covering all or part of the transaction, explicit mention must be made of any related disclosures (eg by including a copy of the disclosure, or by reporting the allocated DOTAS scheme reference number).

(d)   *Submission of applications* – Postal applications can be submitted to:

HMRC
Trusts & Estates Technical Team (Clearances)
Ferrers House
Castle Meadow Road
Nottingham
NG2 1BB

Email applications can be submitted to the Trusts & Estates Technical Team (Clearances): mailpoint.e@hmrc.gsi.gov.uk.

The following reference should be quoted: BP102/P1/08E. If the application contains commercially sensitive information, HMRC should be emailed (as above) with a contact name and telephone number and they will contact the application.

## *(5)   General advice on specialist technical areas of taxation*

(www.hmrc.gov.uk/cap/gen-advice.htm)

The above webpage lists contact details for general advice on the following specialist topics:

- Inheritance tax

- Non resident trusts, domicile and residence

- Charities and Community Amateur Sports Clubs

- Individual Savings Accounts and the tax deduction scheme for interest

- Reliefs and exemptions available under Double Taxation Treaties and the EU Interest and Royalties Directive

- Pension schemes

- Oil companies

- Stamp Duty, Stamp Duty Land Tax and Stamp Duty Reserve Tax

- Underlying tax

- Venture capital schemes: EIS, CVS VCTs and EMI.

- Research and Development tax credits

- Controlled Foreign Companies (CFCs)

- Arbitrage

## Statutory Clearances and Approvals

(*http://www.hmrc.gov.uk/cap/*)

(1) *General* – Clearances applications may be submitted to HMRC by letter, fax or email, including in respect of the following:

| Clearance category | Statutory reference |
| --- | --- |
| Demergers* | *CTA 2010, s 1091* |
| Demergers: Chargeable payments* | *CTA 2010, s 1092* |
| Purchase of own shares* | *CTA 2010, s 1044* |
| EIS shares: acquisition by new company* | *ITA 2007, s 247(1)(f)* |
| Transactions in securities* | *ITA 2007, s 701; CTA 2010, s 748* |
| Share exchanges* | *TCGA 1992, s 138(1)* |
| Share exchanges: continuity of SEIS relief* | *ITA 2007, s 257HB(1)(f)* |
| Reconstructions involving the transfer of a business* | *TCGA 1992, s 139(5)* |
| Transfer or division of a UK business between EU member states* | *TCGA 1992, s 140B* |
| Transfer or division of non-UK business by a UK company to a company resident in another EU member state | *TCGA 1992, s 140D* |
| Intangible assets* | *CTA 2009, s 831* |
| Loan relationships: transfers* | *CTA 2009, s 427* |
| Loan relationships: mergers* | *CTA 2009, s 437* |
| Derivative contracts: transfers* | *CTA 2009, s 677* |
| Derivative contracts: mergers* | *CTA 2009, s 686* |
| Targeted Anti Avoidance Rule 3 (Capital Gains)* | *TCGA 1992, ss 184G–184H* |
| Company migrations | *TMA 1970, s 109B* |
| Insurance companies: Transfer of business | *TA 1988, s 444AED* |
| Insurance companies: Transfer of long-term business on or after 1 January 2013 | *FA 2012, s 133* |
| Insurance companies: Transitional rules | *FA 2012, Sch 17, para 18* |
| Corporate Venturing Schemes | *FA 2000, Sch 15, Pt X* |
| Assignment of lease at undervalue* | *ITTOIA 2005, s 300; CTA 2009, s 237* |
| Transactions in land* | *ITA 2007, s 770; CTA 2010, s 831* |
| Offshore funds: | |
| (a) Reporting fund status | *SI 2009/3001, reg 54(2)* |
| (b) Equivalence and genuine diversity of ownership requirements | *SI 2009/3001, reg 78* |
| Stamp Duty Adjudication | *SA 1891, s 12A* |

\* See note (2) below

(2) *Submission of applications* – A list of HMRC contact details in respect of each category of statutory clearance application can be found here: www.hmrc.gov.uk/cap/#apa

(3)   *Clearance applications* under more than one of the provisions marked * above may be submitted to HMRC as a single application, by email, fax or letter, as follows:

By letter:

Clearance and Counteraction Team, Anti-Avoidance Group
SO528
PO Box 194
Bootle
L69 9AA

Mark the application 'Market sensitive' or 'Non market sensitive'.

*By Fax:* 020 7438 4409

Note: If faxing market sensitive information, call the HMRC team leader on Tel: 020 7438 7474 beforehand.

*By Email:* reconstructions@hmrc.gsi.gov.uk

*For general enquiries to the unit: Tel: 020 7438 7474*

# Index